W9-DHW-385

A set of six

Joseph Conrad

Nabu Public Domain Reprints:

You are holding a reproduction of an original work published before 1923 that is in the public domain in the United States of America, and possibly other countries. You may freely copy and distribute this work as no entity (individual or corporate) has a copyright on the body of the work. This book may contain prior copyright references, and library stamps (as most of these works were scanned from library copies). These have been scanned and retained as part of the historical artifact.

This book may have occasional imperfections such as missing or blurred pages, poor pictures, errant marks, etc. that were either part of the original artifact, or were introduced by the scanning process. We believe this work is culturally important, and despite the imperfections, have elected to bring it back into print as part of our continuing commitment to the preservation of printed works worldwide. We appreciate your understanding of the imperfections in the preservation process, and hope you enjoy this valuable book.

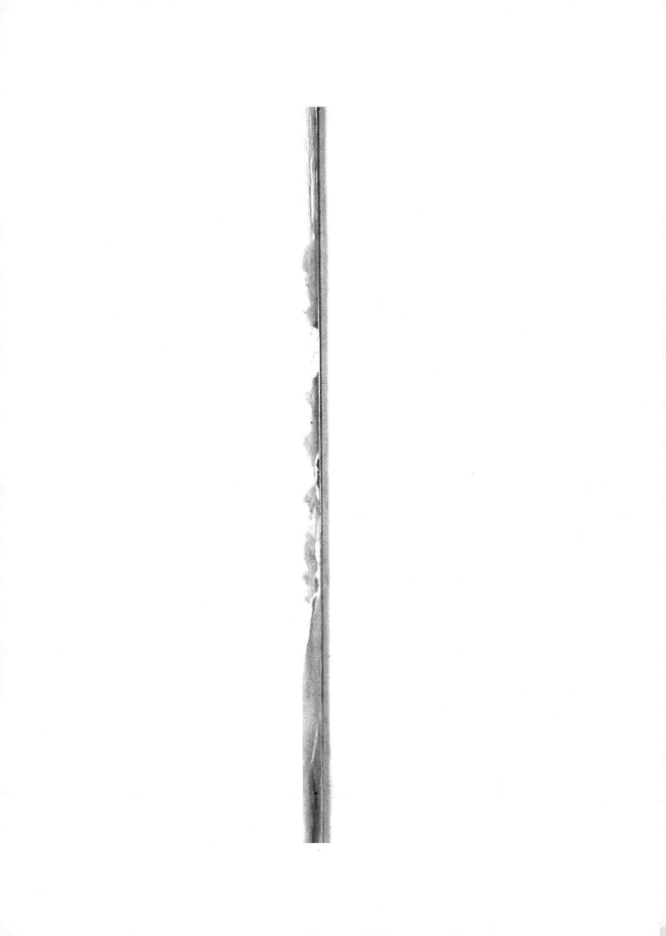

A SET OF SIX

BY THE SAME AUTHOR.

ALMAYER'S FOLLY

AN OUTCAST OF THE ISLANDS

THE NIGGER OF THE " NARCISSUS "

TALES OF UNREST

LORD JIM

YOUTH : A NARRATIVE

TYPHOON

NOSTROMO : A TALE OF THE SEABOARD

THE MIRROR OF THE SEA

THE SECRET AGENT

UNDER WESTERN EYES

SOME REMINISCENCES

'TWIXT LAND AND SEA

CHANCE

WITHIN THE TIDES

VICTORY

WITH FORD M. HUEFFER

ROMANCE : A NOVEL

THE INHERITORS : AN EXTRAVAGANT STORY

A SET OF SIX

BY

JOSEPH CONRAD

Les petites marionnettes
Font, font, font.
Trois petits tours
Et puis s'en vont.
NURSERY RHYMES.

SIXTH EDITION

180804.
25.5.23.

METHUEN & CO. LTD.
36 ESSEX STREET W.C.
LONDON

First Published (Crown 8vo) . . . . August 6th 1903
Second Edition . . . . . . September 1908
Third Edition . . . . . . March 1909
Fourth Edition . . . . . June 1919
Fifth Edition (Cheap Form) . . . March 11th 1920
Sixth Edition (Crown 8vo) 1920

PR
6005
O4S45
1920
cop. 2

TO

MISS M. H. M. CAPES

CONTENTS

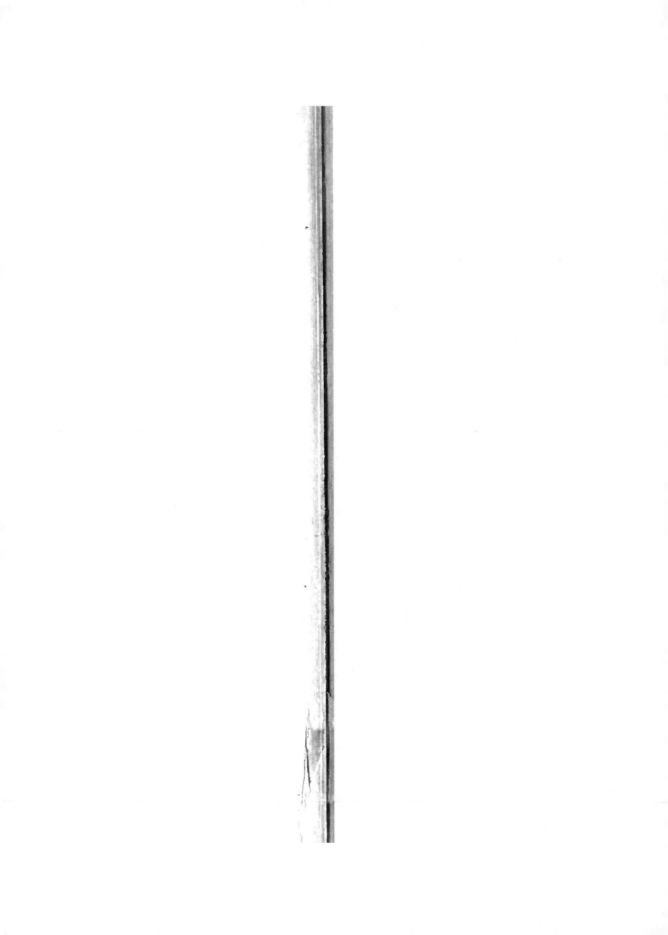

A SET OF SIX

GASPAR RUIZ

I

A REVOLUTIONARY war raises many strange characters out of the obscurity which is the common lot of humble lives in an undisturbed state of society.

Certain individualities grow into fame through their vices and their virtues, or simply by their actions, which may have a temporary importance; and then they become forgotten. The names of a few leaders alone survive the end of armed strife and are further preserved in history; so that, vanishing from men's active memories, they still exist in books.

The name of General Santierra attained that cold paper-and-ink immortality. He was a South American of good family, and the books published in his lifetime numbered him amongst the liberators of that continent from the oppressive rule of Spain.

That long contest, waged for independence on one side and for dominion on the other, developed in the course of years and the vicissitudes of changing fortune the fierceness and inhumanity of a struggle for life. All feelings of pity and compassion disappeared in the growth of political hatred. And, as is usual in war, the mass of the people, who had the least to gain by the issue, suffered most in their obscure persons and their humble fortunes.

General Santierra began his service as lieutenant in the patriot army raised and commanded by the famous San Martin, afterwards conqueror of Lima and liberator of Peru. A great battle had just been fought on the banks of the river Bio-Bio. Amongst the prisoners made upon the routed Royalist troops there was a soldier called Gaspar Ruiz. His powerful build and his big head rendered him remarkable amongst his fellow-captives. The personality of the man was unmistakable. Some months before he had been missed from the ranks of Republican troops after one of the many skirmishes which preceded the great battle. And now, having been captured arms in hand amongst Royalists, he could expect no other fate but to be shot as a deserter.

Gaspar Ruiz, however, was not a deserter; his mind was hardly active enough to take a discriminating view of the advantages or perils of treachery. Why should he change sides ? He had really been made a prisoner, had suffered ill-usage and many privations. Neither side showed tenderness to its adversaries. There came a day when he was ordered, together with some other captured rebels, to march in the front rank of the Royal troops. A musket had been thrust into his hands. He had taken it. He had marched. He did not want to be killed with circumstances of peculiar atrocity for refusing to march. He did not understand heroism, but it was his intention to throw his musket away at the first opportunity. Meantime he had gone on loading and firing, from fear of having his brains blown out at the first sign of unwillingness, by some non-commissioned officer of the King of Spain. He tried to set forth these elementary considerations before the sergeant of the guard set over him and some twenty other such deserters, who had been condemned summarily to be shot.

It was in the quadrangle of the fort at the back of the batteries which command the roadstead of Valparaiso. The officer who had identified him had gone on without listening to his protestations. His doom was sealed ; his hands were tied very tightly together behind his back ; his body was sore all over from the many blows with sticks and butts of muskets which had hurried him along on the painful road from the place of his capture to the gate of the fort. This was the only kind of systematic attention the prisoners had received from their escort during a four days' journey across a scantily watered tract of country. At the crossings of rare streams they were permitted to quench their thirst by lapping hurriedly like dogs. In the evening a few scraps of meat were thrown amongst them as they dropped down dead-beat upon the stony ground of the halting-place.

As he stood in the courtyard of the castle in the early morning, after having been driven hard all night, Gaspar Ruiz's throat was parched, and his tongue felt very large and dry in his mouth.

And Gaspar Ruiz, besides being very thirsty, was stirred by a feeling of sluggish anger, which he could not very well express, as though the vigour of his spirit were by no means equal to the strength of his body.

The other prisoners in the batch of the condemned hung their heads, looking obstinately on the ground. But Gaspar Ruiz kept on repeating : " What should I desert for to the Royalists ? Why should I desert ? Tell me, Estaban ! "

He addressed himself to the sergeant, who happened to belong to the same part of the country as himself. But the sergeant, after shrugging his meagre shoulders once, paid no further attention to the deep murmuring voice at his back. It was indeed strange that Gaspar Ruiz should desert. His people were in too humble a station to feel much the disadvantages of any form of government. There was no reason why Gaspar Ruiz should wish to uphold in his own person the rule of the King of Spain. Neither had he been anxious to exert himself for its subversion. He had joined the side of Independence in an extremely reasonable and natural manner. A band of patriots appeared one morning early, surrounding his father's ranche, spearing the watch-dogs and hamstringing a fat cow all in the twinkling of an eye, to the cries of " *Viva la Libertad !* " Their officer discoursed of Liberty with enthusiasm and eloquence after a long and refreshing sleep. When they left in the evening, taking with them some of Ruiz, the father's, best horses to replace their own lamed animals, Gaspar Ruiz went away with them, having been invited pressingly to do so by the eloquent officer.

Shortly afterwards a detachment of Royalist troops coming to pacify the district, burnt the ranche, carried off the remaining horses and cattle, and having thus deprived the old people of all their worldly possessions, left them sitting under a bush in the enjoyment of the insatiable boon of life.

II

GASPAR RUIZ, condemned to death as a deserter, was not thinking either of his native place or of his parents, to whom he had been a good son on account of the mildness of his character and the great strength of his limbs. The practical advantage of this last was made still more valuable to his father by his obedient disposition. Gaspar Ruiz had an acquiescent soul.

But it was stirred now to a sort of dim revolt by his dislike to die the death of a traitor. He was not a traitor. He said again to the sergeant : " You know I did not desert, Estaban. You know I remained behind amongst the trees with three others to keep the enemy back while the detachment was running away ! "

Lieutenant Santierra, little more than a boy at the time, and unused as yet to the sanguinary inbecilities of a state of war, had lingered near-by, as if fascinated by the sight of these men who were to be shot presently—"for an example "—as the *Commandante* had said.

The sergeant, without deigning to look at the prisoner, addressed himself to the young officer with a superior smile.

"Ten men would not have been enough to make him a prisoner, *mi teniente*. Moreover, the other three rejoined the detachment after dark. Why should he unwounded and the strongest of them all, have failed to do so ? "

"My strength is as nothing against a mounted man with a lasso," Gaspar Ruiz protested eagerly. "He dragged me behind his horse for half a mile."

At this excellent reason the sergeant only laughed contemptuously. The young officer hurried away after the *Commandante*.

Presently the adjutant of the castle came by. He was a truculent, raw-boned man in a ragged uniform. His spluttering voice issued out of a flat, yellow face. The sergeant learned from him that the condemned men would not be shot till sunset. He begged then to know what he was to do with them meantime.

The adjutant looked savagely round the courtyard, and, pointing to the door of a small dungeon-like guardroom, receiving light and air through one heavily-barred window, said : "Drive the scoundrels in there."

The sergeant, tightening his grip upon the stick he carried in virtue of his rank, executed this order with alacrity and zeal. He hit Gaspar Ruiz, whose movements were slow, over his head and shoulders. Gaspar Ruiz stood still for a moment under the shower of blows, biting his lip thoughtfully as if absorbed by a perplexing mental process—then followed the others without haste. The door was locked, and the adjutant carried off the key.

By noon the heat of that low vaulted place crammed to suffocation had become unbearable. The prisoners crowded towards the window, begging their guards for a drop of water ; but the soldiers remained lying in indolent attitudes wherever there was a little shade under a wall, while the sentry sat with his back against the door smoking a cigarette, and raising his eyebrows philosophically from time to time. Gaspar Ruiz had pushed his way to the window with irresistible force. His capacious chest needed more air than the others; his big face, resting with its chin on the ledge, pressed close to the bars, seemed to support the other faces crowding up for breath. From moaned entreaties they had passed to desperate cries, and the tumultuous howling of those thirsty men obliged a young officer who was just then crossing the courtyard to shout in order to make himself heard.

"Why don't you give some water to these prisoners ! "

The sergeant, with an air of surprised innocence, excused himself by the remark that all those men were condemned to die in a very few hours.

Lieutenant Santierra stamped his foot. "They are condemned to death, not to torture," he shouted. "Give them some water at once."

Impressed by this appearance of anger, the soldiers bestirred themselves, and the sentry, snatching up his musket, stood to attention.

But when a couple of buckets were found and filled from the well, it was discovered that they could not be passed through the bars, which were set too close. At the prospect of quenching their thirst, the shrieks of those trampled down in the struggle to get near the opening became very heartrending. But when the soldiers who had lifted the buckets towards the window put them to the ground again helplessly, the yell of disappointment was still more terrible.

The soldiers of the army of Independence were not equipped with canteens. A small tin cup was found, but its approach to the opening caused such a commotion, such yells of rage and pain in the vague mass of limbs behind the straining faces at the window, that Lieutenant Santierra cried out hurriedly, "No, no—you must open the door, sergeant."

The sergeant, shrugging his shoulders, explained that he had no right to open the door even if he had had the key. But he had not the key. The adjutant of the garrison kept the key. Those men were giving much unnecessary trouble, since they had to die at sunset in any case. Why they had not been shot at once early in the morning he could not understand.

Lieutenant Santierra kept his back studiously to the window. It was at his earnest solicitations that the *Commandante* had delayed the execution. This favour had been granted to him in consideration of his distinguished family and of his father's high position amongst the chiefs of the Republican party. Lieutenant Santierra believed that the General commanding would visit the fort some time in the afternoon, and he ingenuously hoped that his naïve intercession would induce that severe man to pardon some, at least, of those criminals. In the revulsion of his feeling his interference stood revealed now as guilty and futile meddling. It appeared to him obvious that the general would never even consent to listen to his petition. He could never save those men, and he had only made himself responsible for the sufferings added to the cruelty of their fate.

" Then go at once and get the key from the adjutant," said Lieutenant Santierra.

The sergeant shook his head with a sort of bashful smile, while his eyes glanced sideways at Gaspar Ruiz's face, motionless and silent, staring through the bars at the bottom of a heap of other haggard, distorted, yelling faces.

His worship the adjutant de Plaza, the sergeant murmured, was having his siesta ; and supposing that he, the sergeant, would be allowed access to him, the only result he expected would be to have his soul flogged out of his body for presuming to disturb his worship's repose. He made a deprecatory movement with his hands, and stood stock-still, looking down modestly upon his brown toes.

Lieutenant Santierra glared with indignation, but hesitated. His handsome oval face, as smooth as a girl's, flushed with the shame of his perplexity. Its nature humiliated his spirit. His hairless upper lip trembled ; he seemed on the point of either bursting into a fit of rage or into tears of dismay.

2

Fifty years later, General Santierra, the venerable relic of revolutionary times, was well able to remember the feelings of the young lieutenant. Since he had given up riding altogether, and found it difficult to walk beyond the limits of his garden, the general's greatest delight was to entertain in his house the officers of the foreign men-of-war visiting the harbour. For Englishmen he had a preference, as for old companions in arms. English naval men of all ranks accepted his hospitality with curiosity, because he had known Lord Cochrane and had taken part, on board the patriot squadron commanded by that marvellous seaman, in the cutting out and blockading operations before Callao—an episode of unalloyed glory in the wars of Independence and of endless honour in the fighting tradition of Englishmen. He was a fair linguist, this ancient survivor of the Liberating armies. A trick of smoothing his long white beard whenever he was short of a word in French or English imparted an air of leisurely dignity to the tone of his reminiscences.

III

"Yes, my friends," he used to say to his guests, "what would you have? A youth of seventeen summers, without worldly experience, and owing my rank only to the glorious patriotism of my father, may God rest his soul. I suffered immense humiliation, not so much from the disobedience of that subordinate, who, after all, was responsible for those prisoners; but I suffered because, like the boy I was, I myself dreaded going to the adjutant for the key. I had felt, before, his rough and cutting tongue. Being quite a common fellow, with no merit except his savage valour, he made me feel his contempt and dislike from the first day I joined my battalion in garrison at the fort. It was only a fortnight before! I would have confronted him sword in hand, but I shrank from the mocking brutality of his sneers.

"I don't remember having been so miserable in my

life before or since. The torment of my sensibility was so great that I wished the sergeant to fall dead at my feet, and the stupid soldiers who stared at me to turn into corpses; and even those wretches for whom my entreaties had procured a reprieve I wished dead also, because I could not face them without shame. A mephitic heat like a whiff of air from hell came out of that dark place in which they were confined. Those at the window who had heard what was going on jeered at me in very desperation : one of these fellows, gone mad no doubt, kept on urging me volubly to order the soldiers to fire through the window. His insane loquacity made my heart turn faint. And my feet were like lead. There was no higher officer to whom I could appeal. I had not even the firmness of spirit to simply go away.

"Benumbed by my remorse, I stood with my back to the window. You must not suppose that all this lasted a long time. How long could it have been ? A minute ? If you measured by mental suffering it was like a hundred years ; a longer time than all my life has been since. No, certainly, it was not so much as a minute. The hoarse screaming of those miserable wretches died out in their dry throats, and then suddenly a voice spoke, a deep voice muttering calmly. It called upon me to turn round.

"That voice, Señores, proceeded from the head of Gaspar Ruiz. Of his body I could see nothing. Some of his fellow-captives had clambered upon his back. He was holding them up. His eyes blinked without looking at me. That and the moving of his lips was all he seemed able to manage in his overloaded state. And when I turned round, this head, that seemed more than human size resting on its chin under a multitude of other heads, asked me whether I really desired to quench the thirst of the captives.

"I said, 'Yes, yes!' eagerly, and came up quite close to the window. I was like a child, and did not know what would happen. I was anxious to be comforted in my helplessness and remorse.

"'Have you the authority, Señor teniente, to release

my wrists from their bonds ? ' Gaspar Ruiz's head asked me.

"His features expressed no anxiety, no hope; his heavy eyelids blinked upon his eyes that looked past me straight into the courtyard.

"As if in an ugly dream, I spoke, stammering: 'What do you mean ? And how can I reach the bonds on your wrists ? '

" ' I will try what I can do,' he said ; and then that large staring head moved at last, and all the wild faces piled up in that window disappeared, tumbling down. He had shaken his load off with one movement, so strong he was.

"And he had not only shaken it off, but he got free of the crush and vanished from my sight. For a moment there was no one at all to be seen at the window. He had swung about, butting and shouldering, clearing a space for himself in the only way he could do it with his hands tied behind his back.

"Finally, backing to the opening, he pushed out to me between the bars his wrists, lashed with many turns of rope. His hands, very swollen, with knotted veins, looked enormous and unwieldy. I saw his bent back. It was very broad. His voice was like the muttering of a bull.

" ' Cut, *Señor teniente.* Cut ! '

"I drew my sword, my new unblunted sword that had seen no service as yet, and severed the many turns of the hide rope. I did this without knowing the why and the wherefore of my action, but as it were compelled by my faith in that man. The sergeant made as if to cry out, but astonishment deprived him of his voice, and he remained standing with his mouth open as if overtaken by sudden imbecility.

"I sheathed my sword and faced the soldiers. An air of awestruck expectation had replaced their usual listless apathy. I heard the voice of Gaspar Ruiz shouting inside, but the words I could not make out plainly. I suppose that to see him with his arms free augmented the influence of his strength : I mean by this, the spiritual influence that with ignorant people attaches to an exceptional degree of bodily vigour. In fact, he was no more to be feared than before, on account of the numbness of his arms and hands, which lasted for some time.

"The sergeant had recovered his power of speech. 'By all the saints!' he cried, 'we shall have to get a cavalry man with a lasso to secure him again, if he is to be led to the place of execution. Nothing less than a good *enlazador* on a good horse can subdue him. Your worship was pleased to perform a very mad thing.'

"I had nothing to say. I was surprised myself, and I felt a childish curiosity to see what would happen. But the sergeant was thinking of the difficulty of controlling Gaspar Ruiz when the time for making an example would come.

"'Or perhaps,' the sergeant pursued vexedly, 'we shall be obliged to shoot him down as he dashes out when the door is opened.' He was going to give further vent to his anxieties as to the proper carrying out of the sentence; but he interrupted himself with a sudden exclamation, snatched a musket from a soldier, and stood watchful with his eyes fixed on the window.

IV

"GASPAR RUIZ had clambered up on the sill, and sat down there with his feet against the thickness of the wall and his knees slightly bent. The window was not quite broad enough for the length of his legs. It appeared to my crestfallen perception that he meant to keep the window all to himself. He seemed to be taking up a comfortable position. Nobody inside dared to approach him now he could strike with his hands.

"'*Por Dios!*' I heard the sergeant muttering at my elbow, 'I shall shoot him through the head now, and get rid of that trouble. He is a condemned man.'

"At that I looked at him angrily. 'The general has not confirmed the sentence,' I said—though I knew well in my heart that these were but vain words. The sentence required no confirmation. ' You have no right to shoot him unless he tries to escape,' I added firmly.

" ' But *sangre de Dios!* ' the sergeant yelled out, bringing his musket up to the shoulder, ' he is escaping now. Look ! '

" But I, as if that Gaspar Ruiz had cast a spell upon me, struck the musket upward, and the bullet flew over the roofs somewhere. The sergeant dashed his arm to the ground and stared. He might have commanded the soldiers to fire, but he did not. And if he had he would not have been obeyed, I think, just then.

" With his feet against the thickness of the wall, and his hairy hands grasping the iron bar, Gaspar sat still. It was an attitude. Nothing happened for a time. And suddenly it dawned upon us that he was straightening his bowed back and contracting his arms. His lips were twisted into a snarl. Next thing we perceived was that the bar of forged iron was being bent slowly by the mightiness of his pull. The sun was beating full upon his cramped, unquivering figure. A shower of sweat-drops burst out of his forehead. Watching the bar grow crooked, I saw a little blood ooze from under his finger-nails. Then he let go. For a moment he remained all huddled up, with a hanging head, looking drowsily into the upturned palms of his mighty hands. Indeed he seemed to have dozed off. Suddenly he flung himself backwards on the sill, and setting the soles of his bare feet against the other middle bar, he bent that one too, but in the opposite direction from the first.

" Such was his strength, which in this case relieved my painful feelings. And the man seemed to have done nothing. Except for the change of position in order to use his feet, which made us all start by its swift-ness, my recollection is that of immobility. But he had bent the bars wide apart. And now he could get out if he liked ; but he dropped his legs inwards, and looking over his shoulder beckoned to the soldiers. ' Hand up the water,' he said. ' I will give them all a drink.'

" He was obeyed. For a moment I expected man and bucket to disappear, overwhelmed by the rush of eagerness ; I thought they would pull him down with their teeth. There was a rush, but holding the bucket on his lap he repulsed the assault of those wretches by the mere swinging of his feet. They flew backwards at every kick, yelling with pain ; and the soldiers laughed, gazing at the window.

"They all laughed, holding their sides, except the sergeant, who was gloomy and morose. He was afraid the prisoners would rise and break out—which would have been a bad example. But there was no fear of that, and I stood myself before the window with my drawn sword. When sufficiently tamed by the strength of Gaspar Ruiz they came up one by one, stretching their necks and presenting their lips to the edge of the bucket which the strong man tilted towards them from his knees with an extraordinary air of charity, gentleness and compassion. That benevolent appearance was of course the effect of his care in not spilling the water and of his attitude as he sat on the sill ; for, if a man lingered with his lips glued to the rim of the bucket after Gaspar Ruiz had said ' You have had enough,' there would be no tenderness or mercy in the shove of the foot which would send him groaning and doubled up far into the interior of the prison, where he would knock down two or three others before he fell himself. They came up to him again and again ; it looked as if they meant to drink the well dry before going to their death ; but the soldiers were so amused by Gaspar Ruiz's systematic proceedings that they carried the water up to the window cheerfully.

"When the adjutant came out after his siesta there was some trouble over this affair, I can assure you. And the worst of it was that the general whom we expected never came to the castle that day."

The guests of General Santierra unanimously expressed their regret that the man of such strength and patience had not been saved.

"He was not saved by my interference," said the General. "The prisoners were led to execution half an hour before sunset. Gaspar Ruiz, contrary to the sergeant's apprehensions, gave no trouble.   There was no necessity to get a cavalry man with a lasso in order to subdue him, as if he were a wild bull of the *campo*.   I believe he marched out with his arms free amongst the others who were bound.   I did not see.   I was not there. I had been put under arrest for interfering with the prisoner's guard.   About dusk, sitting dismally in my quarters, I heard three volleys fired, and thought that I should never hear of Gaspar Ruiz again.   He fell with the others.   But we were to hear of him nevertheless, though the sergeant boasted that, as he lay on his face expiring or dead in the heap of the slain, he had slashed his neck with a sword.   He had done this, he said, to make sure of ridding the world of a dangerous traitor.

"I confess to you, señores, that I thought of that strong man with a sort of gratitude, and with some admiration.   He had used his strength honourably. There dwelt, then, in his soul no fierceness corresponding to the vigour of his body."

V

GASPAR RUIZ, who could with ease bend apart the heavy iron bars of the prison, was led out with others to summary execution.   "Every bullet has its billet," runs the proverb.   All the merit of proverbs consists in the concise and picturesque expression.   In the surprise of our minds is found their persuasiveness.   In other words, we are struck and convinced by the shock.

What surprises us is the form, not the substance. Proverbs are art—cheap art.   As a general rule they are not true ;   unless indeed they happen to be mere platitudes, as for instance the proverb, "Half a loaf is better than no bread," or "A miss is as good as a mile." Some proverbs are simply imbecile, others are immoral. That one evolved out of the naïve heart of the great Russian people, "Man discharges the piece, but God carries the bullet," is piously atrocious, and at bitter variance with the accepted conception of a compassionate God.   It would indeed be an inconsistent occupation for the Guardian of the poor, the innocent and the helpless, to carry the bullet, for instance, into the heart of a father.

Gaspar Ruiz was childless, he had no wife, he had never been in love.   He had hardly ever spoken to a woman, beyond his mother and the ancient negress of the household, whose wrinkled skin was the colour of cinders, and whose lean body was bent double from age. If some bullets from those muskets fired off at fifteen paces were specifically destined for the heart of Gaspar Ruiz, they all missed their billet.   One, however, carried away a small piece of his ear, and another a fragment of flesh from his shoulder.

A red and unclouded sun setting into a purple ocean looked with a fiery stare upon the enormous wall of the Cordilleras, worthy witnesses of his glorious extinction. But it is inconceivable that it should have seen the ant-like men busy with their absurd and insignificant trials of killing and dying for reasons that, apart from being generally childish, were also imperfectly understood. It did light up, however, the backs of the firing party and the faces of the condemned men.   Some of them had fallen on their knees, others remained standing, a few averted their heads from the levelled barrels of muskets.   Gaspar Ruiz, upright, the burliest of them all, hung his big shock head.   The low sun dazzled him a little, and he counted himself a dead man already.

He fell at the first discharge.   He fell because he thought he was a dead man.   He struck the ground heavily.   The jar of the fall surprised him.   "I am not dead apparently," he thought to himself, when he heard the execution platoon reloading its arms at the word of command.   It was then that the hope of escape dawned upon him for the first time.   He remained lying stretched out with rigid limbs under the weight of two bodies collapsed crosswise upon his back.

By the time the soldiers had fired a third volley into the slightly stirring heaps of the slain, the sun had gone out of sight, and almost immediately with the darkening of the ocean dusk fell upon the coasts of the young Republic. Above the gloom of the lowlands the snowy peaks of the Cordillera remained luminous and crimson for a long time. The soldiers before marching back to the fort sat down to smoke.

The sergeant with a naked sword in his hand strolled away by himself along the heap of the dead. He was a humane man, and watched for any stir or twitch of limb in the merciful idea of plunging the point of his blade into any body giving the slightest sign of life. But none of the bodies afforded him an opportunity for the display of this charitable intention. Not a muscle twitched amongst them, not even the powerful muscles of Gaspar Ruiz, who, deluged with the blood of his neighbours and shamming death, strove to appear more lifeless than the others.

He was lying face down. The sergeant recognized him by his stature, and being himself a very small man, looked with envy and contempt at the prostration of so much strength. He had always disliked that particular soldier. Moved by an obscure animosity, he inflicted a long gash across the neck of Gaspar Ruiz, with some vague notion of making sure of that strong man's death, as if a powerful physique were more able to resist the bullets. For the sergeant had no doubt that Gaspar Ruiz had been shot through in many places. Then he passed on, and shortly afterwards marched off with his men, leaving the bodies to the care of crows and vultures.

Gaspar Ruiz had restrained a cry, though it had seemed to him that his head was cut off at a blow ; and when darkness came, shaking off the dead, whose weight had oppressed him, he crawled away over the plain on his hands and knees. After- drinking deeply, like a wounded beast, at a shallow stream, he assumed an upright posture, and staggered on light-headed and aimless, as if lost amongst the stars of the clear night. A small house seemed to rise out of the ground before him. He stumbled into the porch and struck at the door with his fist. There was not a gleam of light. Gaspar Ruiz might have thought that the inhabitants had fled from it, as from many others in the neighbourhood, had it not been for the shouts of abuse that answered his thumping. In his feverish and enfeebled state the angry screaming seemed to him part of a hallucination belonging to the weird dreamlike feeling of his unexpected condemnation to death, of the thirst suffered, of the volleys fired at him within fifteen paces, of his head being cut off at a blow. " Open the door ! " he cried. " Open in the name of God ! "

An infuriated voice from within jeered at him : " Come in, come in. This house belongs to you. All this land belongs to you. Come and take it."

"For the love of God," Gaspar Ruiz murmured.

"Does not all the land belong to you patriots ? " the voice on the other side of the door screamed on. "Are you not a patriot ? "

Gaspar Ruiz did not know. " I am a wounded man," he said apathetically.

All became still inside. Gaspar Ruiz lost the hope of being admitted, and lay down under the porch just outside the door. He was utterly careless of what was going to happen to him. All his consciousness seemed to be concentrated in his neck, where he felt a severe pain. His indifference as to his fate was genuine.

The day was breaking when he awoke from a feverish doze ; the door at which he had knocked in the dark stood wide open now, and a girl, steadying herself with her outspread arms, leaned over the threshold. Lying on his back, he stared up at her. Her face was pale and her eyes were very dark ; her hair hung down black as ebony against her white cheeks ; her lips were full and red. Beyond her he saw another head with long grey hair, and a thin old face with a pair of anxiously clasped hands under the chin.

VI

" I KNEW those people by sight," General Santierra would tell his guests at the dining-table. " I mean the

people with whom Gaspar Ruiz found shelter. The
father was an old Spaniard, a man of property ruined
by the revolution. His estates, his house in town, his
money, everything he had in the world had been con-
fiscated by proclamation, for he was a bitter foe of our
independence. From a position of great dignity and
influence on the Viceroy's Council he became of less
importance than his own negro slaves made free by our
glorious revolution. He had not even the means to flee
the country, as other Spaniards had managed to do.
It may be that, wandering ruined and houseless, and
burdened with nothing but his life, which was left to
him by the clemency of the Provisional Government, he
had simply walked under that broken roof of old tiles.
It was a lonely spot. There did not seem to be even a
dog belonging to the place. But though the roof had
holes, as if a cannon-ball or two had dropped through
it, the wooden shutters were thick and tight-closed all
the time.

"My way took me frequently along the path in
front of that miserable rancho. I rode from the fort to
the town almost every evening, to sigh at the window
of a lady I was in love with, then. When one is young,
you understand. . . . She was a good patriot, you may
be sure. *Caballeros*, credit me or not, political feeling
ran so high in those days that I do not believe I could
have been fascinated by the charms of a woman of
Royalist opinions. . . ."

Murmurs of amused incredulity all round the table
interrupted the General ; and while they lasted he
stroked his white beard gravely.

"Señores," he protested, "a Royalist was a monster
to our overwrought feelings. I am telling you this in
order not to be suspected of the slightest tenderness
towards that old Royalist's daughter. Moreover, as you
know, my affections were engaged elsewhere. But I
could not help noticing her on rare occasions when with
the front door open she stood in the porch.

"You must know that this old Royalist was as crazy
as a man can be. His political misfortunes, his total

downfall and ruin, had disordered his mind. To show his contempt for what we patriots could do, he affected to laugh at his imprisonment, at the confiscation of his lands, the burning of his houses, and the misery to which he and his womenfolk were reduced. This habit of laughing had grown upon him, so that he would begin to laugh and shout directly he caught sight of any stranger. That was the form of his madness.

"I, of course, disregarded the noise of that madman with that feeling of superiority the success of our cause inspired in us Americans. I suppose I really despised him because he was an old Castilian, a Spaniard born, and a Royalist. Those were certainly no reasons to scorn a man; but for centuries Spaniards born had shown their contempt of us Americans, men as well descended as themselves, simply because we were what they called colonists. We had been kept in abasement and made to feel our inferiority in social intercourse. And now it was our turn. It was safe for us patriots to display the same sentiments; and I being a young patriot, son of a patriot, despised that old Spaniard, and despising him I naturally disregarded his abuse, though it was annoying to my feelings. Others perhaps would not have been so forbearing.

"He would begin with a great yell—'I see a patriot. Another of them!' long before I came abreast of the house. The tone of his senseless revilings, mingled with bursts of laughter, was sometimes piercingly shrill and sometimes grave. It was all very mad; but I felt it incumbent upon my dignity to check my horse to a walk without even glancing towards the house, as if that man's abusive clamour in the porch were less than the barking of a cur. I rode by preserving an expression of haughty indifference on my face.

"It was no doubt very dignified; but I should have done better if I had kept my eyes open. A military man in war time should never consider himself off duty; and especially so if the war is a revolutionary war, when the enemy is not at the door, but within your very house. At such times the heat of passionate

convictions passing into hatred, removes the restraints
of honour and humanity from many men and of delicacy
and fear from some women. These last, when once they
throw off the timidity and reserve of their sex, become
by the vivacity of their intelligence and the violence
of their merciless resentment more dangerous than so
many armed giants."

The General's voice rose, but his big hand stroked
his white beard twice with an effect of venerable calmness. "Si, Señores! Women are ready to rise to the
heights of devotion unattainable by us men, or to sink
into the depths of abasement which amazes our masculine prejudices. I am speaking now of exceptional
women, you understand. . . ."

Here one of the guests observed that he had never
met a woman yet who was not capable of turning out
quite exceptional under circumstances that would en-
gage her feelings strongly. "That sort of superiority
in recklessness they have over us," he concluded, " makes
of them the more interesting half of mankind."

The General, who bore the interruption with gravity,
nodded courteous assent. "Si. Si. Under circumstances. . . . Precisely. They can do an infinite deal
of mischief sometimes in quite unexpected ways. For
who could have imagined that a young girl, daughter
of a ruined Royalist whose life itself was held only by
the contempt of his enemies, would have had the power
to bring death and devastation upon two flourishing
provinces and cause serious anxiety to the leaders of
the revolution in the very hour of its success! " He
paused to let the wonder of it penetrate our minds.

"Death and devastation," somebody murmured in
surprise: " how shocking! "

The old General gave a glance in the direction of
the murmur and went on. "Yes. That is, war—
calamity. But the means by which she obtained the
power to work this havoc on our southern frontier seem
to me, who have seen her and spoken to her, still more
shocking. That particular thing left on my mind a
dreadful amazement which the further experience of life,

of more than fifty years, has done nothing to diminish."
He looked round as if to make sure of our attention,
and, in a changed voice : "I am, as you know, a republican, son of a Liberator," he declared. "My incom-
parable mother, God rest her soul, was a Frenchwoman,
the daughter of an ardent republican. As a boy I
fought for liberty ; I've always believed in the equality
of men ; and as to their brotherhood, that, to my
mind, is even more certain. Look at the fierce animosity they display in their differences. And what in
the world do you know that is more bitterly fierce than
brothers' quarrels ? "

All absence of cynicism checked an inclination to
smile at this view of human brotherhood. On the
contrary there was in the tone the melancholy natural
to a man profoundly humane at heart who from duty,
from conviction and from necessity, had played his
part in scenes of ruthless violence.

The General had seen much of fratricidal strife.
"Certainly. There is no doubt of their brotherhood,"
he insisted. "All men are brothers, and as such know
almost too much of each other. But "—and here in
the old patriarchal head, white as silver, the black eyes
humorously twinkled—"if we are all brothers, all the
women are not our sisters."

One of the younger guests was heard murmuring
his satisfaction at the fact. But the General continued,
with deliberate earnestness : "They are so different !
The tale of a king who took a beggar-maid for a partner
of his throne may be pretty enough as we men look
upon ourselves and upon love. But that a young girl,
famous for her haughty beauty and, only a short time
before, the admired of all at the balls in the Viceroy's
palace, should take by the hand a guasso, a common
peasant, is intolerable to our sentiment of women and
their love. It is madness. Nevertheless it happened.
But it must be said that in her case it was the madness
of hate—not of love."

After presenting this excuse in a spirit of chivalrous
justice, the General remained silent for a time. "I

rode past the house every day almost," he began again,
" and this was what was going on within. But how it
was going on no mind of man can conceive. Her
desperation must have been extreme, and Gaspar Ruiz
was a docile fellow. He had been an obedient soldier.
His strength was like an enormous stone lying on the
ground, ready to be hurled this way or that by the hand
that picks it up.

"It is clear that he would tell his story to the people
who gave him the shelter he needed. And he needed
assistance badly. His wound was not dangerous, but
his life was forfeited. The old Royalist being wrapped
up in his laughing madness, the two women arranged
a hiding-place for the wounded man in one of the huts
amongst the fruit trees at the back of the house. That
hovel, an abundance of clear water while the fever was
on him, and some words of pity were all they could give.
I suppose he had a share of what food there was. And
it would be but little : a handful of roasted corn, perhaps
a dish of beans, or a piece of bread with a few figs. To
such misery were those proud and once wealthy people
reduced."

VII

GENERAL SANTIERRA was right in his surmise. Such
was the exact nature of the assistance which Gaspar
Ruiz, peasant son of peasants, received from the
Royalist family whose daughter had opened the door of
their miserable refuge to his extreme distress. Her
sombre resolution ruled the madness of her father and
the trembling bewilderment of her mother.

She had asked the strange man on the doorstep,
" Who wounded you ? "

" The soldiers, señora," Gaspar Ruiz had answered,
in a faint voice.

" Patriots ? "

" Si."

" What for ? "

" Deserter," he gasped, leaning against the wall

under the scrutiny of her black eyes. "I was left for dead over there."

She led him through the house out to a small hut of clay and reeds, lost in the long grass of the overgrown orchard. He sank on a heap of maize straw in a corner, and sighed profoundly.

"No one will look for you here," she said, looking down at him. "Nobody comes near us. We too have been left for dead—here."

He stirred uneasily on his heap of dirty straw, and the pain in his neck made him groan deliriously.

"I shall show Estaban some day that I am alive yet," he mumbled.

He accepted her assistance in silence, and the many days of pain went by. Her appearances in the hut brought him relief and became connected with the feverish dreams of angels which visited his couch; for Gaspar Ruiz was instructed in the mysteries of his religion, and had even been taught to read and write a little by the priest of his village. He waited for her with impatience, and saw her pass out of the dark hut and disappear in the brilliant sunshine with poignant regret. He discovered that, while he lay there feeling so very weak, he could, by closing his eyes, evoke her face with considerable distinctness. And this discovered faculty charmed the long solitary hours of his convalescence. Later, when he began to regain his strength, he would creep at dusk from his hut to the house and sit on the step of the garden door.

In one of the rooms the mad father paced to and fro, muttering to himself with short abrupt laughs. In the passage, sitting on a stool, the mother sighed and moaned. The daughter, in rough threadbare clothing, and her white haggard face half hidden by a coarse manta, stood leaning against the lintel of the door. Gaspar Ruiz, with his elbows propped on his knees and his head resting in his hands, talked to the two women in an undertone.

The common misery of destitution would have made a bitter mockery of a marked insistence on social differ-

3

ences. Gaspar Ruiz understood this in his simplicity. From his captivity amongst the Royalists he could give them news of people they knew. He described their appearance; and when he related the story of the battle in which he was recaptured the two women lamented the blow to their cause and the ruin of their secret hopes.

He had no feeling either way. But he felt a great devotion for that young girl. In his desire to appear worthy of her condescension, he boasted a little of his bodily strength. He had nothing else to boast of. Because of that quality his comrades treated him with as great a deference, he explained, as though he had been a sergeant, both in camp and in battle.

"I could always get as many as I wanted to follow me anywhere, Señorita. I ought to have been made an officer, because I can read and write."

Behind him the silent old lady fetched a moaning sigh from time to time; the distracted father muttered to himself, pacing the sala; and Gaspar Ruiz would raise his eyes now and then to look at the daughter of these people.

He would look at her with curiosity because she was alive, and also with that feeling of familiarity and awe with which he had contemplated in churches the inanimate and powerful statues of the saints, whose protection is invoked in dangers and difficulties. His difficulty was very great.

He could not remain hiding in an orchard for ever and ever. He knew also very well that before he had gone half a day's journey in any direction, he would be picked up by one of the cavalry patrols scouring the country, and brought into one or another of the camps where the patriot army destined for the liberation of Peru was collected. There he would in the end be recognized as Gaspar Ruiz—the deserter to the Royalists —and no doubt shot very effectually this time. There did not seem any place in the world for the innocent Gaspar Ruiz anywhere. And at this thought his simple soul surrendered itself to gloom and resentment as black as night.

They had made him a soldier forcibly. He did not mind being a soldier. And he had been a good soldier as he had been a good son, because of his docility and his strength. But now there was no use for either. They had taken him from his parents, and he could no longer be a soldier—not a good soldier at any rate. Nobody would listen to his explanations. What injustice it was! What injustice!

And in a mournful murmur he would go over the story of his capture and recapture for the twentieth time. Then, raising his eyes to the silent girl in the doorway, " Si, Señorita," he would say with a deep sigh, "injustice has made this poor breath in my body quite worthless to me and to anybody else. And I do not care who robs me of it."

One evening, as he exhaled thus the plaint of his wounded soul, she condescended to say that, if she were a man, she would consider no life worthless which held the possibility of revenge.

She seemed to be speaking to herself. Her voice was low. He drank in the gentle, as if dreamy sound, with a consciousness of peculiar delight, of something warming his breast like a draught of generous wine.

"True, Señorita," he said, raising his face up to hers slowly : "there is Estaban, who must be shown that I am not dead after all."

The mutterings of the mad father had ceased long before ; the sighing mother had withdrawn somewhere into one of the empty rooms. All was still within as well as without, in the moonlight bright as day on the wild orchard full of inky shadows. Gaspar Ruiz saw the dark eyes of Doña Erminia look down at him.

"Ah! The sergeant," she muttered disdainfully.

"Why! He has wounded me with his sword," he protested, bewildered by the contempt that seemed to shine livid on her pale face.

She crushed him with her glance. The power of her will to be understood was so strong that it kindled in him the intelligence of unexpressed things.

"What else did you expect me to do ? " he cried, as

if suddenly driven to despair. "Have I the power to do
more ? Am I a general with an army at my back ?—
miserable sinner that I am to be despised by you at last."

VIII

"Señores," related the General to his guests, " though
my thoughts were of love then, and therefore enchanting,
the sight of that house always affected me disagreeably,
especially in the moonlight, when its close shutters and
its air of lonely neglect appeared sinister. Still I went
on using the bridle-path by the ravine, because it was
a short cut. The mad Royalist howled and laughed at
me every evening to his complete satisfaction ; but
after a time, as if wearied with my indifference, he ceased
to appear in the porch. How they persuaded him to
leave off I do not know. However, with Gaspar Ruiz
in the house there would have been no difficulty in
restraining him by force. It was now part of their policy
in there to avoid anything which could provoke me.
At least, so I suppose.

" Notwithstanding my infatuation with the brightest
pair of eyes in Chile, I noticed the absence of the old
man after a week or so. A few more days passed. I
began to think that perhaps these Royalists had gone
away somewhere else. But one evening, as I was
hastening towards the city, I saw again somebody in the
porch. It was not the madman ; it was the girl. She
stood holding on to one of the wooden columns, tall and
white-faced, her big eyes sunk deep with privation and
sorrow. I looked hard at her, and she met my stare
with a strange, inquisitive look. Then, as I turned my
head after riding past, she seemed to gather courage for
the act, and absolutely beckoned me back.

" I obeyed, señores, almost without thinking, so great
was my astonishment. It was greater still when I heard
what she had to say. She began by thanking me for
my forbearance of her father's infirmity, so that I felt
ashamed of myself. I had meant to show disdain, not

forbearance! Every word must have burnt her lips, but she never departed from a gentle and melancholy dignity which filled me with respect against my will. Señores, we are no match for women. But I could hardly believe my ears when she began her tale. Providence, she concluded, seemed to have preserved the life of that wronged soldier, who now trusted to my honour as a *caballero* and to my compassion for his sufferings.

" ' Wronged man,' I observed coldly. ' Well, I think so too : and you have been harbouring an enemy of your cause.'

" ' He was a poor Christian crying for help at our door in the name of God, señor,' she answered simply.

" I began to admire her. ' Where is he now ? ' I asked stiffly.

" But she would not answer that question. With extreme cunning, and an almost fiendish delicacy, she managed to remind me of my failure in saving the lives of the prisoners in the guard-room, without wounding my pride. She knew, of course, the whole story. Gaspar Ruiz, she said, entreated me to procure for him a safe-conduct from General San Martin himself. He had an important communication to make to the commander-in-chief.

" *Por Dios*, señores, she made me swallow all that, pretending to be only the mouthpiece of that poor man. Overcome by injustice, he expected to find, she said, as much generosity in me as had been shown to him by the Royalist family which had given him a refuge.

" Ha ! It was well and nobly said to a youngster like me. I thought her great. Alas! she was only implacable.

" In the end I rode away very enthusiastic about the business, without demanding even to see Gaspar Ruiz, who I was confident was in the house.

" But on calm reflection I began to see some difficulties which I had not confidence enough in myself to encounter. It was not easy to approach a commander-in-chief with such a story. I feared failure. At last I thought it better to lay the matter before my general-of-division, Robles, a friend of my family, who had appointed me his aide-de-camp lately.

"He took it out of my hands at once without any ceremony.

"'In the house! of course he is in the house,' he said contemptuously. 'You ought to have gone sword in hand inside and demanded his surrender, instead of chatting with a Royalist girl in the porch. Those people should have been hunted out of that long ago. Who knows how many spies they have harboured right in the very midst of our camps? A safe-conduct from the Commander-in-Chief! The audacity of the fellow! Ha! ha! Now we shall catch him to-night, and then we shall find out, without any safe-conduct, what he has got to say, that is so very important. Ha! ha! ha!'

"General Robles, peace to his soul, was a short, thick man, with round, staring eyes, fierce and jovial. Seeing my distress he added:

"'Come, come, *Chico*. I promise you his life if he does not resist. And that is not likely. We are not going to break up a good soldier if it can be helped. I tell you what! I am curious to see your strong man. Nothing but a general will do for the picaro—well, he shall have a general to talk to. Ha! ha! I shall go myself to the catching, and you are coming with me, of course.'

"And it was done that same night. Early in the evening the house and the orchard were surrounded quietly. Later on the general and I left a ball we were attending in town and rode out at an easy gallop. At some little distance from the house we pulled up. A mounted orderly held our horses. A low whistle warned the men watching all along the ravine, and we walked up to the porch softly. The barricaded house in the moonlight seemed empty.

"The general knocked at the door. After a time a woman's voice within asked who was there. My chief nudged me hard. I gasped.

"'It is I, Lieutenant Santierra,' I stammered out, as if choked. 'Open the door.'

"It came open slowly. The girl, holding a thin taper in her hand, seeing another man with me, began to back away before us slowly, shading the light with her hand. Her impassive white face looked ghostly. I followed behind General Robles. Her eyes were fixed on mine. I made a gesture of helplessness behind my chief's back, trying at the same time to give a reassuring expression to my face. Neither of us three uttered a sound.

"We found ourselves in a room with bare floor and walls. There was a rough table and a couple of stools in it, nothing else whatever. An old woman with her grey hair hanging loose wrung her hands when we appeared. A peal of loud laughter resounded through the empty house, very amazing and weird. At this the old woman tried to get past us.

"'Nobody to leave the room,' said General Robles to me.

"I swung the door to, heard the latch click, and the laughter became faint in our ears.

"Before another word could be spoken in that room I was amazed by hearing the sound of distant thunder.

"I had carried in with me into the house a vivid impression of a beautiful clear moonlight night, without a speck of cloud in the sky. I could not believe my ears. Sent early abroad for my education, I was not familiar with the most dreaded natural phenomenon of my native land. I saw, with inexpressible astonishment, a look of terror in my chief's eyes. Suddenly I felt giddy! The general staggered against me heavily; the girl seemed to reel in the middle of the room, the taper fell out of her hand and the light went out; a shrill cry of 'Misericordia!' from the old woman pierced my ears. In the pitchy darkness I heard the plaster off the walls falling on the floor. It is a mercy there was no ceiling. Holding on to the latch of the door, I heard the grinding of the roof-tiles cease above my head. The shock was over.

"'Out of the house! The door! Fly, Santierra, fly!'

howled the general. You know, señores, in our country the bravest are not ashamed of the fear an earthquake strikes into all the senses of man. One never gets used to it. Repeated experience only augments the mastery of that nameless terror.

"It was my first earthquake, and I was the calmest of them all. I understood that the crash outside was caused by the porch, with its wooden pillars and tiled roof projection, falling down. The next shock would destroy the house, maybe. That rumble as of thunder was approaching again. The general was rushing round the room, to find the door perhaps. He made a noise as though he were trying to climb the walls, and I heard him distinctly invoke the names of several saints. 'Out, out, San tierra!' he yelled.

"The girl's voice was the only one I did not hear.

"'General,' I cried, 'I cannot move the door. We must be locked in.'

"I did not recognize his voice in the shout of malediction and despair he let out. Señores, I know many men in my country, especially in the provinces most subject to earthquakes, who will neither eat, sleep, pray, nor even sit down to cards with closed doors. The danger is not in the loss of time, but in this—that the movement of the walls may prevent a door being opened at all. This was what had happened to us. We were trapped, and we had no help to expect from anybody. There is no man in my country who will go into a house when the earth trembles. There never was—except one: Gaspar Ruiz.

"He had come out of whatever hole he had been hiding in outside, and had clambered over the timbers of the destroyed porch. Above the awful subterranean groan of coming destruction I heard a mighty voice shouting the word 'Erminia!' with the lungs of a giant. An earthquake is a great leveller of distinctions. I collected all my resolution against the terror of the scene. 'She is here,' I shouted back. A roar as of a furious wild beast answered me—while my head swam, my heart sank, and the sweat of anguish streamed like rain off my brow.

"He had the strength to pick up one of the heavy posts of the porch. Holding it under his armpit like a lance, but with both hands, he charged madly the rocking house with the force of a battering-ram, bursting open the door and rushing in, headlong, over our prostrate bodies. I and the general picking ourselves up, bolted out together, without looking round once till we got across the road. Then, clinging to each other, we beheld the house change suddenly into a heap of formless rubbish behind the back of a man, who staggered towards us bearing the form of a woman clasped in his arms. Her long black hair hung nearly to his feet. He laid her down reverently on the heaving earth, and the moonlight shone on her closed eyes.

"Señores, we mounted with difficulty. Our horses getting up plunged madly, held by the soldiers who had come running from all sides. Nobody thought of catching Gaspar Ruiz then. The eyes of men and animals shone with wild fear. My general approached Gaspar Ruiz, who stood motionless as a statue above the girl. He let himself be shaken by the shoulder without detaching his eyes from her face.

"'*Que guape!*' shouted the general in his ear. 'You are the bravest man living. You have saved my life. I am General Robles. Come to my quarters to-morrow, if God gives us the grace to see another day.'

"He never stirred—as if deaf, without feeling, insensible.

"We rode away for the town, full of our relations, of our friends, of whose fate we hardly dared to think. The soldiers ran by the side of our horses. Everything was forgotten in the immensity of the catastrophe overtaking a whole country."

. . . .

Gaspar Ruiz saw the girl open her eyes. The raising of her eyelids seemed to recall him from a trance. They were alone ; the cries of terror and distress from homeless people filled the plains of the coast remote and immense, coming like a whisper into their loneliness.

She rose swiftly to her feet, darting fearful glances on all sides. "What is it ?" she cried out low, and peering into his face. "Where am I ?"

He bowed his head sadly, without a word.

". . . Who are you ?"

He knelt down slowly before her, and touched the hem of her coarse black baize skirt. "Your slave," he said.

She caught sight then of the heap of rubbish that had been the house, all misty in the cloud of dust. "Ah !" she cried, pressing her hand to her forehead.

"I carried you out from there," he whispered at her feet.

"And they ?" she asked in a great sob.

He rose, and taking her by the arms, led her gently towards the shapeless ruin half overwhelmed by a landslide. "Come and listen," he said.

The serene moon saw them clambering over that heap of stones, joists and tiles, which was a grave. They pressed their ears to the interstices, listening for the sound of a groan, for a sigh of pain.

At last he said, "They died swiftly. You are alone."

She sat down on a piece of broken timber and put one arm across her face. He waited—then approaching his lips to her ear. "Let us go," he whispered.

"Never—never from here," she cried out, flinging her arms above her head.

He stooped over her, and her raised arms fell upon his shoulders. He lifted her up, steadied himself and began to walk, looking straight before him.

"What are you doing ?" she asked feebly.

"I am escaping from my enemies," he said, never once glancing at his light burden.

"With me ?" she sighed helplessly.

"Never without you," he said. "You are my strength."

He pressed her close to him. His face was grave and his footsteps steady. The conflagrations bursting out in

the ruins of destroyed villages dotted the plain with red
fires ; and the sounds of distant lamentations, the cries
of Misericordia ! Misericordia ! made a desolate murmur
in his ears. He walked on, solemn and collected, as if
carrying something holy, fragile and precious.

The earth rocked at times under his feet.

IX

WITH movements of mechanical care and an air of ab-
straction old General Santierra lighted a long and thick
cigar.

"It was a good many hours before we could send a
party back to the ravine," he said to his guests. "We
had found one-third of the town laid low, the rest shaken
up ; and the inhabitants, rich and poor, reduced to the
same state of distraction by the universal disaster. The
affected cheerfulness of some contrasted with the despair
of others. In the general confusion a number of reckless thieves, without fear of God or man, became a danger
to those who from the downfall of their homes had managed to save some valuables. Crying 'Misericordia'
louder than any at every tremor, and beating their breasts
with one hand, these scoundrels robbed the poor victims
with the other, not even stopping short of murder.

"General Robles' division was occupied entirely in
guarding the destroyed quarters of the town from the
depredations of these inhuman monsters. Taken up
with my duties of orderly officer, it was only in the
morning that I could assure myself of the safety of my
own family. My mother and my sisters had escaped
with their lives from that ball-room, where I had left
them early in the evening. I remember those two
beautiful young women—God rest their souls—as if I
saw them this moment, in the garden of our destroyed
house, pale but active, assisting some of our poor neighbours, in their soiled ball-dresses and with the dust of
fallen walls on their hair. As to my mother, she had a
stoical soul in her frail body. Half-covered by a costly
shawl, she was lying on a rustic seat by the side of an

ornamental basin whose fountain had ceased to play for ever on that night.

"I had hardly had time to embrace them all with transports of joy when my chief, coming along, dispatched me to the ravine with a few soldiers, to bring in my strong man, as he called him, and that pale girl.

"But there was no one for us to bring in. A landslide had covered the ruins of the house; and it was like a large mound of earth with only the ends of some timbers visible here and there—nothing more.

"Thus were the tribulations of the old Royalist couple ended. An enormous and unconsecrated grave had swallowed them up alive, in their unhappy obstinacy against the will of a people to be free. And their daughter was gone.

"That Gaspar Ruiz had carried her off I understood very well. But as the case was not foreseen, I had no instructions to pursue them. And certainly I had no desire to do so. I had grown mistrustful of my interference. It had never been successful, and had not even appeared creditable. He was gone. Well, let him go. And he had carried off the Royalist girl! Nothing better. *Vaya con Dios*. This was not the time to bother about a deserter who, justly or unjustly, ought to have been dead, and a girl for whom it would have been better to have never been born.

"So I marched my men back to the town.

"After a few days, order having been re-established, all the principal families, including my own, left for Santiago. We had a fine house there. At the same time the division of Robles was moved to new cantonments near the capital. This change suited very well the state of my domestic and amorous feelings.

"One night, rather late, I was called to my chief. I found General Robles in his quarters, at ease, with his uniform off, drinking neat brandy out of a tumbler—as a precaution, he used to say, against the sleeplessness induced by the bites of mosquitoes. He was a good soldier, and he taught me the art and practice of war. No doubt God has been merciful to his soul; for his motives were never other than patriotic, if his character was irascible. As to the use of mosquito nets, he considered it effeminate, shameful—unworthy of a soldier.

"I noticed at the first glance that his face, already very red, wore an expression of high good-humour.

"'Aha! *Señor teniente,*' he cried loudly, as I saluted at the door. 'Behold! Your strong man has turned up again.'

"He extended to me a folded letter, which I saw was superscribed 'To the Commander-in-Chief of the Republican Armies.'

"'This,' General Robles went on in his loud voice, 'was thrust by a boy into the hand of a sentry at the Quartel General, while the fellow stood there thinking of his girl, no doubt—for before he could gather his wits together the boy had disappeared amongst the market people, and he protests he could not recognize him to save his life.'

"My chief told me further that the soldier had given the letter to the sergeant of the guard, and that ultimately it had reached the hands of our generalissimo. His Excellency had deigned to take cognisance of it with his own eyes. After that he had referred the matter in confidence to General Robles.

"The letter, señores, I cannot now recollect textually. I saw the signature of Gaspar Ruiz. He was an audacious fellow. He had snatched a soul for himself out of a cataclysm, remember. And now it was that soul which had dictated the terms of his letter. Its tone was very independent. I remember it struck me at the time as noble—dignified. It was, no doubt, her letter. Now I shudder at the depth of its duplicity. Gaspar Ruiz was made to complain of the injustice of which he had been a victim. He invoked his previous record of fidelity and courage. Having been saved from death by the miraculous interposition of Providence, he could think of nothing but of retrieving his character. This, he wrote, he could not hope to do in the ranks as a discredited soldier still under suspicion. He had the means to give a striking proof of his fidelity. And he ended by proposing to the General-in-Chief a meeting at midnight in the middle of the Plaza before the Moneta. The signal would be to strike fire with flint and steel three times, which was not too conspicuous and yet distinctive enough for recognition.

"San Martin, the great Liberator, loved men of audacity and courage. Besides, he was just and compassionate. I told him as much of the man's story as I knew, and was ordered to accompany him on the appointed night. The signals were duly exchanged. It was midnight, and the whole town was dark and silent. Their two cloaked figures came together in the centre of the vast Plaza, and, keeping discreetly at a distance, I listened for an hour or more to the murmur of their voices. Then the general motioned me to approach; and as I did so I heard San Martin, who was courteous to gentle and simple alike, offer Gaspar Ruiz the hospitality of the headquarters for the night. But the soldier refused, saying that he would not be worthy of that honour till he had done something.

" ' You cannot have a common deserter for your guest, Excellency,' he protested with a low laugh, and stepping backwards merged slowly into the night.

"The Commander-in-Chief observed to me, as we turned away : ' He had somebody with him, our friend Ruiz. I saw two figures for a moment. It was an unobtrusive companion.'

"I too had observed another figure join the vanishing form of Gaspar Ruiz. It had the appearance of a short fellow in a poncho and a big hat. And I wondered stupidly who it could be he had dared take into his confidence. I might have guessed it could be no one but that fatal girl—alas !

"Where he kept her concealed I do not know. He had—it was known afterwards—an uncle, his mother's brother, a small shopkeeper in Santiago. Perhaps it was there that she found a roof and food. Whatever she found, it was poor enough to exasperate her pride and keep up her anger and hate. It is certain she did not accompany him on the feat he undertook to accomplish first of all. It was nothing less than the destruction of a store of war material collected secretly by the Spanish authorities in the south, in a town called Linares. Gaspar Ruiz was entrusted with a small party only, but they proved themselves worthy of San Martin's confidence. The season was not propitious. They had to swim swollen rivers. They seemed, however, to have galloped night and day, outriding the news of their foray, and holding straight for the town, a hundred miles into the enemy's country, till at break of day they rode into it sword in hand, surprising the little garrison. It fled without making a stand, leaving most of its officers in Gaspar Ruiz' hands.

"A great explosion of gunpowder ended the conflagration of the magazines the raiders had set on fire without loss of time. In less than six hours they were riding away at the same mad speed, without the loss of a single man. Good as they were, such an exploit is not performed without a still better leadership.

"I was dining at the headquarters when Gaspar Ruiz himself brought the news of his success. And it was a great blow to the Royalist troops. For a proof he displayed to us the garrison's flag. He took it from under his poncho and flung it on the table. The man was transfigured ; there was something exulting and menacing in the expression of his face. He stood behind General San Martin's chair and looked proudly at us all. He had a round blue cap edged with silver braid on his head, and we all could see a large white scar on the nape of his sunburnt neck.

"Somebody asked him what he had done with the captured Spanish officers.

"He shrugged his shoulders scornfully. 'What a question to ask ! In a partisan war you do not burden yourself with prisoners. I let them go—and here are their sword-knots.'

"He flung a bunch of them on the table upon the flag. Then General Robles, whom I was attending there, spoke up in his loud, thick voice : 'You did ! Then, my brave friend, you do not know yet how a war like ours

ought to be conducted. You should have done—this.'
And he passed the edge of his hand across his own throat.

"Alas, señores! It was only too true that on both
sides this contest, in its nature so heroic, was stained by
ferocity. The murmurs that arose at General Robles'
words were by no means unanimous in tone. But the
generous and brave San Martin praised the humane
action, and pointed out to Ruiz a place on his right
hand. Then rising with a full glass he proposed a
toast : 'Caballeros and comrades-in-arms, let us drink
the health of Captain Gaspar Ruiz.' And when we had
emptied our glasses : 'I intend,' the Commander-in-
Chief continued, 'to entrust him with the guardianship
of our southern frontier, while we go afar to liberate our
brethren in Peru. He whom the enemy could not stop
from striking a blow at his very heart will know how to
protect the peaceful populations we leave behind us to
pursue our sacred task.' And he embraced the silent
Gaspar Ruiz by his side.

"Later on, when we all rose from table, I approached
the latest officer of the army with my congratulations.
'And, Captain Ruiz,' I added, 'perhaps you do not mind
telling a man who has always believed in the upright-
ness of your character what became of Doña Erminia on
that night ? '

"At this friendly question his aspect changed. He
looked at me from under his eyebrows with the heavy,
bull glance of a guasso—of a peasant. '*Senor teniente*,'
he said thickly, and as if very much cast down, 'do not
ask me about the señorita, for I prefer not to think about
her at all when I am amongst you.'

"He looked, with a frown, all about the room, full of
smoking and talking officers. Of course I did not insist.

"These, señores, were the last words I was to hear him
utter for a long, long time. The very next day we em-
barked for our arduous expedition to Peru, and we only
heard of Gaspar Ruiz' doings in the midst of battles of
our own. He had been appointed military guardian of
our southern province. He raised a *partida*. But his
leniency to the conquered foe displeased the Civil

Governor, who was a formal, uneasy man, full of suspicions. He forwarded reports against Gaspar Ruiz to the Supreme Government; one of them being that he had married publicly, with great pomp, a woman of Royalist tendencies. Quarrels were sure to arise between these two men of very different character. At last the Civil Governor began to complain of his inactivity, and to hint at treachery, which, he wrote, would be not surprising in a man of such antecedents. Gaspar Ruiz heard of it. His rage flamed up, and the woman ever by his side knew how to feed it with perfidious words. I do not know whether really the Supreme Government ever did—as he complained afterwards—send orders for his arrest. It seems certain that the Civil Governor began to tamper with his officers, and that Gaspar Ruiz discovered the fact.

"One evening, when the Governor was giving a *tertullia*, Gaspar Ruiz, followed by six men he could trust, appeared riding through the town to the door of the Government House, and entered the sala armed, his hat on his head. As the Governor, displeased, advanced to meet him, he seized the wretched man round the body, carried him off from the midst of the appalled guests, as though he were a child, and flung him down the outer steps into the street. An angry hug from Gaspar Ruiz was enough to crush the life out of a giant; but in addition Gaspar Ruiz' horsemen fired their pistols at the body of the Governor as it lay motionless at the bottom of the stairs.

X

"AFTER this—as he called it—act of justice, Ruiz crossed the Rio Blanco, followed by the greater part of his band, and entrenched himself upon a hill. A company of regular troops sent out foolishly against him was surrounded, and destroyed almost to a man. Other expeditions, though better organized, were equally unsuccessful.

"It was during these sanguinary skirmishes that his

4

wife first began to appear on horseback at his right hand. Rendered proud and self-confident by his successes, Ruiz no longer charged at the head of his *partida*, but presumptuously, like a general directing the movements of an army, he remained in the rear, well mounted and motionless on an eminence, sending out his orders. She was seen repeatedly at his side, and for a long time was mistaken for a man. There was much talk then of a mysterious white-faced chief, to whom the defeats of our troops were ascribed. She rode like an Indian woman, astride, wearing a broad-rimmed man's hat and a dark poncho. Afterwards, in the day of their greatest prosperity, this poncho was embroidered in gold, and she wore then, also, the sword of poor Don Antonio de Leyva. This veteran Chilian officer, having the misfortune to be surrounded with his small force, and running short of ammunition, found his death at the hands of the Arauco Indians, the allies and auxiliaries of Gaspar Ruiz. This was the fatal affair long remembered afterwards as the 'Massacre of the Island.' The sword of the unhappy officer was presented to her by Peneleo, the Araucanian chief; for these Indians, struck by her aspect, the deathly pallor of her face, which no exposure to the weather seemed to affect, and her calm indifference under fire, looked upon her as a supernatural being, or at least as a witch. By this superstition the prestige and authority of Gaspar Ruiz amongst these ignorant people were greatly augmented. She must have savoured her vengeance to the full on that day when she buckled on the sword of Don Antonio de Leyva. It never left her side, unless she put on her woman's clothes—not that she would or could ever use it, but she loved to feel it beating upon her thigh as a perpetual reminder and symbol of the dishonour to the arms of the Republic. She was insatiable. Moreover, on the path she had led Gaspar Ruiz upon, there is no stopping Escaped prisoners—and they were not many—used to relate how with a few whispered words she could change the expression of his face and revive his flagging animosity. They told how after every skirmish, after every raid, after every successful action, he would ride up to her and look into her face. Its haughty calm was never relaxed. Her embrace, señores, must have been as cold as the embrace of a statue. He tried to melt her icy heart in a stream of warm blood. Some English naval officers who visited him at that time noticed the strange character of his infatuation."

At the movement of surprise and curiosity in his audience General Santierra paused for a moment.

"Yes—English naval officers," he repeated. "Ruiz had consented to receive them to arrange for the liberation of some prisoners of your nationality. In the territory upon which he ranged, from sea coast to the Cordillera, there was a bay where the ships of that time, after rounding Cape Horn, used to resort for wood and water. There, decoying the crew on shore, he captured first the whaling brig *Hersalia*, and afterwards made himself master by surprise of two more ships, one English and one American.

"It was rumoured at the time that he dreamed of setting up a navy of his own. But that, of course, was impossible. Still, manning the brig with part of her own crew, and putting an officer and a good many men of his own on board, he sent her off to the Spanish Governor of the island of Chiloe with a report of his exploits, and a demand for assistance in the war against the rebels. The Governor could not do much for him; but he sent in return two light field-pieces, a letter of compliments, with a colonel's commission in the royal forces, and a great Spanish flag. This standard with much ceremony was hoisted over his house in the heart of the Arauco country. Surely on that day she may have smiled on her guasso husband with a less haughty reserve.

"The senior officer of the English squadron on our coast made representations to our Government as to these captures. But Gaspar Ruiz refused to treat with us. Then an English frigate proceeded to the bay, and her captain, doctor, and two lieutenants travelled inland under a safe-conduct. They were well received, and

spent three days as guests of the partisan chief. A sort
of military barbaric state was kept up at the residence.
It was furnished with the loot of frontier towns. When
first admitted to the principal sala, they saw his wife
lying down (she was not in good health then), with
Gaspar Ruiz sitting at the foot of the couch. His hat
was lying on the floor, and his hands reposed on the
hilt of his sword.

" During that first conversation he never removed his
big hands from the sword-hilt, except once, to arrange
the coverings about her, with gentle, careful touches.
They noticed that whenever she spoke he would fix his
eyes upon her in a kind of expectant, breathless attention, and seemingly forget the existence of the world and
his own existence too. In the course of the farewell
banquet, at which she was present reclining on her couch,
he burst forth into complaints of the treatment he had
received. After General San Martin's departure he had
been beset by spies, slandered by civil officials, his
services ignored, his liberty and even his life threatened
by the Chilian Government. He got up from the table,
thundered execrations pacing the room wildly, then sat
down on the couch at his wife's feet, his breast heaving,
his eyes fixed on the floor. She reclined on her back,
her head on the cushions, her eyes nearly closed.

" ' And now I am an honoured Spanish officer,' he
added in a calm voice.

" The captain of the English frigate then took the
opportunity to inform him gently that Lima had fallen,
and that by the terms of a convention the Spaniards
were withdrawing from the whole continent.

" Gaspar Ruiz raised his head, and without hesitation,
speaking with suppressed vehemence, declared that if not
a single Spanish soldier were left in the whole of South
America he would persist in carrying on the contest
against Chile to the last drop of blood. When he finished
that mad tirade his wife's long white hand was raised,
and she just caressed his knee with the tips of her fingers
for a fraction of a second.

" For the rest of the officers' stay, which did not

extend for more than half an hour after the banquet, that
ferocious chieftain of a desperate *partida* overflowed with
amiability and kindness.   He had been hospitable before,
but now it seemed as though he could not do enough
for the comfort and safety of his visitors' journey back
to their ship.

"Nothing, I have been told, could have presented a
greater contrast to his late violence or the habitual
taciturn reserve of his manner.   Like a man elated
beyond measure by an unexpected happiness, he overflowed with good-will, amiability, and attentions.   He
embraced the officers like brothers, almost with tears in
his eyes.   The released prisoners were presented each
with a piece of gold.   At the last moment, suddenly, he
declared he could do no less than restore to the masters
of the merchant vessels all their private property.   This
unexpected generosity caused some delay in the departure
of the party, and their first march was very short.

"Late in the evening Gaspar Ruiz rode up with an
escort, to their camp fires, bringing along with him a mule
loaded with cases of wine.   He had come, he said, to drink
a stirrup cup with his English friends, whom he would
never see again.   He was mellow and joyous in his temper.   He told stories of his own exploits, laughed like
a boy, borrowed a guitar from the Englishmen's chief
muleteer, and sitting cross-legged on his superfine poncho
spread before the glow of the embers, sang a guasso
love-song in a tender voice.   Then his head dropped on
his breast, his hands fell to the ground ; the guitar rolled
off his knees—and a great hush fell over the camp after
the love-song of the implacable partisan who had made
so many of our people weep for destroyed homes and for
loves cut short.

"Before anybody could make a sound he sprang up
from the ground and called for his horse.

"'Adios, my friends ! ' he cried.   'Go with God.   I
love you.   And tell them well in Santiago that between
Gaspar Ruiz, colonel of the King of Spain, and the
republican carrion-crows of Chile there is war to the last
breath—war ! war ! war ! '

"With a great yell of 'War! war! war!' which his escort took up, they rode away, and the sound of hoofs and of voices died out in the distance between the slopes of the hills.

"The two young English officers were convinced that Ruiz was mad. How do you say that ?—tile loose—eh ? But the doctor, an observant Scotsman with much shrewdness and philosophy in his character, told me that it was a very curious case of possession. I met him many years afterwards, but he remembered the experience very well. He told me too that in his opinion that woman did not lead Gaspar Ruiz into the practice of sanguinary treachery by direct persuasion, but by the subtle way of awakening and keeping alive in his simple mind a burning sense of an irreparable wrong. Maybe, maybe. But I would say that she poured half of her vengeful soul into the strong clay of that man, as you may pour intoxication, madness, poison into an empty cup.

"If he wanted war he got it in earnest when our victorious army began to return from Peru. Systematic operations were planned against this blot on the honour and prosperity of our hardly-won independence. General Robles commanded, with his well-known ruthless severity. Savage reprisals were exercised on both sides, and no quarter was given in the field. Having won my promotion in the Peru campaign, I was a captain on the staff.

"Gaspar Ruiz found himself hard pressed ; at the same time we heard by means of a fugitive priest who had been carried off from his village presbytery, and galloped eighty miles into the hills to perform the christening ceremony, that a daughter was born to them. To celebrate the event, I suppose, Ruiz executed one or two brilliant forays clear away at the rear of our forces, and defeated the detachments sent out to cut off his retreat. General Robles nearly had a stroke of apoplexy from rage. He found another cause of insomnia than the bites of mosquitoes ; but against this one, señores, tumblers of raw brandy had no more effect than so much water.

He took to railing and storming at me about my strong
man. And from our impatience to end this inglorious
campaign I am afraid that we young officers became
reckless and apt to take undue risks on service.

"Nevertheless, slowly, inch by inch as it were, our
columns were closing upon Gaspar Ruiz, though he had
managed to raise all the Araucanian nation of wild
Indians against us. Then a year or more later our
Government became aware through its agents and spies
that he had actually entered into alliance with Carreras,
the so-called dictator of the so-called republic of Mendoza,
on the other side of the mountains. Whether Gaspar
Ruiz had a deep political intention, or whether he wished
only to secure a safe retreat for his wife and child while
he pursued remorselessly against us his war of surprises
and massacres, I cannot tell. The alliance, however, was
a fact. Defeated in his attempt to check our advance
from the sea, he retreated with his usual swiftness, and
preparing for another hard and hazardous tussle, began
by sending his wife with the little girl across the Pequeña
range of mountains, on the frontier of Mendoza.

XI

"Now Carreras, under the guise of politics and liberal-
ism, was a scoundrel of the deepest dye, and the unhappy
state of Mendoza was the prey of thieves, robbers,
traitors and murderers, who formed his party. He was
under a noble exterior a man without heart, pity, honour,
or conscience. He aspired to nothing but tyranny, and
though he would have made use of Gaspar Ruiz for his
nefarious designs, yet he soon became aware that to
propitiate the Chilian Government would answer his
purpose better. I blush to say that he made proposals
to our Government to deliver up on certain conditions
the wife and child of the man who had trusted to his
honour, and that this offer was accepted.

"While on her way to Mendoza over the Pequeña
Pass she was betrayed by her escort of Carreras' men,
and given up to the officer in command of a Chilian fort

on the upland at the foot of the main Cordillera range. This atrocious transaction might have cost me dear, for as a matter of fact I was a prisoner in Gaspar Ruiz' camp when he received the news. I had been captured during a reconnaissance, my escort of a few troopers being speared by the Indians of his bodyguard. I was saved from the same fate because he recognized my features just in time. No doubt my friends thought I was dead, and I would not have given much for my life at any time. But the strong man treated me very well, because, he said, I had always believed in his innocence and had tried to serve him when he was a victim of injustice.

"'And now,' was his speech to me, 'you shall see that I always speak the truth. You are safe.'

"I did not think I was very safe when I was called up to go to him one night. He paced up and down like a wild beast, exclaiming, 'Betrayed! Betrayed!'

"He walked up to me clenching his fists. 'I could cut your throat.'

"'Will that give your wife back to you?' I said as quietly as I could.

"'And the child!' he yelled out, as if mad. He fell into a chair and laughed in a frightful, boisterous manner. 'Oh, no, you are safe.'

"I assured him that his wife's life was safe too; but I did not say what I was convinced of—that he would never see her again. He wanted war to the death, and the war could only end with his death.

"He gave me a strange, inexplicable look, and sat muttering blankly, 'In their hands. In their hands.'

"I kept as still as a mouse before a cat.

"Suddenly he jumped up. 'What am I doing here?' he cried; and opening the door, he yelled out orders to saddle and mount. 'What is it?' he stammered, coming up to me. 'The Pequeña fort; a fort of palisades! Nothing. I would get her back if she were hidden in the very heart of the mountain.' He amazed me by adding, with an effort: 'I carried her off in my two arms while the earth trembled. And the child at least is mine. She at least is mine!'

"Those were bizarre words; but I had no time for wonder.

"'You shall go with me,' he said violently. 'I may want to parley, and any other messenger from Ruiz, the outlaw, would have his throat cut.'

"This was true enough. Between him and the rest of incensed mankind there could be no communication, according to the customs of honourable warfare.

"In less than half an hour we were in the saddle, flying wildly through the night. He had only an escort of twenty men at his quarters, but would not wait for more. He sent, however, messengers to Pencleo, the Indian chief then ranging in the foothills, directing him to bring his warriors to the uplands and meet him at the lake called the Eye of Water, near whose shores the frontier fort of Pequeña was built.

"We crossed the lowlands with that untired rapidity of movement which had made Gaspar Ruiz' raids so famous. We followed the lower valleys up to their precipitous heads. The ride was not without its dangers. A cornice road on a perpendicular wall of basalt wound itself around a buttressing rock, and at last we emerged from the gloom of a deep gorge upon the upland of Pequeña.

"It was a plain of green wiry grass and thin flowering bushes; but high above our heads patches of snow hung in the folds and crevices of the great walls of rock. The little lake was as round as a staring eye. The garrison of the fort were just driving in their small herd of cattle when we appeared. Then the great wooden gates swung to, and that four-square enclosure of broad blackened stakes pointed at the top and barely hiding the grass roofs of the huts inside seemed deserted, empty, without a single soul.

"But when summoned to surrender, by a man who at Gaspar Ruiz' order rode fearlessly forward, those inside answered by a volley which rolled him and his horse over. I heard Ruiz by my side grind his teeth. 'It does not matter,' he said. 'Now you go.'

"Torn and faded as its rags were, the vestiges of my uniform were recognized, and I was allowed to approach within speaking distance; and then I had to wait, because a voice clamouring through a loophole with joy and astonishment would not allow me to place a word. It was the voice of Major Pajol, an old friend. He, like my other comrades, had thought me killed a long time ago.

"'Put spurs to your horse, man!' he yelled, in the greatest excitement; 'we will swing the gate open for you.'

"I let the reins fall out of my hand and shook my head. 'I am on my honour,' I cried.

"'To him!' he shouted, with infinite disgust.

"'He promises you your life.'

"'Our life is our own. And do you, Santierra, advise us to surrender to that *rastrero*?'

"'No!' I shouted. 'But he wants his wife and child, and he can cut you off from water.'

"'Then she would be the first to suffer. You may tell him that. Look here—this is all nonsense: we shall dash out and capture you.'

"'You shall not catch me alive,' I said firmly.

"'Imbecile!'

"'For God's sake,' I continued hastily, 'do not open the gate.' And I pointed at the multitude of Peneleo's Indians who covered the shores of the lake.

"I had never seen so many of these savages together. Their lances seemed as numerous as stalks of grass. Their hoarse voices made a vast, inarticulate sound like the murmur of the sea.

"My friend Pajol was swearing to himself. 'Well, then—go to the devil!' he shouted, exasperated. But as I swung round he repented, for I heard him say hurriedly, 'Shoot the fool's horse before he gets away.'

"He had good marksmen. Two shots rang out, and in the very act of turning my horse staggered, fell and lay still as if struck by lightning. I had my feet out of the stirrups and rolled clear of him; but I did

not attempt to rise. Neither dared they rush out to
drag me in.

"The masses of Indians had begun to move upon the
fort. They rode up in squadrons, trailing their long
chusos ; then dismounted out of musket-shot, and, throwing off their fur mantles, advanced naked to the attack,
stamping their feet and shouting in cadence. A sheet
of flame ran three times along the face of the fort without
checking their steady march. They crowded right up
to the very stakes, flourishing their broad knives.
But this palisade was not fastened together with hide
lashings in the usual way, but with long iron nails,
which they could not cut. Dismayed at the failure of
their usual method of forcing an entrance, the heathen,
who had marched so steadily against the musketry
fire, broke and fled under the volleys of the besieged.

"Directly they had passed me on their advance I
got up and rejoined Gaspar Ruiz on a low ridge which
jutted out upon the plain. The musketry of his own
men had covered the attack, but now at a sign from
him a trumpet sounded the 'Cease fire.' Together
we looked in silence at the hopeless rout of the savages.

"'It must be a siege, then,' he muttered. And I
detected him wringing his hands stealthily.

"But what sort of siege could it be ? Without any
need for me to repeat my friend Pajol's message, he
dared not cut the water off from the besieged. They
had plenty of meat. And, indeed, if they had been short,
he would have been too anxious to send food into the
stockade had he been able. But, as a matter of fact, it
was we on the plain who were beginning to feel the pinch
of hunger.

"Peneleo, the Indian chief, sat by our fire folded in
his ample mantle of guanaco skins. He was an athletic
savage, with an enormous square shock head of hair resembling a straw beehive in shape and size, and with
grave, surly, much-lined features. In his broken Spanish
he repeated, growling like a bad-tempered wild beast, that
if an opening ever so small were made in the stockade

his men would march in and get the señora—not otherwise.

" Gaspar Ruiz, sitting opposite him, kept his eyes fixed on the fort night and day as it were, in awful silence and immobility. Meantime, by runners from the lowlands that arrived nearly every day, we heard of the defeat of one of his lieutenants in the Maipu valley. Scouts sent afar brought news of a column of infantry advancing through distant passes to the relief of the fort. They were slow, but we could trace their toilful progress up the lower valleys. I wondered why Ruiz did not march to attack and destroy this threatening force, in some wild gorge fit for an ambuscade, in accordance with his genius for guerilla warfare. But his genius seemed to have abandoned him to his despair.

" It was obvious to me that he could not tear himself away from the sight of the fort. I protest to you, señores, that I was moved almost to pity by the sight of this powerless strong man sitting on the ridge, indifferent to sun, to rain, to cold, to wind ; with his hands clasped round his legs and his chin resting on his knees, gazing —gazing—gazing.

" And the fort he kept his eyes fastened on was as still and silent as himself. The garrison gave no sign of life. They did not even answer the desultory fire directed at the loopholes.

" One night, as I strolled past him, he, without changing his attitude, spoke to me unexpectedly. 'I have sent for a gun,' he said. ' I shall have time to get her back and retreat before your Robles manages to crawl up here.'

" He had sent for a gun to the plains.

" It was long in coming, but at last it came. It was a seven-pounder field-gun. Dismounted and lashed crosswise to two long poles, it had been carried up the narrow paths between two mules with ease. His wild cry of exultation at daybreak when he saw the gun escort emerge from the valley rings in my ears now.

" But, señores, I have no words to depict his amazement, his fury, his despair and distraction, when he heard that the animal loaded with the gun-carriage had, during the last night march, somehow or other tumbled down a precipice. He broke into menaces of death and torture against the escort. I kept out of his way all that day, lying behind some bushes, and wondering what he would do now. Retreat was left for him; but he could not retreat.

"I saw below me his artillerist, Jorge, an old Spanish soldier, building up a sort of structure with heaped-up saddles. The gun, ready loaded, was lifted on to that, but in the act of firing the whole thing collapsed and the shot flew high above the stockade.

"Nothing more was attempted. One of the ammunition mules had been lost too, and they had no more than six shots to fire; amply enough to batter down the gate providing the gun was well laid. This was impossible without it being properly mounted. There was no time nor means to construct a carriage. Already every moment I expected to hear Robles' bugle-calls echo amongst the crags.

"Penelco, wandering about uneasily, draped in his skins, sat down for a moment near me growling his usual tale.

"'Make an *entrada*—a hole. If make a hole, *bueno*. If not make a hole, them vamos—we must go away.'

"After sunset I observed with surprise the Indians making preparations as if for another assault. Their lines stood ranged in the shadows of the mountains. On the plain in front of the fort gate I saw a group of men swaying about in the same place.

"I walked down the ridge disregarded. The moonlight in the clear air of the uplands was as bright as day, but the intense shadows confused my sight, and I could not make out what they were doing. I heard the voice of Jorge, the artillerist, say in a queer, doubtful tone, 'It is loaded, señors.'

"Then another voice in that group pronounced firmly the words, 'Bring the riata here.' It was the voice of Gaspar Ruiz.

"A silence fell, in which the popping shots of the

besieged garrison rang out sharply. They too had
observed the group. But the distance was too great
and in the spatter of spent musket-balls cutting up
the ground, the group opened, closed, swayed, giving me
a glimpse of busy stooping figures in its midst. I drew
nearer, doubting whether this was a weird vision, a
suggestive and insensate dream.

"A strangely stifled voice commanded, 'Haul the
hitches tighter.'

"'*Si, señor*,' several other voices answered in tones
of awed alacrity.

"Then the stifled voice said: 'Like this. I must
be free to breathe.'

"Then there was a concerned noise of many men
together. 'Help him up, *hombres*. Steady! Under the
other arm.'

"That deadened voice ordered: '*Bueno*! Stand
away from me, men.'

"I pushed my way through the recoiling circle, and
heard once more that same oppressed voice saying
earnestly: 'Forget that I am a living man, Jorge. Forget me altogether, and think of what you have to do.'

"'Be without fear, señor. You are nothing to me
but a gun carriage, and I shall not waste a shot.'

"I heard the spluttering of a port-fire, and smelt the
saltpetre of the match. I saw suddenly before me a
nondescript shape on all fours like a beast, but with a
man's head drooping below a tubular projection over the
nape of the neck, and the gleam of a rounded mass of
bronze on its back.

"In front of a silent semicircle of men it squatted
alone with Jorge behind it and a trumpeter motionless,
his trumpet in his hand, by its side.

"Jorge, bent double, muttered, port-fire in hand:
'An inch to the left, señor. Too much. So. Now, if
you let yourself down a little by letting your elbows
bend, I will . . .'

"He leaped aside, lowering his port-fire, and a burst
of flame darted out of the muzzle of the gun lashed on the
man's back.

"Then Gaspar Ruiz lowered himself slowly. 'Good shot?' he asked.

"'Full on, señor.'

"'Then load again.'

"He lay there before me on his breast under the darkly glittering bronze of his monstrous burden, such as no love or strength of man had ever had to bear in the lamentable history of the world. His arms were spread out, and he resembled a prostrate penitent on the moonlit ground.

"Again I saw him raised to his hands and knees, and the men stand away from him, and old Jorge stoop, glancing along the gun.

"'Left a little. Right an inch. *Por Dios, señor,* stop this trembling. Where is your strength?'

"The old gunner's voice was cracked with emotion. He stepped aside, and quick as lightning brought the spark to the touch-hole.

"'Excellent!' he cried tearfully; but Gaspar Ruiz lay for a long time silent, flattened on the ground.

"'I am tired,' he murmured at last. 'Will another shot do it?'

"'Without doubt,' said Jorge, bending down to his ear.

"'Then—load,' I heard him utter distinctly. 'Trumpeter!'

"'I am here, señor, ready for your word.'

"'Blow a blast at this word that shall be heard from one end of Chile to the other,' he said, in an extraordinarily strong voice. 'And you others stand ready to cut this accursed riata, for then will be the time for me to lead you in your rush. Now raise me up, and, you, Jorge—be quick with your aim.'

"The rattle of musketry from the fort nearly drowned his voice. The palisade was wreathed in smoke and flame.

"'Exert your force forward against the recoil, *mi amo,*' said the old gunner shakily. 'Dig your fingers into the ground. So. Now!'

"A cry of exultation escaped him after the shot,

The trumpeter raised his trumpet nearly to his lips, and waited. But no word came from the prostrate man. I fell on one knee, and heard all he had to say then.

" 'Something broken,' he whispered, lifting his head a little, and turning his eyes towards me in his hopelessly crushed attitude.

" 'The gate hangs only by the splinters,' yelled Jorge.

"Gaspar Ruiz tried to speak, but his voice died out in his throat, and I helped to roll the gun off his broken back. He was insensible.

"I kept my lips shut, of course. The signal for the Indians to attack was never given. Instead, the bugle-calls of the relieving force, for which my ears had thirsted so long, burst out, terrifying like the call of the Last Day to our surprised enemies.

"A tornado, señores, a real hurricane of stampeded men, wild horses, mounted Indians, swept over me as I cowered on the ground by the side of Gaspar Ruiz, still stretched out on his face in the shape of a cross. Peneleo, galloping for life, jabbed at me with his long *chuso* in passing—for the sake of old acquaintance, I suppose. How I escaped the flying lead is more difficult to explain. Venturing to rise on my knees too soon, some soldiers of the 17th Taltal regiment, in their hurry to get at something alive, nearly bayonetted me on the spot. They looked very disappointed too when some officers galloping up drove them away with the flat of their swords.

"It was General Robles with his staff. He wanted badly to make some prisoners. He, too, seemed disappointed for a moment. 'What? Is it you?' he cried. But he dismounted at once to embrace me, for he was an old friend of my family. I pointed to the body at our feet, and said only these two words:

" 'Gaspar Ruiz.'

"He threw his arms up in astonishment.

" 'Aha! Your strong man! Always to the last with your strong man. No matter. He saved our lives when the earth trembled enough to make the bravest faint with fear. I was frightened out of my wits. But he—no! *Que guape!* Where's the hero who got the best of him? Ha! ha! ha! What killed him, *chico?*'

"'His own strength, general,' I answered.

XII

"But Gaspar Ruiz breathed yet. I had him carried in his poncho under the shelter of some bushes on the very ridge from which he had been gazing so fixedly at the fort while unseen death was hovering already over his head.

"Our troops had bivouacked round the fort. Towards daybreak I was not surprised to hear that I was designated to command the escort of a prisoner who was to be sent down at once to Santiago. Of course the prisoner was Gaspar Ruiz' wife.

"'I have named you out of regard for your feelings,' General Robles remarked. 'Though the woman really ought to be shot for all the harm she has done to the Republic.'

"And as I made a movement of shocked protest, he continued :

"'Now he is as well as dead, she is of no importance. Nobody will know what to do with her. However, the Government wants her.' He shrugged his shoulders. 'I suppose he must have buried large quantities of his loot in places that she alone knows of.'

"At dawn I saw her coming up the ridge, guarded by two soldiers, and carrying her child on her arm.

"I walked to meet her.

"'Is he living yet?' she asked, confronting me with that white, impassive face he used to look at in an adoring way.

"I bent my head, and led her round a clump of bushes without a word. His eyes were open. He breathed with difficulty, and uttered her name with a great effort.

5

" ' Erminia ! '

" She knelt at his head. The little girl, unconscious of him, and with her big eyes looking about, began to chatter suddenly, in a joyous, thin voice. She pointed a tiny finger at the rosy glow of sunrise behind the black shapes of the peaks. And while that child-talk, incomprehensible and sweet to the ear, lasted, those two, the dying man and the kneeling woman, remained silent, looking into each other's eyes, listening to the frail sound. Then the prattle stopped. The child laid its head against its mother's breast and was still.

" ' It was for you,' he began. ' Forgive.' His voice failed him. Presently I heard a mutter, and caught the pitiful words : ' Not strong enough.'

" She looked at him with an extraordinary intensity. He tried to smile, and in a humble tone, ' Forgive me,' he repeated. ' Leaving you . . .'

" She bent down, dry-eyed and in a steady voice : ' On all the earth I have loved nothing but you, Gaspar,' she said.

" His head made a movement. His eyes revived. ' At last ! ' he sighed out. Then, anxiously, ' But is this true . . . is this true ? '

" ' As true as that there is no mercy and justice in this world,' she answered him passionately. She stooped over his face. He tried to raise his head, but it fell back, and when she kissed his lips he was already dead. His glazed eyes stared at the sky, on which pink clouds floated very high. But I noticed the eyelids of the child, pressed to its mother's breast, droop and close slowly. She had gone to sleep.

" The widow of Gaspar Ruiz, the strong man, allowed me to lead her away without shedding a tear.

" For travelling we had arranged for her a side-saddle very much like a chair, with a board swung beneath to rest her feet on. And the first day she rode without uttering a word, and hardly for one moment turning her eyes away from the little girl, whom she held on her knees. At our first camp I saw her during the night walking about, rocking the child in her arms and gazing down at it by the light of the moon. After we had started on our second day's march she asked me how soon we should come to the first village of the inhabited country.

"I said we should be there about noon.

"'And will there be women there?' she inquired.

"I told her that it was a large village. 'There will be men and women there, señora,' I said, 'whose hearts shall be made glad by the news that all the unrest and war is over now.'

"'Yes, it is all over now,' she repeated. Then, after a time: 'Señor officer, what will your Government do with me?'

"'I do not know, señora,' I said. 'They will treat you well, no doubt. We republicans are not savages, and take no vengeance on women.'

"She gave me a look at the word 'republicans' which I imagined full of undying hate. But an hour or so afterwards, as we drew up to let the baggage mules go first along a narrow path skirting a precipice, she looked at me with such a white, troubled face that I felt a great pity for her.

"'Señor officer,' she said, 'I am weak, I tremble. It is an insensate fear.' And indeed her lips did tremble, while she tried to smile glancing at the beginning of the narrow path which was not so dangerous after all. 'I am afraid I shall drop the child. Gaspar saved your life, you remember. . . . Take her from me.'

"I took the child out of her extended arms. 'Shut your eyes, señora, and trust to your mule,' I recommended.

"She did so, and with her pallor and her wasted thin face she looked deathlike. At a turn of the path, where a great crag of purple porphyry closes the view of the lowlands, I saw her open her eyes. I rode just behind her holding the little girl with my right arm. 'The child is all right,' I cried encouragingly.

"'Yes,' she answered faintly; and then, to my intense terror, I saw her stand up on the foot-rest, staring horribly, and throw herself forward into the chasm on our right.

"I cannot describe to you the sudden and abject fear that came over me at that dreadful sight. It was a dread of the abyss, the dread of the crags which seemed to nod upon me. My head swam. I pressed the child to my side and sat my horse as still as a statue. I was speechless and cold all over. Her mule staggered, sidling close to the rock, and then went on. My horse only pricked up his ears with a slight snort. My heart stood still, and from the depths of the precipice the stones rattling in the bed of the furious stream made me almost insane with their sound.

"Next moment we were round the turn and on a broad and grassy slope. And then I yelled. My men came running back to me in great alarm. It seems that at first I did nothing but shout 'She has given the child into my hands! She has given the child into my hands!' The escort thought I had gone mad."

General Santierra ceased and got up from the table. "And that is all, señores," he concluded, with a courteous glance at his rising guests.

"But what became of the child, General?" we asked.

"Ah, the child, the child."

He walked to one of the windows opening on his beautiful garden, the refuge of his old days. Its fame was great in the land. Keeping us back with a raised arm, he called out, "Erminia, Erminia!" and waited. Then his cautioning arm dropped, and we crowded to the windows.

From a clump of trees a woman had come upon the broad walk bordered with flowers. We could hear the rustle of her starched petticoats and observed the ample spread of her old-fashioned black silk skirt. She looked up, and seeing all these eyes staring at her, stopped, frowned, smiled, shook her finger at the General, who was laughing boisterously, and drawing the black lace on her head so as to partly conceal her haughty profile, passed out of our sight, walking with stiff dignity.

"You have beheld the guardian angel of the old man —and her to whom you owe all that is seemly and comfortable in my hospitality. Somehow, señores, though the flame of love has been kindled early in my breast, I have never married. And because of that perhaps the sparks of the sacred fire are not yet extinct here." He struck his broad chest. "Still alive, still alive," he said, with serio-comic emphasis. "But I shall not marry now. She is General Santierra's adopted daughter and heiress."

One of our fellow-guests, a young naval officer, described her afterwards as a "short, stout, old girl of forty or thereabouts." We had all noticed that her hair was turning grey, and that she had very fine black eyes.

"And," General Santierra continued, "neither would she ever hear of marrying any one. A real calamity ! Good, patient, devoted to the old man. A simple soul. But I would not advise any of you to ask for her hand, for if she took yours into hers it would be only to crush your bones. Ah ! she does not jest on that subject. And she is the own daughter of her father, the strong man who perished through his own strength : the strength of his body, of his simplicity—of his love !"

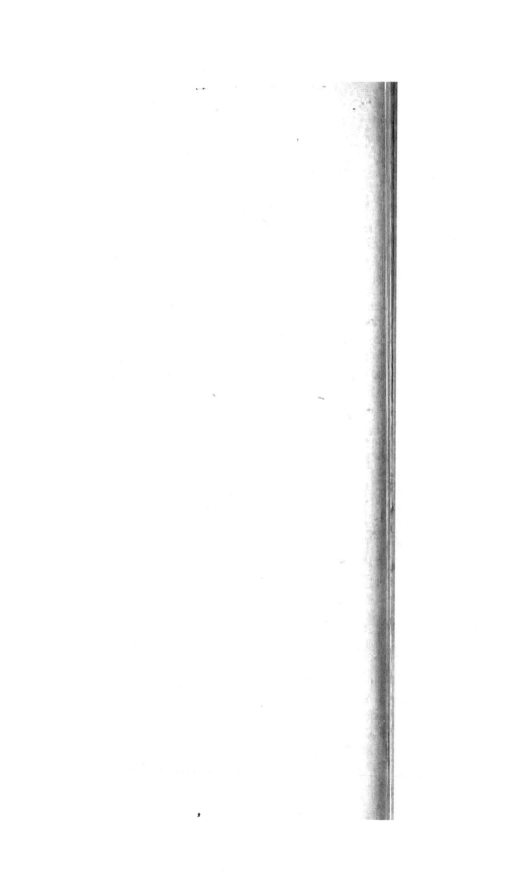

THE INFORMER

MR. X came to me, preceded by a letter of introduction from a good friend of mine in Paris,
specifically to see my collection of Chinese bronzes and
porcelain.

My friend in Paris is a collector too. He collects
neither porcelain, nor bronzes, nor pictures, nor medals,
nor stamps, nor anything that could be profitably dis-
persed under an auctioneer's hammer. He would reject,
with genuine surprise, the name of a collector. Nevertheless, that's what he is by temperament. He collects
acquaintances. It is delicate work. He brings to it
the patience, the passion, the determination of a true
collector of curiosities. His collection does not contain
any royal personages. I don't think he considers them
sufficiently rare and interesting; but, with that excep-
tion, he has met with and talked to every one worth knowing on any conceivable ground. He observes them,
listens to them, penetrates them, measures them, and
puts the memory away in the galleries of his mind. He
has schemed, plotted, and travelled all over Europe in
order to add to his collection of distinguished personal
acquaintances.

As he is wealthy, well connected and unprejudiced,
his collection is pretty complete, including objects (or
should I say subjects ?) whose value is unappreciated by
the vulgar, and often unknown to popular fame. Of
those specimens my friend is naturally the most proud.

71

He wrote to me of X. "He is the greatest rebel (*révolté*) of modern times. The world knows him as a revolutionary writer whose savage irony has laid bare the rottenness of the most respectable institutions. He has scalped every venerated head, and has mangled at the stake of his wit every received opinion and every recognised principle of conduct and policy. Who does not remember his flaming red revolutionary pamphlets. Their sudden swarmings used to overwhelm the powers of every Continental police like a plague of crimson gadflies. But this extreme writer has been also the active inspirer of secret societies, the mysterious unknown Number One of desperate conspiracies suspected and unsuspected, matured or baffled. And the world at large has never had an inkling of that fact! This accounts for him going about amongst us to this day, a veteran of many subterranean campaigns, standing aside now, safe within his reputation of merely the greatest destructive publicist that ever lived."

Thus wrote my friend, adding that Mr. X was an enlightened connoisseur of bronzes and china, and asking me to show him my collection.

X turned up in due course. My treasures are disposed in three large rooms without carpets and curtains. There is no other furniture than the étagères and the glass cases whose contents shall be worth a fortune to my heirs. I allow no fires to be lighted, for fear of accidents, and a fire-proof door separates them from the rest of the house.

It was a bitter cold day. We kept on our overcoats and hats. Middle-sized and spare, his eyes alert in a long, Roman-nosed countenance, X walked on his neat little feet, with short steps, and looked at my collection intelligently. I hope I looked at him intelligently too. A snow-white moustache and imperial made his nut-brown complexion appear darker than it really was. In his fur coat and shiny tall hat that terrible man looked fashionable. I believe he belonged to a noble family, and could have called himself Vicomte X de la Z if he chose. We talked nothing but bronzes and porcelain.

He was remarkably appreciative. We parted on cordial terms.

Where he was staying I don't know. I imagine he must have been a lonely man. Anarchists, I suppose, have no families—not, at any rate, as we understand that social relation. Organization into families may answer to a need of human nature, but in the last instance it is based on law, and therefore must be something odious and impossible to an anarchist. But, indeed, I don't understand anarchists. Does a man of that—of that—persuasion still remain an anarchist when alone, quite alone and going to bed, for instance ? Does he lay his head on the pillow, pull his bedclothes over him, and go to sleep with the necessity of the *chambardement général*, as the French slang has it, of the general blow-up, always present to his mind ? And if so, how can he ? I am sure that if such a faith (or such a fanaticism) once mastered my thoughts I would never be able to compose myself sufficiently to sleep or eat or perform any of the routine acts of daily life. I would want no wife, no children ; I could have no friends, it seems to me ; and as to collecting bronzes or china, that, I should say, would be quite out of the question. But I don't know. All I know is that Mr. X took his meals in a very good restaurant which I frequented also.

With his head uncovered, the silver top-knot of his brushed-up hair completed the character of his physiognomy, all bony ridges and sunken hollows, clothed in a perfect impassiveness of expression. His meagre brown hands emerging from large white cuffs came and went breaking bread, pouring wine, and so on, with quiet mechanical precision. His head and body above the tablecloth had a rigid immobility. This firebrand, this great agitator, exhibited the least possible amount of warmth and animation. His voice was rasping, cold, and monotonous in a low key. He could not be called a talkative personality ; but with his detached calm manner he appeared as ready to keep the conversation going as to drop it at any moment.

And his conversation was by no means commonplace. To me, I own, there was some excitement in talking quietly across the dinner-table with a man whose venomous pen-stabs had sapped the vitality of at least one monarchy. That much was a matter of public knowledge. But I knew more. I knew of him—from my friend—as a certainty what the guardians of social order in Europe had at most only suspected, or dimly guessed at.

He had had what I may call his underground life. And as I sat, evening after evening, facing him at dinner, a curiosity in that direction would naturally arise in my mind. I am a quiet and peaceable product of civilization, and know no passion other than the passion for collecting things which are rare, and must remain exquisite even if approaching to the monstrous. Some Chinese bronzes are monstrously precious. And here (out of my friend's collection), here I had before me a kind of rare monster. It is true that this monster was polished and in a sense even exquisite. His beautiful unruffled manner was that. But then he was not of bronze. He was not even Chinese, which would have enabled one to contemplate him calmly across the gulf of racial difference. He was alive and European; he had the manner of good society, wore a coat and hat like mine, and had pretty near the same taste in cooking. It was too frightful to think of.

One evening he remarked, casually, in the course of conversation, "There's no amendment to be got out of mankind except by terror and violence."

You can imagine the effect of such a phrase out of such a man's mouth upon a person like myself, whose whole scheme of life had been based upon a suave and delicate discrimination of social and artistic values. Just imagine! Upon me, to whom all sorts and forms of violence appeared as unreal as the giants, ogres, and seven-headed hydras whose activities affect, fantastically, the course of legends and fairy-tales!

I seemed suddenly to hear above the festive bustle and clatter of the brilliant restaurant the mutter of a hungry and seditious multitude.

I suppose I am impressionable and imaginative. I had a disturbing vision of darkness, full of lean jaws and wild eyes, amongst the hundred electric lights of the place. But somehow this vision made me angry, too. The sight of that man, so calm, breaking bits of white bread, exasperated me. And I had the audacity to ask him how it was that the starving proletariat of Europe to whom he had been preaching revolt and violence had not been made indignant by his openly luxurious life. "At all this," I said, pointedly, with a glance round the room and at a bottle of champagne we generally shared between us at dinner.

He remained unmoved.

"Do I feed on their toil and their heart's blood? Am I a speculator or a capitalist? Did I steal my fortune from a starving people? No! They know this very well. And they envy me nothing. The miserable mass of the people is generous to its leaders. What I have acquired has come to me through my writings; not from the millions of pamphlets distributed gratis to the hungry and the oppressed, but from the hundreds of thousands of copies sold to the well-fed bourgeois. You know that my writings were at one time the rage, the fashion—the thing to read with wonder, and horror, to turn your eyes up at my pathos . . . or else to laugh in ecstasies at my wit."

"Yes," I admitted, "I remember, of course; and I confess frankly that I could never understand that infatuation."

"Don't you know yet," he said, "that an idle and selfish class loves to see mischief being made, even if it is made at its own expense? Its own life being all a matter of pose and gesture, it is unable to realize the power and the danger of a real movement and of words that have no sham meaning. It is all fun and sentiment. It is sufficient, for instance, to point out the attitude of the old French aristocracy towards the philosophers whose words were preparing the Great Revolution. Even in England, where you have some common-sense, a demagogue has only to shout loud enough and long enough to find some backing in the very class he is shouting at. You too like to see mischief being made. The demagogue carries the amateurs of emotion with him. Amateurism in this, that, and the other thing is a delightfully easy way of killing time, and of feeding one's own vanity—the silly vanity of being abreast with the ideas of the day after to-morrow. Just as good and otherwise harmless people will join you in ecstasies over your collection without having the slightest notion in what its marvellousness really consists."

I hung my head. It was a crushing illustration of the sad truth he advanced. The world is full of such people. And that instance of the French aristocracy before the Revolution was extremely telling, too. I could not traverse his statement, though its cynicism— always a distasteful trait—took off much of its value, to my mind. However, I admit I was impressed. I felt the need to say something which would not be in the nature of assent and yet would not invite discussion.

"You don't mean to say," I observed, airily, "that extreme revolutionists have ever been actively assisted by the infatuation of such people ? "

"I did not mean exactly that by what I said just now. I generalized. But since you ask me, I may tell you that such help has been given to revolutionary activities, more or less consciously, in various countries. And even in this country."

"Impossible ! " I protested with firmness. "We don't play with fire to that extent."

"And yet you can better afford it than others, perhaps. But let me observe that most women, if not always ready to play with fire, are generally eager to play with a loose spark or so."

"Is this a joke ? " I asked, smiling.

"If it is, I am not aware of it," he said, woodenly, " I was thinking of an instance. Oh ! mild enough in a way . . ."

I became all expectation at this. I had tried many times to approach him on his underground side, so to speak. The very word had been pronounced between us. But he had always met me with his impenetrable calm.

"And at the same time," Mr. X continued, "it will give you a notion of the difficulties that may arise in what you are pleased to call underground work. It is sometimes difficult to deal with them. Of course there is no hierarchy amongst the affiliated. No rigid system."

My surprise was great, but short-lived. Clearly, amongst extreme anarchists there could be no hierarchy; nothing in the nature of a law of precedence. The idea of anarchy ruling among anarchists was comforting, too. It could not possibly make for efficiency.

Mr. X startled me by asking, abruptly, "You know Hermione Street?"

I nodded doubtful assent. Hermione Street has been, within the last three years, improved out of any man's knowledge. The name exists still, but not one brick or stone of the old Hermione Street is left now. It was the old street he meant, for he said:

"There was a row of two-storied brick houses on the left, with their backs against the wing of a great public building—you remember. Would it surprise you very much to hear that one of these houses was for a time the centre of anarchist propaganda and of what you would call underground action?"

"Not at all," I declared. Hermione Street had never been particularly respectable, as I remembered it.

"The house was the property of a distinguished government official," he added, sipping his champagne.

"Oh, indeed!" I said, this time not believing a word of it.

"Of course he was not living there," Mr. X continued. "But from ten till four he sat next door to it, the dear man, in his well-appointed private room in the wing of the public building I've mentioned. To be strictly accurate, I must explain that the house in Hermione Street did not really belong to him. It belonged to his grown-up children—a daughter and a son. The girl, a fine figure, was by no means vulgarly pretty. To

more personal charm than mere youth could account
for, she added the seductive appearance of enthusiasm,
of independence, of courageous thought.   I suppose she
put on these appearances as she put on her picturesque
dresses and for the same reason : to assert her individuality at any cost.   You know, women would go to any
length almost for such a purpose.   She went to a great
length.   She had acquired all the appropriate gestures
of revolutionary convictions ;—the gestures of pity, of
anger, of indignation against the anti-humanitarian vices
of the social class to which she belonged herself.   All this
sat on her striking personality as becomingly as her slightly original costumes.   Very slightly original ; just enough
to mark a protest against the philistinism of the overfed
taskmasters of the poor.   Just enough, and no more.   It
would not have done to go too far in that direction—you
understand.   But she was of age, and nothing stood in
the way of her offering her house to the revolutionary
workers."

"You don't mean it ! " I cried.

" I assure you," he affirmed, " that she made that very
practical gesture.   How else could they have got hold
of it ?   The cause is not rich.   And, moreover, there
would have been difficulties with any ordinary house-
agent, who would have wanted references and so on.
The group she came in contact with while exploring
the poor quarters of the town (you know the gesture
of charity and personal service which was so fashionable
some years ago) accepted with gratitude.   The first
advantage was that Hermione Street is, as you know,
well away from the suspect part of the town, specially
watched by the police.

" The ground floor consisted of a little Italian restaurant, of the flyblown sort.   There was no difficulty
in buying the proprietor out.   A woman and a man
belonging to the group took it on.   The man had been
a cook.   The comrades could get their meals there,
unnoticed amongst the other customers.   This was
another advantage.   The first floor was occupied by
a shabby Variety Artists' Agency—an agency for per-

formers in inferior music-halls, you know. A fellow called Bomm, I remember. He was not disturbed. It was rather favourable than otherwise to have a lot of foreign-looking people, jugglers, acrobats, singers of both sexes, and so on, going in and out all day long. The police paid no attention to new faces, you see. The top floor happened, most conveniently, to stand empty then."

X interrupted himself to attack impassively, with measured movements, a *bombe glacée* which the waiter had just set down on the table. He swallowed carefully a few spoonfuls of the iced sweet, and asked me, " Did you ever hear of Stone's Dried Soup ? "

" Hear of *what.*' "

" It was," X pursued evenly, " a comestible article, once rather prominently advertised in the dailies, but which never, somehow, gained the favour of the public. The enterprise fizzled out, as you say here. Parcels of their stock could be picked up at auctions at considerably less than a penny a pound. The group bought some of it, and an agency for Stone's Dried Soup was started on the top floor. A perfectly respectable business. The stuff, a yellow powder of extremely unappetising aspect, was put up in large square tins, of which six went to a case. If anybody ever came to give an order, it was, of course, executed. But the advantage of the powder was this, that things could be concealed in it very conveniently. Now and then a special case got put on a van and sent off to be exported abroad under the very nose of the policeman on duty at the corner. You understand ? "

" I think I do," I said, with an expressive nod at the remnants of the *bombe* melting slowly in the dish.

" Exactly. But the cases were useful in another way, too. In the basement, or in the cellar at the back, rather, two printing-presses were established. A lot of revolutionary literature of the most inflammatory kind was got away from the house in Stone's Dried Soup cases. The brother of our anarchist young lady found some occupation there. He wrote articles, helped to set up type and pull off the sheets, and generally assisted the man in charge, a very able young fellow called Sevrin.

"The guiding spirit of that group was a fanatic of social revolution. He is dead now. He was an engraver and etcher of genius. You must have seen his work. It is much sought after by certain amateurs now. He began by being revolutionary in his art, and ended by becoming a revolutionist, after his wife and child had died in want and misery. He used to say that the bourgeois, the smug overfed lot, had killed them. That was his real belief. He still worked at his art and led a double life. He was tall, gaunt and swarthy, with a long, brown beard and deep-set eyes, you must have seen him. His name was Horne."

At this I was really startled. Of course years ago I used to meet Horne about. He looked like a powerful, rough gipsy, in an old top hat, with a red muffler round his throat and buttoned up in a long, shabby overcoat. He talked of his art with exaltation, and gave one the impression of being strung up to the verge of insanity. A small group of connoisseurs appreciated his work. Who would have thought that this man. . . . Amazing! And yet it was not, after all, so difficult to believe.

"As you see," X went on, "this group was in a position to pursue its work of propaganda, and the other kind of work too, under very advantageous conditions. They were all resolute, experienced men of a superior stamp. And yet we became struck at length by the fact that plans prepared in Hermione Street almost invariably failed."

"Who were ' we ' ? " I asked pointedly.

"Some of us in Brussels—at the centre," he said hastily. " Whatever vigorous action originated in Hermione Street seemed doomed to failure. Something always happened to baffle the best-planned manifestations in every part of Europe. It was a time of general activity. You must not imagine that all our failures are of a loud sort, with arrests and trials. That is not so. Often the police work quietly, almost secretly, defeating our combinations by clever counter-plotting.

No arrests, no noise, no alarming of the public mind and inflating the passions. It is a wise procedure. But at that time the police were too uniformly successful from the Mediterranean to the Baltic. It was annoying and began to look dangerous. At last we came to the conclusion that there must be some untrustworthy elements amongst the London groups. And I came over to see what could be done quietly.

"My first step was to call upon our young Lady Amateur of anarchism at her private house. She received me in a flattering way. I judged that she knew nothing of the chemical and other operations going on at the top of the house in Hermione Street. The printing of anarchist literature was the only ' activity ' she seemed to be aware of there. She was displaying very strikingly the usual signs of severe enthusiasm, and had already written many sentimental articles with ferocious conclusions. I could see she was enjoying herself hugely, with all the gestures and grimaces of deadly earnestness. They suited her big-eyed, broad-browed face and the good carriage of her shapely head, crowned by a magnificent lot of brown hair done in an unusual and becoming style. Her brother was in the room too, a serious youth, with arched eyebrows and wearing a red necktie, who struck me as being absolutely in the dark about everything in the world, including himself. By and by a tall young man came in. He was clean-shaved, with a strong bluish jaw and something of the air of a taciturn actor or of a fanatical priest: the type with thick black eyebrows—you know. But he was very presentable indeed. He shook hands at once vigorously with each of us. The young lady came up to me and murmured sweetly, ' Comrade Sevrin.'

"I had never seen him before. He had little to say to us, but sat down by the side of the girl, and they fell at once into earnest conversation. She leaned forward in her deep arm-chair, and took her nicely rounded chin in her beautiful white hand. He looked attentively into her eyes. It was the attitude of love-making, serious, intense, as if on the brink of the grave. I suppose

6

she felt it necessary to round and complete her assumption of advanced ideas, of revolutionary lawlessness, by making believe to be in love with an anarchist. And this one, I repeat, was extremely presentable, notwithstanding his fanatical black-browed aspect. After a few stolen glances in their direction, I had no doubt that he was in earnest. As to the lady, her gestures were unapproachable, better than the very thing itself in the blended suggestion of dignity, sweetness, condescension, fascination, surrender, and reserve. She interpreted her conception of what that precise sort of love-making should be with consummate art. And so far, she too, no doubt, was in earnest. Gestures—but so perfect !

" After I had been left alone with our Lady Amateur I informed her guardedly of the object of my visit. I hinted at our suspicions. I wanted to hear what she would have to say, and half expected some perhaps unconscious revelation. All she said was 'That's serious,' looking delightfully concerned and grave. But there was a sparkle in her eyes which meant plainly, 'How exciting !' After all, she knew little of anything except of words. Still, she undertook to put me in communication with Horne, who was not easy to find unless in Hermione Street, where I did not wish to show myself just then.

" I met Horne, This was another kind of a fanatic altogether. I exposed to him the conclusion we in Brussels had arrived at, and pointed out the significant series of failures. To this he answered with irrelevant exaltation.

" ' I have something in hand that shall strike terror into the heart of these gorged brutes.'

" And then I learned that, by excavating in one of the cellars of the house, he and some companions had made their way into the vaults under the great public building I have mentoned before. The blowing up of a a whole wing was a certainty as soon as the materials were ready.

" I was not so appalled at the stupidity of that move as I might have been had not the usefulness of our centre in Hermione Street become already very problematical. In fact, in my opinion it was much more of a police trap by this time than anything else.

"What was necessary now was to discover what, or rather who, was wrong, and I managed at last to get that idea into Horne's head. He glared, perplexed, his nostrils working as if sniffing treachery in the air.

"And here comes a piece of work which will no doubt strike you as a sort of theatrical expedient. And yet what else could have been done? The problem was to find out the untrustworthy member of the group. But no suspicion could be fastened on one more than another. To set a watch upon them all was not very practicable. Besides, that proceeding often fails. In any case, it takes time, and the danger was pressing. I felt certain that the premises in Hermione Street would be ultimately raided, though the police had evidently such confidence in the informer that the house, for the time being, was not even watched. Horne was positive on that point. Under the circumstances it was an unfavourable symptom. Something had to be done quickly.

"I decided to organize a raid myself upon the group. Do you understand? A raid of other trusty comrades personating the police. A conspiracy within a conspiracy. You see the object of it, of course. When apparently about to be arrested I hoped the informer would betray himself in some way or other; either by some unguarded act or simply by his unconcerned demeanour, for instance. Of course there was the risk of complete failure and the no lesser risk of some fatal accident in the course of resistance, perhaps, or in the efforts at escape. For, as you will easily see, the Hermione Street group had to be actually and completely taken unawares, as I was sure they would be by the real police before very long. The informer was amongst them, and Horne alone could be let into the secret of my plan.

"I will not enter into the detail of my preparations. It was not very easy to arrange, but it was done very well, with a really convincing effect. The sham police invaded the restaurant, whose shutters were immediately put up. The surprise was perfect. Most of the Hermione Street party were found in the second cellar, enlarging the hole communicating with the vaults of the great public building. At the first alarm, several comrades bolted through impulsively into the aforesaid vault, where, of course, had this been a genuine raid, they would have been hopelessly trapped. We did not bother about them for the moment. They were harmless enough. The top floor caused considerable anxiety to Horne and myself. There, surrounded by tins of Stone's Dried Soup, a comrade, nick-named the Professor (he was an ex-science student) was engaged in perfecting some new detonators. He was an abstracted, self-confident, sallow little man, armed with large round spectacles, and we were afraid that under a mistaken impression he would blow himself up and wreck the house about our ears. I rushed upstairs and found him already at the door, on the alert, listening, as he said, to 'suspicious noises down below.' Before I had quite finished explaining to him what was going on, he shrugged his shoulders disdainfully and turned away to his balances and test-tubes. His was the true spirit of an extreme revolutionist. Explosives were his faith, his hope, his weapon, and his shield. He perished a couple of years afterwards in a secret laboratory through the premature explosion of one of his improved detonators.

"Hurrying down again, I found an impressive scene in the gloom of the big cellar. The man who personated the inspector (he was no stranger to the part) was speaking harshly, and giving bogus orders to his bogus subordinates for the removal of his prisoners. Evidently nothing enlightening had happened so far. Horne, saturnine and swarthy, waited with folded arms, and his patient, moody expectation had an air of stoicism well in keeping with the situation. I detected in the shadows one of the Hermione Street group surreptitiously chewing up and swallowing a small piece of paper. Some compromising scrap, I suppose; perhaps just a note of a few names and addresses. He was a true and faithful 'companion.' But the fund of secret malice which lurks at the bottom of our sympathies caused me to feel amused at that perfectly uncalled-for performance.

"In every other respect the risky experiment, the theatrical *coup*, if you like to call it so, seemed to have failed. The deception could not be kept up much longer; the explanation would bring about a very embarrassing and even grave situation. The man who had eaten the paper would be furious. The fellows who had bolted away would be angry too.

"To add to my vexation, the door communicating with the other cellar, where the printing-presses were, flew open, and our young lady revolutionist appeared, a black silhouette in a close-fitting dress and a large hat, with the blaze of gas flaring in there at her back. Over her shoulder I perceived the arched eyebrows and the red necktie of her brother.

"The last people in the world I wanted to see then! They had gone that evening to some amateur concert for the delectation of the poor people, you know; but she had insisted on leaving early, on purpose to call in Hermione Street on the way home, under the pretext of having some work to do. Her usual task was to correct the proofs of the Italian and French editions of the *Alarm Bell* and the *Firebrand*." . . .

"Heavens!" I murmured. I had been shown once a few copies of these publications. Nothing, in my opinion, could have been less fit for the eyes of a young lady. They were the most advanced things of the sort; advanced, I mean, beyond all bounds of reason and decency. One of them preached the dissolution of all social and domestic ties; the other advocated systematic murder. To think of a young girl calmly tracking printers' errors all along the sort of abominable sentences I remembered was intolerable to my sentiment of womanhood. Mr X, after giving me a glance, pursued steadily:

"I think, however, that she came mostly to exercise her fascinations upon Sevrin, and to receive his homage in her queenly and condescending way. She was aware

of both—her power and his homage—and enjoyed them
with, I dare say, complete innocence. We have no
ground in expediency or morals to quarrel with her on
that account. Charm in woman and exceptional
intelligence in man are a law unto themselves. Is it
not so ? "

I refrained from expressing my abhorrence of that
licentious doctrine because of my curiosity.

" But what happened then ? " I hastened to ask.

X went on crumbling slowly a small piece of bread
with a careless left hand.

" What happened, in effect," he confessed, " is that
she saved the situation."

" She gave you an opportunity to end your rather
sinister farce," I suggested.

" Yes," he said, preserving his impassive bearing.
" The farce was bound to end soon. And it ended in a
very few minutes. And it ended well. Had she not
come in, it might have ended badly. Her brother, of
course, did not count. They had slipped into the house
quietly some time before. The printing-cellar had an
entrance of its own. Not finding any one there, she
sat down to her proofs, expecting Sevrin to return to his
work at any moment. He did not do so. She grew
impatient, heard through the door the sounds of a
disturbance in the other cellar and naturally came in to
see what was the matter.

" Sevrin had been with us. At first he had seemed
to me the most amazed of the whole raided lot. He
appeared for an instant as if paralyzed with astonishment, He stood rooted to the spot. He never moved
a limb. A solitary gas-jet flared near his head ; all
the other lights had been put out at the first alarm.
And presently, from my dark corner, I observed on his
shaven actor's face an expression of puzzled, vexed
watchfulness. He knitted his heavy eyebrows. The
corners of his mouth dropped scornfully. He was
angry. Most likely he had seen through the game, and
I regretted I had not taken him from the first into my
complete confidence.

" But with the appearance of the girl he became obviously alarmed. It was plain. I could see it grow. The change of his expression was swift and startling. And I did not know why. The reason never occurred to me. I was merely astonished at the extreme alteration of the man's face. Of course he had not been aware of her presence in the other cellar. But that did not explain the shock her advent had given him. For a moment he seemed to have been reduced to imbecility. He opened his mouth as if to shout, or perhaps only to gasp. At any rate, it was somebody else who shouted. This somebody else was the heroic comrade whom I had detected swallowing a piece of paper. With laudable presence of mind he let out a warning yell.

" ' It's the police ! Back ! Back ! Run back, and bolt the door behind you.'

" It was an excellent hint ; but instead of retreating, the girl continued to advance, followed by her long-faced brother in his knicker-bocker suit, in which he had been singing comic songs for the entertainment of a joyless proletariat. She advanced not as if she had failed to understand—the word ' police ' has an unmistakable sound—but rather as if she could not help herself. She did not advance with the free gait and expanding presence of a distinguished amateur anarchist amongst poor, struggling professionals, but with slightly raised shoulders, and her elbows pressed close to her body, as if trying to shrink within herself. Her eyes were fixed immovably upon Sevrin. Sevrin the man, I fancy ; not Sevrin the anarchist. But she advanced. And that was natural. For all their assumption of independence, girls of that class are used to the feeling of being specially protected, as, in fact, they are. This feeling accounts for nine-tenths of their audacious gestures. Her face had gone completely colourless. Ghastly. Fancy having it brought home to her so brutally that she was the sort of person who must run away from the police ! I believe she was pale with indignation, mostly, though there was, of course, also the concern for her intact personality, a vague dread of some sort of rudeness. And naturally, she turned to a man, to the man on whom she had a claim of fascination and homage—the man who could not conceivably fail her at any juncture."

"But," I cried, amazed at this analysis, "if it had been serious, real, I mean—as she thought it was—what could she expect him to do for her ? "

X never moved a muscle of his face.

"Goodness knows. I imagine that this charming, generous, and independent creature had never known in her life a single genuine thought; I mean a single thought detached from small human vanities, or whose source was not in some conventional perception. All I know is that after advancing a few steps she extended her hand towards the motionless Sevrin. And that at least was no gesture. It was a natural movement. As to what she expected him to do, who can tell ? The impossible. But whatever she expected, it could not have come up, I am safe to say, to what he had made up his mind to do, even before that entreating hand had appealed to him so directly. It had not been necessary. From the moment he had seen her enter that cellar, he had made up his mind to sacrifice his future usefulness, to throw off the impenetrable solidly-fastened mask it had been his pride to wear——'

"What do you mean ? " I interrupted, puzzled. "Was it Sevrin, then who was——"

"He was. The most persistent, the most dangerous, the craftiest, the most systematic of informers. A genius amongst betrayers. Fortunately for us, he was unique. The man was a fanatic, I have told you. Fortunately, again for us, he had fallen in love with the accomplished and innocent gestures of that girl. An actor in desperate earnest himself, he must have believed in the absolute value of conventional signs. As to the grossness of the trap into which he fell, the explanation must be that two sentiments of such absorbing magnitude cannot exist simultaneously in one heart. The danger of that other and unconscious comedian robbed him of his vision, of his perspicacity, of his judgment.

Indeed, it did at first rob him of his self-possession. But he regained that through the necessity—as it appeared to him imperiously—to do something at once. To do what ? Why, to get her out of the house as quickly as possible. He was desperately anxious to do that. I have told you he was terrified. It could not be about himself. He had been surprised and annoyed at a move quite unforeseen and premature, I may even say he had been furious. He was accustomed to arrange the last scene of his betrayals with a deep, subtle art which left his revolutionist reputation untouched. But it seems clear to me that at the same time he had resolved to make the best of it, to keep his mask resolutely on. It was only with the discovery of her being in the house that everything—the forced calm, the restraint of his fanaticism, the mask—all came off together in a kind of panic. Why panic, do you ask ? The answer is very simple. He remembered—or, I dare say, he had never forgotten the Professor alone at the top of the house, pursuing his researches, surrounded by tins upon tins of Stones Dried Soup. There was enough in some few of them to bury us all where we stood under a heap of bricks. Servin of course, was aware of that. And we must believe, also, that he knew the exact character of the man, apparently. He had gauged so many such characters! Or perhaps he only gave the Professor credit for what he himself was capable of. But, in any case, the effect was produced. And suddenly he raised his voice in authority.

" ' Get the lady away at once.'

" It turned out that he was as hoarse as a crow ; result, no doubt, of the intense emotion. It passed off in a moment. But these fateful words issued forth from his contracted throat in a discordant, ridiculous croak. They required no answer. The thing was done. However, the man personating the inspector judged it expedient to say roughly :

" ' She shall go soon enough, together with the rest of you.'

" These were the last words belonging to the comedy part of this affair.

" Oblivious of everything and everybody, Sevrin strode towards him and seized the lapels of his coat. Under his thin bluish cheeks one could see his jaws working with passion.

" ' You have men posted outside. Get the lady taken home at once. Do you hear ? Now. Before you try to get hold of the man upstairs.'

" ' Oh ! There is a man upstairs,' scoffed the other openly, ' Well, he shall be brought down in time to see the end of this.'

" But Sevrin, beside himself, took no heed of the tone.

" ' Who's the imbecile meddler who sent you blundering here ? Didn't you understand your instructions ? Don't you know anything ? It's incredible. Here——'

" He dropped the lapels of the coat and, plunging his hand into his breast, jerked feverishly at something under his shirt. At last he produced a small square pocket of soft leather, which must have been hanging like a scapulary from his neck by the tape, whose broken ends dangled from his fist.

" 'Look inside,' he spluttered, flinging it in the other's face. And instantly he turned round towards the girl. She stood just behind him, perfectly still and silent. Her set, white face gave an illusion of placidity. Only her staring eyes seemed bigger and darker.

" He spoke rapidly, with a nervous assurance. I heard him distinctly promise her to make everything as clear as daylight presently. But that was all I caught. He stood close to her, never attempting to touch her even with the tip of his little finger—and she stared at him stupidly. For a moment, however, her eyelids descended slowly, pathetically, and then, with the long black eyelashes lying on her white cheeks, she looked as if she were about to fall down in a swoon. But she never even swayed where she stood. He urged her loudly to follow him at once, and walked towards the door at the bottom of the cellar stairs without looking behind him. And, as a matter of fact, she did move after him a pace or two. But, of course, he was not allowed to reach the door.

There were angry exclamations, the tumult of a short fierce scuffle. Flung away violently, he came flying backwards upon her, and fell. She threw out her arms in a gesture of dismay and stepped aside, just clear of his head, which struck the ground heavily near her shoe.

"He grunted with the shock. By this time he had picked himself up, slowly, dazedly, he was awake to the reality of things. The man into whose hands he had thrust the leather case had extracted therefrom a narrow strip of bluish paper. He held it up above his head, and, as after the scuffle an expectant uneasy stillness reigned once more, he threw it down disdainfully with the words, 'I think, comrades, that this proof was hardly necessary.'

"Quick as thought, the girl stooped after the fluttering slip. Holding it spread out in both hands, she looked at it; then, without raising her eyes, opened her fingers slowly and let it fall.

"I examined that curious document afterwards. It was signed by a very high personage, and stamped and countersigned by other high officials in various countries of Europe. In his trade—or shall I say, in his mission?—that sort of talisman might have been necessary, no doubt. Even to the police itself—all but the heads—he had been known only as Sevrin the noted anarchist.

"He hung his head, biting his lower lip, A change had come over him, a sort of thoughtful, absorbed calmness. Nevertheless, he panted. His sides worked visibly, and his nostrils expanded and collapsed in weird contrast with his sombre aspect of a fanatical monk in a meditative attitude, but with something, too, in his face of an actor intent upon the terrible exigencies of his part. Before him Horne declaimed, haggard and bearded like an inspired denunciatory prophet from a wilderness. Two fanatics. They were made to understand each other. Does this surprise you? I suppose you think that such people would be foaming at the mouth and snarling at each other?"

"I protested hastily that I was not surprised in the least; that I thought nothing of the kind; that anarchists in general were simply inconceivable to me mentally, morally, logically, sentimentally, and even physically. Mr. X received this declaration with his usual woodenness and went on.

"Horne had burst out into eloquence. While pouring out scornful invective, he let tears escape from his eyes and roll down his black beard unheeded. Sevrin panted quicker and quicker. When he opened his mouth to speak, everyone hung on his word.

"'Don't be a fool, Horne,' he began. 'You know very well that I have done this for none of the reasons you are throwing at me.' And in a moment he became outwardly as steady as a rock under the other's lurid stare. 'I have been thwarting, deceiving and betraying you—from conviction.'

"He turned his back on Horne, and addressing the girl, repeated the words : 'From conviction.'

"It's extraordinary how cold she looked. I suppose she could not think of an appropriate gesture. There can have been few precedents indeed for such a situation.

"'Clear as daylight,' he added. 'Do you understand what that means ? From conviction.'

"And still she did not stir. She did not know what to do. But the luckless wretch was about to give her the opportunity for a beautiful and correct gesture.

"'I have felt in me the power to make you share this conviction,' he protested, ardently. He had forgotten himself ; he made a step towards her—perhaps he stumbled. To me he seemed to be stooping low as if to touch the hem of her garment. And then the appropriate gesture came. She snatched her skirt away from his polluting contact and averted her head with an upward tilt. It was magnificently done, this gesture of conventionally unstained honour, of an unblemished high-minded amateur.

"Nothing could have been better. And he seemed to think so, too, for once more he turned away. But this time he faced no one. He was again panting frightfully, while he fumbled hurriedly in his waistcoat pocket, and then raised his hand to his lips. There was something furtive in this movement, but directly afterwards his bearing changed. His laboured breathing gave him a resemblance to a man who had just run a desperate race ; but a curious air of detachment, of sudden and profound indifference, replaced the strain of the striving effort. The race was over. I did not want to see what would happen next. I was only too well aware. I tucked the young lady's arm under mine without a word, and made my way with her to the stairs.

" Her brother walked behind us. Half-way up the short flight she seemed unable to lift her feet high enough for the steps, and we had to pull and push to get her to the top. In the passage she dragged herself along, hanging on my arm, helplessly bent like an impotent old woman. We issued into an empty street through a half-open door, staggering like besotted revellers. At the corner we stopped a four-wheeler, and the ancient driver looked round from his box with morose scorn at our efforts to get her in. Twice during the drive I felt her collapse on my shoulder in a half-faint. Facing us, the youth in knickerbockers remained as mute as a fish, and, till he jumped out with the latch-key, sat more still than I would have believed it possible.

" At the door of their drawing-room she left my arm and walked in first, catching at the chairs and tables. She unpinned her hat, then, exhausted with the effort, her cloak still hanging from her shoulders, flung herself into a deep arm-chair, sideways, her face half buried in a cushion. The good brother appeared silently before her with a glass of water. She motioned it away. He drank it himself and walked off to a distant corner— behind the grand piano, somewhere. All was still in this room where I had seen, for the first time, Sevrin, the anti-anarchist, captivated and spellbound by the consummate and hereditary grimaces that in a certain sphere of life take the place of feelings with an excellent effect. I suppose her thoughts were busy with the same memory. Her shoulders shook violently. A pure attack of nerves. When it quieted down she affected

firmness, ' What is done to a man of that sort ? What
will they do to him ? '

" ' Nothing. They can do nothing to him,' I assured
her, with perfect truth. I was pretty certain he had
died in less than twenty minutes from the moment his
hand had gone to his lips. For if his fanatical anti-
anarchism went even as far as carrying poison in his
pocket, only to rob his adversaries of legitimate vengeance, I knew he would take care to provide something
that would not fail him when required.

" She drew an angry breath. There were red spots on
her cheeks and a feverish brilliance in her eyes.

" ' Has ever any one been exposed to such a terrible
experience ? To think that he held my hand ! That
man ! ' Her face twitched, she gulped down a pathetic
sob. ' If I ever felt sure of anything, it was of Sevrin's
high-minded motives.'

" Then she began to weep quietly, which was good
for her. Then through her flood of tears, half resentful,
' What was it he said to me ?—" From conviction ! "
It seemed a vile mockery. What could he mean by it ? '

" ' That, my dear young lady,' I said gently, ' is more
than I or anybody else can ever explain to you '."

Mr. X flicked a crumb off the front of his coat.

" And that was strictly true as to her. Though
Horne, for instance, understood very well ; and so did I,
especially after we had been to Sevrin's lodging in a
dismal back street of an intensely respectable quarter.
Horne was known there as a friend, and we had no
difficulty in being admitted, the slatternly maid merely
remarking, as she let us in, that ' Mr. Sevrin had not
been home that night.' We forced open a couple of
drawers in the way of duty, and found a little useful
information. The most interesting part was his diary ;
for this man, engaged in such deadly work, had the weakness to keep a record of the most damnatory kind. There
were his acts and also his thoughts laid bare to us. But
the dead don't mind that. They don't mind anything.

" ' From conviction.' Yes. A vague but ardent
humanitarianism had urged him in his first youth into

the bitterest extremity of negation and revolt. Afterwards his optimism flinched. He doubted and became lost. You have heard of converted atheists. These turn often into dangerous fanatics, but the soul remains the same. After he had got acquainted with the girl, there are to be met in that diary of his very queer politico-amorous rhapsodies. He took her sovereign grimaces with deadly seriousness. He longed to convert her. But all this cannot interest you. For the rest, I don't know if you remember—it is a good many years ago now—the journalistic sensation of the ' Hermione Street Mystery '; the finding of a man's body in the cellar of an empty house; the inquest; some arrests; many surmises—then silence—the usual end for many obscure martyrs and confessors. The fact is, he was not enough of an optimist. You must be a savage, tyrannical, pitiless, thick-and-thin optimist, like Horne, for instance, to make a good social rebel of the extreme type."

He rose from the table. A waiter hurried up with his overcoat; another held his hat in readiness.

" But what became of the young lady ? " I asked.

" Do you really want to know ? " he said, buttoning himself in his fur coat carefully. " I confess to the small malice of sending her Sevrin's diary. She went into retirement; then she went to Florence; then she went into retreat in a convent. I can't tell where she will go next. What does it matter ? Gestures ! Gestures ! Mere gestures of her class."

He fitted on his glossy high hat with extreme precision, and casting a rapid glance round the room, full of well-dressed people, innocently dining, muttered between his teeth :

" And nothing else ! That is why their kind is fated to perish."

I never met Mr. X again after that evening. I took to dining at my club. On my next visit to Paris I found my friend all impatience to hear of the effect produced on me by this rare item of his collection. I told him all the story, and he beamed on me with the pride of his distinguished specimen.

" Isn't X well worth knowing ? " he bubbled over in great delight. " He's unique, amazing, absolutely terrific."

His enthusiasm grated upon my finer feelings. I told him curtly that the man's cynicism was simply abominable.

" Oh, abominable ! abominable ! " assented my friend effusively. " And then, you know, he likes to have his little joke sometimes," he added in a confidential tone.

I fail to understand the connexion of this last remark. I have been utterly unable to discover where in all this the joke comes in.

THE BRUTE

DODGING in from the rain-swept street, I exchanged a smile and a glance with Miss Blank in the bar of the Three Crows. This exchange was effected with extreme propriety. It is a shock to think that, if still alive, Miss Blank must be something over sixty now. How time passes!

Noticing my gaze directed inquiringly at the partition of glass and varnished wood, Miss Blank was good enough to say, encouragingly:

"Only Mr. Jermyn and Mr. Stonor in the parlour, with another gentleman I've never seen before."

I moved towards the parlour door. A voice discoursing on the other side (it was but a matchboard partition), rose so loudly that the concluding words became quite plain in all their atrocity.

"That fellow Wilmot fairly dashed her brains out, and a good job too!"

This inhuman sentiment, since there was nothing profane or improper in it, failed to do as much as to check the slight yawn Miss Blank was achieving behind her hand. And she remained gazing fixedly at the window-panes, which streamed with rain.

As I opened the parlour door the same voice went on in the same cruel strain:

"I was glad when I heard she got the knock from somebody at last. Sorry enough for poor Wilmot, though. That man and I used to be chums at one time.

7   ⸱ 7

Of course that was the end of him. A clear case if there
ever was one. No way out of it. None at all."

The voice belonged to the gentleman Miss Blank had
never seen before. He straddled his long legs on the
hearth-rug. Jermyn, leaning forward, held his pocket-
handkerchief spread out before the grate. He looked
back dismally over his shoulder, and as I slipped behind
one of the little wooden tables. I nodded to him. On
the other side of the fire, imposingly calm and large,
sat Mr. Stonor, jammed tight into a capacious Windsor
arm-chair. There was nothing small about him but
his short, white side-whiskers. Yards and yards of
extra superfine blue cloth (made up into an overcoat)
reposed on a chair by his side. And he must just have
brought some liner from sea. because another chair was
smothered under his black waterproof, ample as a pall,
and made of three-fold oiled silk, double-stitched
throughout. A man's handbag of the usual size looked
like a child's toy on the floor near his feet.

I did not nod to him. He was too big to be nodded to
in that parlour. He was a senior Trinity pilot and
condescended to take his turn in the cutter only during
the summer months. He had been many times in charge
of royal yachts in and out of Port Victoria. Besides,
it's no use nodding to a monument. And he was like
one. He didn't speak, he didn't budge. He just sat
there, holding his handsome old head up, immovable,
and almost bigger than life. It was extremely fine.
Mr. Stonor's presence reduced old Jermyn to a mere
shabby wisp of a man, and made the talkative stranger
in tweeds on the hearthrug look absurdly boyish. The
latter must have been a few years over thirty, and was
certainly not the sort of individual that gets abashed
at the sound of his own voice, because gathering me in,
as it were, by a friendly glance, he kept it going without
a check.

" I was glad of it," he repeated emphatically. " You
may be surprised at it, but then you haven't gone
through the experience I've had of her. I can tell you, it
was something to remember. Of course, I got off scot

free myself—as you can see. She did her best to break up my pluck for me tho'. She jolly near drove as fine a fellow as ever lived into a madhouse. What do you say to that—eh ?"

Not an eyelid twitched in Mr. Stonor's enormous face. Monumental! The speaker looked straight into my eyes.

" It used to make me sick to think of her going about the world murdering people."

Jermyn approached the handkerchief a little nearer to the grate and groaned. It was simply a habit he had.

" I've seen her once," he declared, with mournful indifference. " She had a house——"

The stranger in tweeds turned to stare down at him surprised.

" She had three houses," he corrected authoritatively. But Jermyn was not to be contradicted.

" She had a house, I say," he repeated, with dismal obstinacy. " A great, big, ugly, white thing. You could see it from miles away—sticking up."

" So you could," assented the other readily. " It was old Colchester's notion, though he was always threatening to give her up. He couldn't stand her racket any more; he declared ; it was too much of a good thing for him ; he would wash his hands of her, if he never got hold of another—and so on. I dare say he would have chucked her, only—it may surprise you—his missus wouldn't hear of it. Funny, eh ? But with women, you never know how they will take a thing, and Mrs. Colchester, with her moustaches and big eyebrows, set up for being as strong-minded as they make them. She used to walk about in a brown silk dress, with a great gold cable flopping about her bosom. You should have heard her snapping out : ' Rubbish ! ' or ' Stuff and nonsense ! ' I daresay she knew when she was well off. They had no children, and had never set up a home anywhere. When in England she just made shift to hang out anyhow in some cheap hotel or boarding-house. I daresay she liked to get back to the comforts she was used to. She knew very well she couldn't gain by any change. And, moreover, Colchester,

though a first-rate man, was not what you may call in
his first youth, and, perhaps, she may have thought
that he wouldn't be able to get hold of another (as he
used to say) so easily. Anyhow, for one reason or
another, it was 'Rubbish' and 'Stuff and nonsense'
for the good lady. I overheard once young Mr. Apse
himself say to her confidentially: "I assure you, Mrs.
Colchester, I am beginning to feel quite unhappy about
the name she's getting for herself.' 'Oh,' says she,
with her deep little hoarse laugh, ' if one took notice of
all the silly talk,' and she showed Apse all her ugly false
teeth at once. ' It would take more than that to make
me lose my confidence in her, I assure you,' says
she."

At this point, without any change of facial expression,
Mr. Stonor emitted a short sardonic laugh. It was very
impressive, but I didn't see the fun. I looked from one
to another. The stranger on the hearthrug had an ugly
smile.

"And Mr. Apse shook both Mrs. Colchester's hands,
he was so pleased to hear a good word said for their
favourite. All these Apses, young and old you know,
were perfectly infatuated with that abominable, dangerous——"

"I beg your pardon," I interrupted, for he seemed
to be addressing himself exclusively to me, " but who
on earth are you talking about ? "

"I am talking of the Apse family," he answered,
courteously.

I nearly let out a damn at this. But just then the
respected Miss Blank put her head in, and said that the
cab was at the door, if Mr. Stonor wanted to catch the
eleven-three up.

At once the senior pilot arose in his mighty bulk and
began to struggle into his coat, with awe-inspiring up-
heavals. The stranger and I hurried impulsively to his
assistance, and directly we laid our hands on him he
became perfectly quiescent. We had to raise our arms
very high, and to make efforts. It was like caparisoning
a docile elephant. With a " Thanks, gentlemen," he

dived under and squeezed himself through the door in a great hurry.

We smiled at each other in a friendly way.

" I wonder how he manages to hoist himself up a ship's side-ladder," said the man in tweeds ; and poor Jermyn, who was a mere North Sea pilot, without official status or recognition of any sort, pilot only by courtesy, groaned.

" He makes eight hundred a year."

" Are you a sailor ? " I asked the stranger, who had gone back to his position on the rug.

" I used to be till a couple of years ago when I got married," answered this communicative individual. " I even went to sea first in that very ship we were speaking of when you came in."

" What ship ? " I asked, puzzled. " I never heard you mention a ship."

" I've just told you her name, my dear sir," he replied. " The *Apse Family*. Surely you've heard of the great firm of Apse & Sons, shipowners. They had a pretty big fleet. There was the *Lucy Apse*, and the *Harold Apse*, and *Anne, John, Malcolm, Clara, Juliet*, and so on —no end of *Apses*. Every brother, sister, aunt, cousin, wife—and grandmother too, for all I know—of the firm had a ship named after them. Good, solid, old-fashioned craft they were too, built to carry and to last. None of your new-fangled, labour-saving appliances in them, but plenty of men and plenty of good salt beef and hard tack put aboard—and off you go to fight your way out and home again."

The miserable Jermyn made a sound of approval, which sounded like a groan of pain. Those were the ships for him. He pointed out in doleful tones that you couldn't say to labour-saving appliances : " Jump lively now, my hearties." No labour-saving appliance would go aloft on a dirty night with the sands under your lee.

" No," assented the stranger, with a wink at me " The Apses didn't believe in them either, apparently. They treated their people well—as people don't get

treated nowadays, and they were awfully proud of their
ships. Nothing ever happened to them. This last one,
the *Apse Family* was to be like the others, only she was
to be still stronger, still safer, still more roomy and comfortable. I believe they meant her to last for ever.
They had her built composite—iron, teak-wood, and
greenheart, and her scantling was something fabulous.
If ever an order was given for a ship in a spirit of pride
this one was. Everything of the best. The commodore
captain of the employ was to command her, and they
planned the accommodation for him like a house on shore
under a big, tall poop that went nearly to the mainmast.
No wonder Mrs. Colchester wouldn't let the old man
give her up. Why, it was the best home she ever had
in all her married days. She had a nerve, that woman.

" The fuss that was made while that ship was building !
Let's have this a little stronger, and that a little heavier ;
and hadn't that other thing better be changed for something a little thicker. The builders entered into the
spirit of the game, and there she was, growing into the
clumsiest, heaviest ship of her size right before all their
eyes, without anybody becoming aware of it somehow.
She was to be 2,000 tons register, or a little over ; no
less on any account. But see what happens. When
they came to measure her she turned out 1,999 tons and
a fraction. General consternation ! And they say old
Mr. Apse was so annoyed, when they told him, that he
took to his bed and died. The old gentleman had
retired from the firm twenty-five years before, and was
ninety-six years old if a day, so his death wasn't, perhaps,
so surprising. Still Mr. Lucian Apse was convinced
that his father would have lived to a hundred. So we
may put him at the head of the list. Next comes the
poor devil of a shipwright that brute caught and squashed
as she went off the ways. They called it the launch of a
ship, but I've heard people say that, from the wailing and
yelling and scrambling out of the way, it was more like
letting a devil loose upon the river. She snapped all her
checks like pack-thread, and went for the tugs in attend-
ance like a fury. Before anybody could see what she

was up to she sent one of them to the bottom, and laid up another for three months' repairs. One of her cables parted, and then, suddenly—you couldn't tell why—she let herself be brought up with the other as quiet as a lamb.

"That's how she was. You could never be sure what she would be up to next. There are ships difficult to handle, but generally you can depend on them behaving rationally. With *that* ship, whatever you did with her, you never knew how it would end. She was a wicked beast. Or, perhaps, she was only just insane."

He uttered this supposition in so earnest a tone that I could not refrain from smiling. He left off biting his lower lip to apostrophize me.

"Eh! Why not? Why couldn't there be something in her build, in her lines corresponding to—What's madness? Only something just a tiny bit wrong in the make of your brain. Why shouldn't there be a mad ship —I mean mad in a ship-like way, so that under no circumstances could you be sure she would do what any other sensible ship would naturally do for you. There are ships that steer wildly, and ships that can't be quite trusted always to stay ; others want careful watching when running in a gale ; and, again, there may be a ship that will make heavy weather of it in every little blow. But then you expect her to be always so. You take it as part of her character, as a ship, just as you take account of a man's peculiarities of temper when you deal with him. But with her you couldn't. She was unaccountable. If she wasn't mad, then she was the most evil-minded, underhand, savage brute that ever went afloat. I've seen her run in a heavy gale beautifully for two days, and on the third broach to twice in the same afternoon. The first time she flung the helmsman clean over the wheel, but as she didn't quite manage to kill him she had another try about three hours afterwards. She swamped herself fore and aft, burst all the canvas we had set, scared all hands into a panic, and even frightened Mrs. Colchester down there in these beautiful stern cabins that she was so proud of. When we mustered the crew there was one man missing. Swept overboard, of course, without being either seen or heard, poor devil! and I only wonder more of us didn't go.

"Always something like that. Always. I heard an old mate tell Captain Colchester once that it had come to this with him, that he was afraid to open his mouth to give any sort of order. She was as much of a terror in harbour as at sea. You could never be certain what would hold her. On the slightest provocation she would start snapping ropes, cables, wire hawsers, like carrots. She was heavy, clumsy, unhandy—but that does not quite explain that power for mischief she had. You know, somehow, when I think of her I can't help remembering what we hear of incurable lunatics breaking loose now and then."

He looked at me inquisitively. But, of course, I couldn't admit that a ship could be mad.

"In the ports where she was known," he went on, "they dreaded the sight of her. She thought nothing of knocking away twenty feet or so of solid stone facing off a quay or wiping off the end of a wooden wharf. She must have lost miles of chain and hundreds of tons of anchors in her time. When she fell aboard some poor unoffending ship it was the very devil of a job to haul her off again. And she never got hurt herself—just a few scratches or so, perhaps. They had wanted to have her strong. And so she was. Strong enough to ram Polar ice with. And as she began so she went on. From the day she was launched she never let a year pass without murdering somebody. I think the owners got very worried about it. But they were a stiff-necked generation all these Apses; they wouldn't admit there could be anything wrong with the *Apse Family*. They wouldn't even change her name. 'Stuff and nonsense,' as Mrs. Colchester used to say. They ought at least to have shut her up for life in some dry dock or other, away up the river, and never let her smell salt water again. I assure you, my dear sir, that she invariably did kill some one every voyage she made. It was perfectly well known. She got a name for it, far and wide."

I expressed my surprise that a ship with such a deadly reputation could ever get a crew.

"Then, you don't know what sailors are, my dear sir. Let me just show you by an instance. One day in dock at home, while loafing on the forecastle head, I noticed two respectable salts come along, one a middle-aged, competent, steady man, evidently, the other a smart, youngish chap. They read the name on the bows and stopped to look at her. Says the elder man : ' *Apse Family*. That's the sanguinary female dog ' (I'm putting it in that way) ' of a ship, Jack, that kills a man every voyage. I wouldn't sign in her—not for Joe, I wouldn't.' And the other says : ' If she were mine, I'd have her towed on the mud and set on fire, blamme if I wouldn't.' Then the first man chimes in : ' Much do they care ! Men are cheap, God knows.' The younger one spat in the water alongside. ' They won't have me—not for double wages.'

"They hung about for some time and then walked up the dock. Half an hour later I saw them both on our deck looking about for the mate, and apparently very anxious to be taken on. And they were."

"How do you account for this ? " I asked.

"What would you say ? " he retorted. "Recklessness ! The vanity of boasting in the evening to all their chums : ' We've just shipped in that there *Apse Family*. Blow her. She ain't going to scare us.' Sheer sailor-like perversity ! A sort of curiosity. Well—a little of all that, no doubt. I put the question to them in the course of the voyage. The answer of the elderly chap was :

"' A man can die but once.' The younger assured me in a mocking tone that he wanted to see ' how she would do it this time.' But I tell you what ; there was a sort of fascination about the brute."

Jermyn, who seemed to have seen every ship in the world, broke in sulkily :

"I saw her once out of this very window towing up the river ; a great black ugly thing, going along like a big hearse."

"Something sinister about her looks, wasn't there ?"
said the man in tweeds, looking down at old Jermyn
with a friendly eye. "I always had a sort of horror of
her. She gave me a beastly shock when I was no more
than fourteen, the very first day—nay, hour—I joined
her. Father came up to see me off, and was to go down
to Gravesend with us. I was his second boy to go to sea.
My big brother was already an officer then. We got on
board about eleven in the morning, and found the ship
ready to drop out of the basin, stern first. She had
not moved three times her own length when, at a little
pluck the tug gave her to enter the dock gates, she made
one of her rampaging starts, and put such a weight on
the check rope—a new six-inch hawser—that forward
there they had no chance to ease it round in time, and
it parted. I saw the broken end fly up high in the air,
and the next moment that brute brought her quarter
against the pier-head with a jar that staggered everybody
about her decks. She didn't hurt herself. Not she !
But one of the boys the mate had sent aloft on the mizzen
to do something, came down on the poop-deck—thump—
right in front of me. He was not much older than
myself. We had been grinning at each other only a
few minutes before. He must have been handling
himself carelessly, not expecting to get such a jerk. I
heard his startled cry—Oh !—in a high treble as he felt
himself going, and looked up in time to see him go limp
all over as he fell. Ough ! Poor father was remarkably
white about the gills when we shook hands in Gravesend.
'Are you all right ? ' he says, looking hard at me. 'Yes,
father.' 'Quite sure ?' 'Yes, father.' 'Well, then,
good-bye, my boy.' He told me afterwards that for
half a word he would have carried me off home with him
there and then. I am the baby of the family—you
know," added the man in tweeds, stroking his moustache with an ingenuous smile.

I acknowledged this interesting communication by a
sympathetic murmur. He waved his hand carelessly.

"This might have utterly spoiled a chap's nerve for
going aloft, you know—utterly. He fell within two feet

of me, cracking his head on a mooring-bitt. Never moved. Stone dead. Nice looking little fellow, he was. I had just been thinking we would be great chums. However, that wasn't yet the worst that brute of a ship could do. I served in her three years of my time, and then I got transferred to the *Lucy Apse*, for a year. The sailmaker we had in the *Apse Family* turned up there, too, and I remember him saying to me one evening, after we had been a week at sea : ' Isn't she a meek little ship ? ' No wonder we thought the *Lucy Apse* a dear, meek, little ship after getting clear of that big rampaging savage brute. It was like heaven. Her officers seemed to me the restfullest lot of men on earth. To me who had known no ship but the *Apse Family*, the *Lucy* was like a sort of magic craft that did what you wanted her to do of her own accord. One evening we got caught aback pretty sharply from right ahead. In about ten minutes we had her full again, sheets aft, tacks down, decks cleared, and the officer of the watch leaning against the weather rail peacefully. It seemed simply marvellous to me. The other would have stuck for half-an-hour in irons, rolling her decks full of water, knocking the men about—spars cracking, braces snapping, yards taking charge, and a confounded scare going on aft because of her beastly rudder, which she had a way of flapping about fit to raise your hair on end. I couldn't get over my wonder for days.

"Well, I finished my last year of apprenticeship in that jolly little ship—she wasn't so little either, but after that other heavy devil she seemed but a plaything to handle. I finished my time and passed ; and then just as I was thinking of having three weeks of real good time on shore I got at breakfast a letter asking me the earliest day I could be ready to join the *Apse Family* as third mate. I gave my plate a shove that shot it into the middle of the table ; dad looked up over his paper ; mother raised her hands in astonishment, and I went out bare-headed into our bit of garden, where I walked round and round for an hour.

"When I came in again mother was out of the dining-room, and dad had shifted berth into his big armchair. The letter was lying on the mantelpiece.

"'It's very creditable to you to get the offer, and very kind of them to make it,' he said. 'And I see also that Charles has been appointed chief mate of that ship for one voyage.'

"There was overleaf a PS. to that effect in Mr. Apse's own handwriting, which I had overlooked. Charley was my big brother.

"'I don't like very much to have two of my boys together in one ship,' father goes on, in his deliberate, solemn way. 'And I may tell you that I would not mind writing Mr. Apse a letter to that effect.'

"Dear old dad! He was a wonderful father. What would you have done? The mere notion of going back (and as an officer, too), to be worried and bothered, and kept on the jump night and day by that brute, made me feel sick. But she wasn't a ship you could afford to fight shy of. Besides, the most genuine excuse could not be given without mortally offending Apse & Sons. The firm, and I believe the whole family down to the old unmarried aunts in Lancashire, had grown desperately touchy about that accursed ship's character. This was the case for answering 'Ready now' from your very death-bed if you wished to die in their good grace. And that's precisely what I did answer—by wire, to have it over and done with at once.

"The prospect of being shipmates with my big brother cheered me up considerably, though it made me a bit anxious, too. Ever since I remember myself as a little chap he had been very good to me, and I looked upon him as the finest fellow in the world. And so he was. No better officer ever walked the deck of a merchant ship. And that's a fact. He was a fine, strong, upstanding, sun-tanned young fellow, with his brown hair curling a little, and an eye like a hawk. He was just splendid. We hadn't seen each other for many years, and even this time, though he had been in England three weeks already, he hadn't showed up at home yet, but had spent his spare time in Surrey somewhere making up to Maggie

Colchester, old Captain Colchester's niece. Her father, a great friend of dad's, was in the sugar-broking business, and Charley made a sort of second home of their house. I wondered what my big brother would think of me. There was a sort of sternness about Charley's face which never left it, not even when he was larking in his rather wild fashion.

"He received me with a great shout of laughter. He seemed to think my joining as an officer the greatest joke in the world. There was a difference of ten years between us, and I suppose he remembered me best in pinafores. I was a kid of four when he first went to sea. It surprised me to find how boisterous he could be.

"'Now we shall see what you are made of,' he cried. And he held me off by the shoulders, and punched my ribs, and hustled me into his berth. 'Sit down, Ned. I am glad of the chance of having you with me. I'll put the finishing touch to you, my young officer, providing you're worth the trouble. And, first of all, get it well into your head that we are not going to let this brute kill anybody this voyage. We'll stop her racket.'

"I perceived he was in dead earnest about it. He talked grimly of the ship, and how we must be careful and never allow this ugly beast to catch us napping with any of her damned tricks.

He gave me a regular lecture on special seamanship for the use of the *Apse Family*; then changing his tone, he began to talk at large, rattling off the wildest, funniest nonsense, till my sides ached with laughing. I could see very well he was a bit above himself with high spirits. It couldn't be because of my coming. Not to that extent. But, of course, I wouldn't have dreamt of asking what was the matter. I had a proper respect for my big brother, I can tell you. But it was all made plain enough a day or two afterwards, when I heard that Miss Maggie Colchester was coming for the voyage. Uncle was giving her a sea-trip for the benefit of her health.

"I don't know what could have been wrong with her health. She had a beautiful colour, and a deuce of a lot of fair hair. She didn't care a rap for wind, or rain, or spray, or sun, or green seas, or anything. She was a blue-eyed, jolly girl of the very best sort, but the way she checked my big brother used to frighten me. I always expected it to end in an awful row. However, nothing decisive happened till after we had been in Sydney for a week. One day, in the men's dinner hour, Charley sticks his head into my cabin. I was stretched out on my back on the settee, smoking in peace.

"'Come ashore with me, Ned,' he says, in his curt way.

"I jumped up, of course, and away after him down the gangway and up George Street. He strode along like a giant, and I at his elbow, panting. It was confoundedly hot. 'Where on earth are you rushing me to, Charley?' I made bold to ask.

"'Here,' he says.

"'Here' was a jeweller's shop. I couldn't imagine what he could want there. It seemed a sort of mad freak. He thrusts under my nose three rings, which looked very tiny on his big, brown palm, growling out—

"'For Maggie! Which?'

"I got a kind of scare at this. I couldn't make a sound, but I pointed at the one that sparkled white and blue. He put it in his waistcoat pocket, paid for it with a lot of sovereigns, and bolted out. When we got on board I was quite out of breath. 'Shake hands, old chap,' I gasped out. He gave me a thump on the back. "Give what orders you like to the boatswain when the hands turn-to,' says he; 'I am off duty this afternoon.'

"Then he vanished from the deck for a while, but presently he came out of the cabin with Maggie, and these two went over the gangway publicly, before all hands, going for a walk together on that awful, blazing, hot day, with clouds of dust flying about. They came back after a few hours looking very staid, but didn't seem to have the slightest idea where they had been. Anyway, that's the answer they both made to Mrs. Colchester's question at tea-time.

"And didn't she turn on Charley, with her voice like

an old night cabman's. 'Rubbish. Don't know where you've been! Stuff and nonsense. You've walked the girl off her legs. Don't do it again.'

"It's surprising how meek Charley could be with that old woman. Only on one occasion he whispered to me, 'I'm jolly glad she isn't Maggie's aunt, except by marriage. That's no sort of relationship.' But I think he let Maggie have too much of her own way. She was hopping all over that ship in her yachting skirt and a red tam-o'-shanter like a bright bird on a dead black tree. The old salts used to grin to themselves when they saw her coming along, and offered to teach her knots or splices. I believe she liked the men, for Charley's sake, I suppose.

"As you may imagine, the diabolic propensities of that cursed ship were never spoken of on board. Not in the cabin, at any rate. Only once on the home-ward passage Charley said, incautiously, something about bringing all her crew home this time. Captain Colchester began to look uncomfortable at once, and that silly, hard-bitten old woman flew out at Charley as though he had said something indecent. I was quite confounded myself; as to Maggie, she sat completely mystified, opening her blue eyes very wide. Of course, before she was a day older she wormed it all out of me. She was a very difficult person to lie to.

"'How awful,' she said, quite solemn. 'So many poor fellows. I am glad the voyage is nearly over. I won't have a moment's peace about Charley now.'

"I assured her Charley was all right. It took more than that ship knew to get over a seaman like Charley. And she agreed with me.

"Next day we got the tug off Dungeness; and when the tow-rope was fast Charley rubbed his hands and said to me in an undertone—

"'We've baffled her, Ned.'

"'Looks like it,' I said, with a grin at him. It was beautiful weather, and the sea as smooth as a millpond. We went up the river without a shadow of trouble except once, when off Hole Haven, the brute took a sudden

sheer and nearly had a barge anchored just clear of the
fairway.   But I was aft, looking after the steering, and
she did not catch me napping that time.   Charley came
up on the poop, looking very concerned.   ' Close shave,'
says he.

" ' Never   mind,   Charley,'   I   answered,   cheerily.
' You've tamed her.'

" We were to tow right up to the dock.   The river
pilot boarded us below Gravesend, and the first words
I heard him say were : ' You may just as well take your
port anchor inboard at once, Mr. Mate.'

" This had been done when I went forward.   I saw
Maggie on the forecastle head enjoying the bustle and I
begged her to go aft, but she took no notice of me, of
course.   Then Charley, who was very busy with the
head gear, caught sight of her and shouted in his biggest
voice : ' Get off the forecastle head, Maggie.   You're in
the way here.'   For all answer she made a funny face at
him, and I saw poor Charley turn away, hiding a smile.
She was flushed with the excitement of getting home
again, and her blue eyes seemed to snap electric sparks
as she looked at the river.   A collier brig had gone round
just ahead of us, and our tug had to stop her engines
in a hurry to avoid running into her.

" In a moment, as is usually the case, all the shipping
in the reach seemed to get into a hopeless tangle.   A
schooner and a ketch got up a small collision all to themselves right in the middle of the river.   It was exciting to
watch, and, meantime, our tug remained stopped.   Any
other ship than that brute could have been coaxed to
keep straight for a couple of minutes—but not she !   Her
head fell off at once, and she began to drift down, taking
her tug along with her.   I noticed a cluster of coasters
at anchor within a quarter of a mile of us, and I thought
I had better speak to the pilot.   " If you let her get
amongst that lot,' I said, quietly, ' she will grind some
of them to bits before we get her out again.'

" ' Don't I know her ! ' cries he, stamping his foot in a
perfect fury.   And he out with his whistle to make that
bothered tug get the ship's head up again as quick as

possible. He blew like mad, waving his arm to port, and presently we could see that the tug's engines had been set going ahead. Her paddles churned the water, but it was as if she had been trying to tow a rock—she couldn't get an inch out of that ship. Again the pilot blew his whistle, and waved his arm to port. We could see the tug's paddles turning faster and faster away, broad on our bow.

"For a moment tug and ship hung motionless in a crowd of moving shipping, and then the terrific strain that evil, stony-hearted brute would always put on everything, tore the towing-chock clean out. The tow-rope surged over, snapping the iron stanchions of the head-rail one after another as if they had been sticks of sealing-wax. It was only then I noticed that in order to have a better view over our heads, Maggie had stepped upon the port anchor as it lay flat on the forecastle deck.

"It had been lowered properly into its hardwood beds, but there had been no time to take a turn with it. Anyway, it was quite secure as it was, for going into dock; but I could see directly that the tow-rope would sweep under the fluke in another second. My heart flew up right into my throat, but not before I had time to yell out: 'Jump clear of that anchor!'

"But I hadn't time to shriek out her name. I don't suppose she heard me at all. The first touch of the hawser against the fluke threw her down; she was up on her feet again as quick as lightning, but she was up on the wrong side. I heard a horrid, scraping sound, and then that anchor, tipping over, rose up like something alive; its great, rough iron arm caught Maggie round the waist, seemed to clasp her close with a dreadful hug, and flung itself with her over and down in a terrific clang of iron, followed by heavy ringing blows that shook the ship from stern to stem—because the ring stopper held!"

"How horrible!" I exclaimed.

"I used to dream for years afterwards of anchors catching hold of girls," said the man in tweeds, a little wildly. He shuddered. "With a most pitiful howl Charley was over after her almost on the instant. But,

8

Lord ! he didn't see as much as a gleam of her red tam-o'-shanter in the water. Nothing ! nothing whatever ! In a moment there were half-a-dozen boats around us, and he got pulled into one. I, with the boatswain and the carpenter, let go the other anchor in a hurry and brought the ship up somehow. The pilot had gone silly. He walked up and down the forecastle head wringing his hands and muttering to himself : ' Killing women, now ! Killing women, now ! ' Not another word could you get out of him.

"Dusk fell, then a night black as pitch ; and peering upon the river I heard a low, mournful hail, ' Ship, ahoy ! ' Two Gravesend watermen came alongside. They had a lantern in their wherry, and looked up the ship's side, holding on to the ladder without a word. I saw in the patch of light a lot of loose, fair hair down there."

He shuddered again.

"After the tide turned poor Maggie's body had floated clear of one of them big mooring buoys," he explained. "I crept aft, feeling half-dead and managed to send a rocket up—to let the other searchers know, on the river. And then I slunk away forward like a cur, and spent the night sitting on the heel of the bowsprit so as to be as far as possible out of Charley's way."

"Poor fellow ! " I murmured.

"Yes. Poor fellow," he repeated musingly. "That brute wouldn't let him—not even him—cheat her of her prey. But he made her fast in dock next morning. He did. We hadn't exchanged a word—not a single look for that matter. I didn't want to look at him. When the last rope was fast he put his hands to his head and stood gazing down at his feet as if trying to remember something. The men waited on the main deck for the words that end the voyage. Perhaps that is what he was trying to remember. I spoke for him. ' That'll do, men.'

"I never saw a crew leave a ship so quietly. They sneaked over the rail one after another, taking care not to bang their sea chests too heavily. They looked our way, but not one had the stomach to come up and offer to shake hands with the mate as is usual.

"I followed him all over the empty ship to and fro, here and there, with no living soul about but the two of us, because the old ship-keeper had locked himself up in the galley—both doors. Suddenly poor Charley mutters, in a crazy voice : 'I'm done here,' and strides down the gangway with me at his heels, up the dock, out at the gate, on towards Tower Hill. He used to take rooms with a decent old landlady in America Square, to be near his work.

"All at once he stops short, turns round, and comes back straight at me. 'Ned,' says he, 'I am going home.' I had the good luck to sight a four-wheeler and got him in just in time. His legs were beginning to give way. In our hall he fell down on a chair, and I'll never forget father's and mother's amazed, perfectly still faces as they stood over him. They couldn't understand what had happened to him till I blubbered out 'Maggie got drowned, yesterday, in the river.'

"Mother let out a little cry. Father looks from him to me, and from me to him, as if comparing our faces— for, upon my soul, Charley did not resemble himself at all. Nobody moved : and the poor fellow raises his big brown hands slowly to his throat, and with one single tug rips everything open—collar, shirt, waistcoat, —a perfect wreck and ruin of a man. Father and I got him upstairs somehow, and mother pretty nearly killed herself nursing him through a brain fever."

The man in tweeds nodded at me significantly.

"Ah ! there was nothing that could be done with that brute. She had a devil in her."

"Where's your brother ?" I asked, expecting to hear he was dead. But he was commanding a smart steamer on the China coast, and never came home now.

Jermyn fetched a heavy sigh, and the handkerchief being now sufficiently dry, put it up tenderly to his red and lamentable nose.

"She was a ravening beast," the man in tweeds started again. "Old Colchester put his foot down and

resigned. And would you believe it ?   Apse & Sons
wrote to ask whether he wouldn't reconsider his decision !
Anything to save the good name of the *Apse Family* !
Old Colchester went to the office then and said that he
would take charge again but only to sail her out into
the North Sea and scuttle her there. He was nearly off
his chump. He used to be darkish iron-grey, but his
hair went snow-white in a fortnight. And Mr. Lucian
Apse (they had known each other as young men) pretended not to notice it.   Eh ?   Here's infatuation if you
like ! Here's pride for you !

" They jumped at the first man they could get to take
her, for fear of the scandal of the *Apse Family* not being
able to find a skipper. He was a festive soul, I believe,
but he stuck to her grim and hard. Wilmot was his
second mate. A harum-scarum fellow, and pretending
to a great scorn for all the girls. The fact is he was really
timid. But let only one of them do as much as lift her
little finger in encouragement, and there was nothing
that could hold the beggar. As apprentice, once, he
deserted abroad after a petticoat, and would have gone to
the dogs then if his skipper hadn't taken the trouble to
find him and lug him by the ears out of some house of
perdition or other.

" It was said that one of the firm had been heard
once to express a hope that this brute of a ship would
get lost soon. I can hardly credit the tale, unless it
might have been Mr. Alfred Apse, whom the family didn't
think much of. They had him in the office, but he was
considered a bad egg altogether, always flying off to race
meetings and coming home drunk. You would have
thought that a ship so full of deadly tricks would run
herself ashore some day out of sheer cussedness. But
not she ! She was going to last for ever. She had a nose
to keep off the bottom."

Jermyn made a grunt of approval.

" A ship after a pilot's own heart, eh ? " jeered the
man in tweeds. " Well, Wilmot managed it. He was the
man for it, but even he, perhaps, couldn't have done the
trick without that green-eyed governess, or nurse, or

whatever she was to the children of Mr. and Mrs. Pamphilius.

"Those people were passengers in her from Port Adelaide to the Cape. Well, the ship went out and anchored outside for the day. The skipper—hospitable soul—had a lot of guests from town to a farewell lunch—as usual with him. It was five in the evening before the last shore boat left the side, and the weather looked ugly and dark in the gulf. There was no reason for him to get under way. However, as he had told everybody he was going that day, he imagined it was proper to do so anyhow. But as he had no mind after all these festivities to tackle the straits in the dark, with a scant wind, he gave orders to keep the ship under lower topsails and foresail as close as she would lie, dodging along the land till the morning. Then he sought his virtuous couch. The mate was on deck, having his face washed very clean with hard rain squalls. Wilmot relieved him at midnight.

"The *Apse Family* had, as you observed, a house on her poop . . ."

"A big, ugly white thing, sticking up," Jermyn murmured sadly, at the fire.

"That's it: a companion for the cabin stairs and a sort of chart-room combined. The rain drove in gusts on the sleepy Wilmot. The ship was then surging slowly to the southward, close hauled, with the coast within three miles or so to windward. There was nothing to look out for in that part of the gulf, and Wilmot went round to dodge the squalls under the lee of that chart-room, whose door on that side was open. The night was black, like a barrel of coal-tar. And then he heard a woman's voice whispering to him.

"That confounded green-eyed girl of the Pamphilius people had put the kids to bed a long time ago, of course, but it seems couldn't get to sleep herself. She heard eight bells struck, and the chief mate come below to turn in. She waited a bit, then got into her dressing-gown and stole across the empty saloon and up the stairs into the chart-room. She sat down on the settee near the open door to cool herself, I daresay.

" I suppose when she whispered to Wilmot it was as if somebody had struck a match in the fellow's brain. I don't know how it was they had got so very thick. I fancy he had met her ashore a few times before. I couldn't make it out, because, when telling the story, Wilmot would break off to swear something awful at every second word. We had met on the quay in Sydney, and he had an apron of sacking up to his chin, a big whip in his hand. A wagon-driver. Glad to do anything not to starve. That's what he had come down to.

" However, there he was, with his head inside the door, on the girl's shoulder as likely as not—officer of the watch ! The helmsman, on giving his evidence afterwards, said that he shouted several times that the binnacle lamp had gone out. It didn't matter to him, because his orders were to ' sail her close.' ' I thought it funny,' he said, ' that the ship should keep on falling off in squalls, but I luffed her up every time as close as I was able. It was so dark I couldn't see my hand before my face, and the rain came in bucketsful on my head.'

" The truth was that at every squall the wind hauled aft a little, till gradually the ship came to be heading straight for the coast, without a single soul in her being aware of it. Wilmot himself confessed that he had not been near the standard compass for an hour. He might well have confessed ! The first thing he knew was the man on the look-out shouting blue murder forward there.

" He tore his neck free, he says, and yelled back at him : ' What do you say ? '

" ' I think I hear breakers ahead, sir,' howled the man and came rushing aft with the rest of the watch, in the ' awfullest blinding deluge that ever fell from the sky,' Wilmot says. For a second or so he was so scared and bewildered that he could not remember on which side of the gulf the ship was. He wasn't a good officer, but he was a seaman all the same. He pulled himself together in a second, and the right orders sprang to his lips without thinking. They were to hard up with the helm and shiver the main and mizzen-topsails.

"It seems that the sails actually fluttered. He couldn't see them, but he heard them rattling and banging above his head. 'No use! She was too slow in going off,' he went on, his dirty face twitching, and the damn'd carter's whip shaking in his hand. 'She seemed to stick fast.' And then the flutter of the canvas above his head ceased. At this critical moment the wind hauled aft again with a gust, filling the sails, and sending the ship with a great way upon the rocks on her lee bow. She had overreached herself in her last little game. Her time had come—the hour, the man, the black night, the treacherous gust of wind—the right woman to put an end to her. The brute deserved nothing better. Strange are the instruments of Providence. There's a sort of poetical justice——"

The man in tweeds looked hard at me.

"The first ledge she went over stripped the false keel off her. Rip! The skipper, rushing out of his berth, found a crazy woman, in a red flannel-dressing-gown, flying round and round the cuddy, screeching like a cockatoo.

"The next bump knocked her clean under the cabin table. It also started the stern-post and carried away the rudder, and then that brute ran up a shelving, rocky shore, tearing her bottom out, till she stopped short, and the foremast dropped over the bows like a gangway."

"Anybody lost?" I asked.

"No one, unless that fellow, Wilmot," answered the gentleman, unknown to Miss Blank, looking round for his cap. "And his case was worse than drowning for a man. Everybody got ashore all right. Gale didn't come on till next day, dead from the West, and broke up that brute in a surprisingly short time. It was as though she had been rotten at heart." . . . He changed his tone. "Rain left off. I must get my bike and rush home to dinner. I live in Herne Bay—came out for a spin this morning."

He nodded at me in a friendly way, and went out with a swagger.

"Do you know who he is, Jermyn?" I asked.

The North Sea pilot shook his head, dismally.
" Fancy losing a ship in that silly fashion !   Oh dear !
oh dear ! " he groaned in lugubrious tones, spreading
his damp handkerchief again like a curtain before the
glowing grate.

On going out I exchanged a glance and a smile (strictly
proper) with the respectable Miss Blank, barmaid of
the Three Crows.

AN ANARCHIST

THAT year I spent the best two months of the dry season on one of the estates—in fact on the principal cattle estate—of a famous meat-extract manufacturing company.

B. O. S. Bos. You have seen the three magic letters on the advertisement pages of magazines and news-papers, in the windows of provision merchants, and on calendars for next year you receive by post in the month of November. They scatter pamphlets also, written in a sickly enthusiastic style and in several languages, giving statistics of slaughter and bloodshed enough to make a Turk turn faint. The " art " illustrating that " literature " represents in vivid and shining colours a large and enraged black bull stamping upon a yellow snake writhing in emerald-green grass, with a cobalt-blue sky for a background. It is atrocious and it is an alle-gory. The snake symbolizes disease, weakness—perhaps mere hunger, which last is the chronic disease of the majority of mankind. Of course everybody knows the B. O. S. Ltd., with its unrivalled products : Vinobos, Jellybos, and the latest unequalled perfection, Tribos, whose nourishment is offered to you not only highly concentrated, but already half digested. Such appar-ently is the love that Limited Company bears to its fellow-men—even as the love of the father and mother penguin for their hungry fledglings.

Of course the capital of a country must be productively employed. I have nothing to say against the company

But being myself animated by feelings of affection towards my fellow-men, I am saddened by the modern system of advertising. Whatever evidence it offers of enterprise, ingenuity, impudence and resource in certain individuals, it proves to my mind the wide prevalence of that form of mental degradation which is called gullibility.

In various parts of the civilised and uncivilised world I have had to swallow B. O. S. with more or less benefit to myself, though without great pleasure. Prepared with hot water and abundantly peppered to bring out the taste, this extract is not really unpalatable. But I have never swallowed its advertisements. Perhaps they have not gone far enough. As far as I can remember they make no promise of everlasting youth to the users of B. O. S., nor yet have they claimed the power of raising the dead for their estimable products. Why this austere reserve, I wonder ! But I don't think they would have had me even on these terms. Whatever form of mental degradation I may (being but human) be suffering from, it is not the popular form. I am not gullible.

I have been at some pains to bring out distinctly this statement about myself in view of the story which follows. I have checked the facts as far as possible. I have turned up the files of French newspapers, and I have also talked with the officer who commands the military guard on the *Ile Royale*, when in the course of my travels I reached Cayenne. I believe the story to be in the main true. It is the sort of story that no man, I think, would ever invent about himself, for it is neither grandiose nor flattering, nor yet funny enough to gratify a perverted vanity.

It concerns the engineer of the steam-launch belonging to the Marañon cattle estate of the B. O. S. Co., Ltd. This estate is also an island—an island as big as a small province, lying in the estuary of a great South American river. It is wild and not beautiful, but the grass growing on its low plains seems to possess exceptionally nourishing and flavouring qualities. It resounds with the lowing of innumerable herds—a deep and distressing sound under the open sky, rising like a monstrous protest of prisoners condemned to death. On the mainland, across twenty miles of discoloured muddy water, there stands a city whose name, let us say, is Horta.

But the most interesting characteristic of this island (which seems like a sort of penal settlement for condemned cattle) consists in its being the only known habitat of an extremely rare and gorgeous butterfly. The species is even more rare than it is beautiful, which is not saying little. I have already alluded to my travels. I travelled at that time, but strictly for myself and with a moderation unknown in our days of round-the-world tickets. I even travelled with a purpose. As a matter of fact, I am —" Ha, ha, ha !—a desperate butterfly-slayer. Ha, ha, ha ! "

This was the tone in which Mr. Harry Gee, the manager of the cattle station, alluded to my pursuits. He seemed to consider me the greatest absurdity in the world. On the other hand, the B. O. S. Co., Ltd., represented to him the acme of the nineteenth century's achievement. I believe that he slept in his leggings and spurs. His days he spent in the saddle flying over the plains, followed by a train of half-wild horsemen, who called him Don Enrique, and who had no definite idea of the B. O. S. Co., Ltd., which paid their wages. He was an excellent manager, but I don't see why, when we met at meals, he should have thumped me on the back, with loud derisive inquiries : " How's the deadly sport to-day ? Butterflies going strong ? Ha, ha, ha ! "—especially as he charged me two dollars per diem for the hospitality of the B. O. S. Co., Ltd. (capital £1,500,000, fully paid up), in whose balance-sheet for that year those monies are no doubt included. " I don't think I can make it anything less in justice to my company," he had remarked, with extreme gravity, when I was arranging with him the terms of my stay on the island.

His chaff would have been harmless enough if intimacy of intercourse in the absence of all friendly feeling were

not a thing detestable in itself.   Moreover, his facetious-
ness was not very amusing.   It consisted in the
wearisome repetition of descriptive phrases applied
to people with a burst of laughter. " Desperate
butterfly-slayer.   Ha, ha, ha ! " was one sample of his
peculiar wit which he himself enjoyed so much.   And
in the same vein of exquisite humour he called my attention to the engineer of the steam-launch, one day, as
we strolled on the path by the side of the creek.

The man's head and shoulders emerged above the
deck, over which were scattered various tools of his
trade and a few pieces of machinery.   He was doing
some repairs to the engines.   At the sound of our footsteps he raised anxiously a grimy face with a pointed
chin and a tiny fair moustache.   What could be seen of
his delicate features under the black smudges appeared
to me wasted and livid in the greenish shade of the
enormous tree spreading its foliage over the launch
moored close to the bank.

To my great surprise, Harry Gee addressed him as
" Crocodile," in that half-jeering, half-bullying tone
which is characteristic of self-satisfaction in his delect-
able kind :

" How does the work get on, Crocodile ? "

I should have said before that the amiable Harry had
picked up French of a sort somewhere—in some colony
or other—and that he pronounced it with a disagreeable,
forced precision as though he meant to guy the language.
The man in the launch answered him quickly in a
pleasant voice.   His eyes had a liquid softness and his
teeth flashed dazzlingly white between his thin drooping
lips.   The manager turned to me, very cheerful and loud,
explaining :

" I call him Crocodile because he lives half in, half
out of the creek.   Amphibious—see ?   There's nothing
else amphibious living on the island except crocodiles ;
so he must belong to the species—eh ?   But in reality he's
nothing less than *un citoyen anarchiste de Barcelone.*"

" A citizen anarchist from Barcelona ? " I repeated,
stupidly, looking down at the man.   He had turned to

his work in the engine-well of the launch and presented his bowed back to us. In that attitude I heard him protest, very audibly:

"I do not even know Spanish."

"Hey? What? You dare to deny you come from over there?" the accomplished manager was down on him truculently.

At this the man straightened himself up, dropping a spanner he had been using, and faced us; but he trembled in all his limbs.

"I deny nothing, nothing, nothing!" he said, excitedly.

He picked up the spanner and went to work again without paying any further attention to us. After looking at him for a minute or so, we went away.

"Is he really an anarchist?" I asked, when out of ear-shot.

"I don't care a hang what he is," answered the humorous official of the B. O. S. Co. "I gave him the name because it suited me to label him in that way. It's good for the company."

"For the company!" I exclaimed, stopping short.

"Aha!" he triumphed, tilting up his hairless pug face and straddling his thin long legs. "That surprises you. I am bound to do my best for my company. They have enormous expenses. Why—our agent in Horta tells me they spend fifty thousand pounds every year in advertising all over the world! One can't be too economical in working the show. Well, just you listen. When I took charge here the estate had no steam-launch. I asked for one, and kept on asking by every mail till I got it; but the man they sent out with it chucked his job at the end of two months, leaving the launch moored at the pontoon in Horta. Got a better screw at a sawmill up the river—blast him! And ever since it has been the same thing. Any Scotch or Yankee vagabond that likes to call himself a mechanic out here gets eighteen pounds a month, and the next you know he's cleared out, after smashing something as likely as not. I give you my word that some of the objects I've had for engine-drivers couldn't tell the boiler from the funnel. But this fellow understands his trade, and I don't mean him to clear out. See ?"

And he struck me lightly on the chest for emphasis. Disregarding his peculiarities of manner, I wanted to know what all this had to do with the man being an anarchist.

"Come !"jeered the manager. "If you saw suddenly a barefooted, unkempt chap slinking amongst the bushes on the sea face of the island, and at the same time observed less than a mile from the beach, a small schooner full of niggers hauling off in a hurry, you wouldn't think the man fell there from the sky, would you ? And it could be nothing else but either that or Cayenne. I've got my wits about me. Directly I sighted this queer game I said to myself—'Escaped Convict.' I was as certain of it as I am of seeing you standing here this minute. So I spurred on straight at him. He stood his ground for a bit on a sand hillock crying out : ' *Monsieur! Monsieur! Arrêtez!* ' then at the last moment broke and ran for life. Says I to my- self, ' I'll tame you before I'm done with you.' So with- out a single word I kept on, heading him off here and there. I rounded him up towards the shore, and at last I had him corralled on a spit, his heels in the water and nothing but sea and sky at his back, with my horse pawing the sand and shaking his head within a yard of him.

" He folded his arms on his breast then and stuck his chin up in a sort of desperate way ; but I wasn't to be impressed by the beggar's posturing.

" Says I, ' You're a runaway convict.'

" When he heard French, his chin went down and his face changed.

" ' I deny nothing,' says he, panting yet, for I had kept him skipping about in the front of my horse pretty smartly. I asked him what he was doing there. He had got his breath by then, and explained that he had meant to make his way to a farm which he understood (from the schooner's people, I suppose) was to be found in the neighbourhood. At that I laughed aloud and he got uneasy. Had he been deceived ? Was there no farm within walking distance ?

" I laughed more and more. He was on foot, and of course the first bunch of cattle he came across would have stamped him to rags under their hoofs. A dismounted man caught on the feeding-grounds hasn't got the ghost of a chance.

" 'My coming upon you like this has certainly saved your life,' I said. He remarked that perhaps it was so ; but that for his part he had imagined I had wanted to kill him under the hoofs of my horse. I assured him that nothing would have been easier had I meant it. And then we came to a sort of dead stop. For the life of me I didn't know what to do with this convict, unless I chucked him into the sea. It occurred to me to ask him what he had been transported for. He hung his head.

" ' What is it ? ' says I. ' Theft, murder, rape, or what ? ' I wanted to hear what he would have to say for himself, though of course I expected it would be some sort of lie. But all he said was—

" ' Make it what you like. I deny nothing. It is no good denying anything.'

" I looked him over carefully and a thought struck me.

" ' They've got anarchists there, too,' I said. ' Perhaps you're one of them.'

" ' I deny nothing whatever, monsieur,' he repeats.

" This answer made me think that perhaps he was not an anarchist. I believe those damned lunatics are rather proud of themselves. If he had been one, he would have probably confessed straight out.

" ' What were you before you became a convict ? '

" ' *Ouvrier*,' he says. ' And a good workman too.'

" At that I began to think he must be an anarchist, after all. That's the class they come mostly from, isn't it ? I hate the cowardly bomb-throwing brutes. I almost made up my mind to turn my horse short round and leave him to starve or drown where he was, which- ever he liked best. As to crossing the island to bother me again, the cattle would see to that. I don't know what induced me to ask—

"'What sort of workman?'

"I didn't care a hang whether he answered me or not. But when he said at once, '*Mécanicien, monsieur*,' I nearly jumped out of the saddle with excitement. The launch had been lying disabled and idle in the creek for three weeks. My duty to the company was clear. He noticed my start, too, and there we were for a minute or so staring at each other as if bewitched.

"'Get up on my horse behind me,' I told him. 'You shall put my steam-launch to rights.'"

These are the words in which the worthy manager of the Marañon estate related to me the coming of the supposed anarchist. He meant to keep him—out of a sense of duty to the company—and the name he had given him would prevent the fellow from obtaining employment anywhere in Horta. The vaqueros of the estate, when they went on leave, spread it all over the town. They did not know what an anarchist was, nor yet what Barcelona meant. They called him Anarchisto de Barcelona, as if it were his Christian name and surname. But the people in town had been reading in their papers about the anarchists in Europe and were very much impressed. Over the jocular addition of "de Barcelona" Mr. Harry Gee chuckled with immense satisfaction. "That breed is particularly murderous, isn't it? It makes the sawmills crowd still more afraid of having anything to do with him—see?" he exulted, candidly. "I hold him by that name better than if I had him chained up by the leg to the deck of the steam-launch.

"And mark," he added, after a pause, "he does not deny it. I am not wronging him in any way. He is a convict of some sort, anyhow."

"But I suppose you pay him some wages, don't you?" I asked.

"Wages! What does he want with money here? He gets his food from my kitchen and his clothing from the store. Of course I'll give him something at the end

of the year, but you don't think I'd employ a convict
and give him the same money I would give an honest
man ? I am looking after the interests of my company
first and last."

I admitted that, for a company spending fifty
thousand pounds every year in advertising, the strictest
economy was obviously necessary. The manager of the
Marañon Estancia grunted approvingly.

"And I'll tell you what," he continued : " if I were
certain he's an anarchist and he had the cheek to ask me
for money, I would give him the toe of my boot. However, let him have the benefit of the doubt. I am perfectly willing to take it that he has done nothing worse
than to stick a knife into somebody—with extenuating
circumstances—French fashion, don't you know. But
that subversive sanguinary rot of doing away with all
law and order in the world makes my blood boil. It's
simply cutting the ground from under the feet of every
decent, respectable, hard-working person. I tell you
that the consciences of people who have them, like you
or I, must be protected in some way ; or else the first
low scoundrel that came along would in every respect be
just as good as myself. Wouldn't he now ? And that's
absurd ! "

He glared at me. I nodded slightly and murmured
that doubtless there was much subtle truth in his view.

The principal truth discoverable in the views of Paul
the engineer was that a little thing may bring about the
undoing of a man.

" *Il ne faut pas beaucoup pour perdre un homme*," he
said to me, thoughtfully, one evening.

I report this reflection in French, since the man was
of Paris, not of Barcelona at all. At the Marañon he lived
apart from the station, in a small shed with a metal roof
and straw walls, which he called *mon atelier*. He had a
work-bench there. They had given him several horse-
blankets and a saddle—not that he ever had occasion
to ride, but because no other bedding was used by the
working-hands, who were all vaqueros—cattlemen.

9

And on this horseman's gear, like a son of the plains, he used to sleep amongst the tools of his trade, in a litter of rusty scrap-iron, with a portable forge at his head, under the work-bench sustaining his grimy mosquito-net.

Now and then I would bring him a few candle ends saved from the scant supply of the manager's house. He was very thankful for these. He did not like to lie awake in the dark, he confessed. He complained that sleep fled from him. " *Le sommeil me fuit,*" he declared, with his habitual air of subdued stoicism, which made him sympathetic and touching. I made it clear to him that I did not attach undue importance to the fact of his having been a convict.

Thus it came about that one evening he was led to talk about himself. As one of the bits of candle on the edge of the bench burned down to the end, he hastened to light another.

He had done his military service in a provincial garrison and returned to Paris to follow his trade. It was a well-paid one. He told me with some pride that in a short time he was earning no less than ten francs a day. He was thinking of setting up for himself by and by and of getting married.

Here he sighed deeply and paused. Then with a return to his stoical note :

" It seems I did not know enough about myself."

On his twenty-fifth birthday two of his friends in the repairing shop where he worked proposed to stand him a dinner. He was immensely touched by this attention.

" I was a steady man," he remarked, " but I am not less sociable than any other body."

The entertainment came off in a little café on the Boulevard de la Chapelle. At dinner they drank some special wine. It was excellent. Everything was excellent ; and the world—in his own words—seemed a very good place to live in. He had good prospects, some little money laid by, and the affection of two excellent friends. He offered to pay for all the drinks after dinner, which was only proper on his part.

They drank more wine ; they drank liqueurs, cognac,

beer, then more liqueurs and more cognac. Two strangers sitting at the next table looked at him, he said, with so much friendliness, that he invited them to join the party.

He had never drunk so much in his life. His elation was extreme, and so pleasurable that whenever it flagged he hastened to order more drinks.

"It seemed to me," he said, in his quiet tone and looking on the ground in the gloomy shed full of shadows, "that I was on the point of just attaining a great and wonderful felicity. Another drink, I felt, would do it. The others were holding out well with me, glass for glass."

But an extraordinary thing happened. At something the strangers said his elation fell. Gloomy ideas—*des idées noires*—rushed into his head. All the world outside the café appeared to him as a dismal evil place where a multitude of poor wretches had to work and slave to the sole end that a few individuals should ride in carriages and live riotously in palaces. He became ashamed of his happiness. The pity of mankind's cruel lot wrung his heart. In a voice choked with sorrow he tried to express these sentiments. He thinks he wept and swore in turns.

The two new acquaintances hastened to applaud his humane indignation. Yes. The amount of injustice in the world was indeed scandalous. There was only one way of dealing with the rotten state of society. Demolish the whole *sacrée boutique*. Blow up the whole iniquitous show.

Their heads hovered over the table. They whispered to him eloquently; I don't think they quite expected the result. He was extremely drunk—mad drunk. With a howl of rage he leaped suddenly upon the table. Kicking over the bottles and glasses, he yelled: "*Vive l'anarchie!* Death to the capitalists!" He yelled this again and again. All round him broken glass was falling, chairs were being swung in the air, people were taking each other by the throat. The police dashed in. He hit, bit, scratched and struggled, till something crashed down upon his head. . .

He came to himself in a police cell, locked up on a charge of assault, seditious cries, and anarchist propaganda.

He looked at me fixedly with his liquid, shining eyes, that seemed very big in the dim light.

" That was bad. But even then I might have got off somehow, perhaps," he said, slowly.

I doubt it. But whatever chance he had was done away with by a young socialist lawyer who volunteered to undertake his defence. In vain he assured him that he was no anarchist ; that he was a quiet, respectable mechanic, only too anxious to work ten hours per day at his trade. He was represented at the trial as the victim of society and his drunken shoutings as the expression of infinite suffering. The young lawyer had his way to make, and this case was just what he wanted for a start. The speech for the defence was pronounced magnificent.

The poor fellow paused, swallowed, and brought out the statement :

" I got the maximum penalty applicable to a first offence."

I made an appropriate murmur. He hung his head and folded his arms.

" When they let me out of prison," he began, gently, " I made tracks, of course, for my old workshop. My *patron* had a particular liking for me before ; but when he saw me he turned green with fright and showed me the door with a shaking hand."

While he stood in the street, uneasy and disconcerted, he was accosted by a middle-aged man who introduced himself as an engineer's fitter, too. " I know who you are," he said. " I have attended your trial. You are a good comrade and your ideas are sound. But the devil of it is that you won't be able to get work anywhere now. These bourgeois 'll conspire to starve you. That's their way. Expect no mercy from the rich."

To be spoken to so kindly in the street had comforted him very much. His seemed to be the sort of nature needing support and sympathy. The idea of not being able to find work had knocked him over completely.

If his *patron*, who knew him so well for a quiet, orderly, competent workman, would have nothing to do with him now—then surely nobody else would. That was clear. The police keeping their eye on him would hasten to warn every employer inclined to give him a chance. He felt suddenly very helpless, alarmed and idle ; and he followed the middle-aged man to the *estaminet* round the corner where he met some other good companions. They assured him that he would not be allowed to starve, work or no work. They had drinks all round to the discomfiture of all employers of labour and to the destruction of society.

He sat biting his lower lip.

"That is, monsieur, how I became a *compagnon*," he said. The hand he passed over his forehead was trembling. "All the same, there's something wrong in a world where a man can get lost for a glass more or less."

He never looked up, though I could see he was getting excited under his dejection. He slapped the bench with his open palm.

"No!" he cried. "It was an impossible existence ! Watched by the police, watched by the comrades, I did not belong to myself any more ! Why, I could not even go to draw a few francs from my savings-bank without a comrade hanging about the door to see that I didn't bolt ! And most of them were neither more nor less than housebreakers. The intelligent, I mean. They robbed the rich ; they were only getting back their own, they said. When I had had some drink I believed them. There were also the fools and the mad. *Des exaltés—quoi!* When I was drunk I loved them. When I got more drink I was angry with the world. That was the best time. I found refuge from misery in rage. But one can't be always drunk—*n'est-ce pas, monsieur*? And when I was sober I was afraid to break away. They would have stuck me like a pig."

He folded his arms again and raised his sharp chin with a bitter smile.

"By and by they told me it was time to go to work. The work was to rob a bank. Afterwards a bomb would be thrown to wreck the place.   My beginner's part would be to keep watch in a street at the back and to take care of a black bag with the bomb inside till it was wanted. After the meeting at which the affair was arranged a trusty comrade did not leave me an inch.   I had not dared to protest ; I was afraid of being done away with quietly in that room ; only, as we were walking together I wondered whether it would not be better for me to throw myself suddenly into the Seine.   But while I was turning it over in my mind we had crossed the bridge, and afterwards I had not the opportunity."

In the light of the candle end, with his sharp features, fluffy little moustache, and oval face, he looked at times delicately and gaily young, and then appeared quite old, decrepit, full of sorrow, pressing his folded arms to his breast.

As he remained silent I felt bound to ask :

" Well !   And how did it end ? "

" Deportation to Cayenne," he answered.

He seemed to think that somebody had given the plot away.   As he was keeping watch in the back street, bag in hand, he was set upon by the police. " These imbeciles," had knocked him down without noticing what he had in his hand.   He wondered how the bomb failed to explode as he fell.   But it didn't explode.

" I tried to tell my story in court," he continued. " The president was amused.   There were in the audience some idiots who laughed."

I expressed the hope that some of his companions had been caught too.   He shuddered slightly before he told me that there were two—Simon, called also Biscuit, the middle-aged fitter who spoke to him in the street, and a fellow of the name of Mafile, one of the sympathetic strangers who had applauded his sentiments and consoled his humanitarian sorrows when he got drunk in the café.

" Yes," he went on with an effort, " I had the advantage of their company over there on St. Joseph's Island, amongst some eighty or ninety other convicts.   We were all classed as dangerous."

St. Joseph's Island is the prettiest of the *Iles de Salut*. It is rocky and green, with shallow ravines, bushes, thickets, groves of mango-trees, and many feathery palms. Six warders armed with revolvers and carbines are in charge of the convicts kept there.

An eight-oared galley keeps up the communication in the daytime, across a channel a quarter of a mile wide, with the *Ile Royale*, where there is a military post. She makes the first trip at six in the morning. At four in the afternoon her service is over, and she is then hauled up into a little dock on the *Ile Royale* and a sentry put over her and a few smaller boats. From that time till next morning the island of St. Joseph remains cut off from the rest of the world, with the warders patrolling in turn the path from the warders' house to the convict huts, and a multitude of sharks patrolling the waters all round.

Under these circumstances the convicts planned a mutiny. Such a thing had never been known in the penitentiary's history before. But their plan was not without some possibility of success. The warders were to be taken by surprise and murdered during the night. Their arms would enable the convicts to shoot down the people in the galley as she came alongside in the morning. The galley once in their possession, other boats were to be captured, and the whole company was to row away up the coast.

At dusk the two warders on duty mustered the convicts as usual. Then they proceeded to inspect the huts to ascertain that everything was in order. In the second they entered they were set upon and absolutely smothered under the numbers of their assailants. The twilight faded rapidly. It was a new moon ; and a heavy black squall gathering over the coast increased the profound darkness of the night. The convicts assembled in the open space, deliberating upon the next step to be taken, argued amongst themselves in low voices."

" You took part in all this ? " I asked.

" No. I knew what was going to be done, of course. But why should I kill these warders ? I had nothing

against them.   But I was afraid of the others.   Whatever happened, I could not escape from them.   I sat
alone on the stump of a tree with my head in my hands,
sick at heart at the thought of a freedom that could be
nothing but a mockery to me.   Suddenly I was startled
to perceive the shape of a man on the path near by.
He stood perfectly still, then his form became effaced in
the night.   It must have been the chief warder coming
to see what had become of his two men.   No one noticed
him.   The convicts kept on quarrelling over their plans.
The leaders could not get themselves obeyed.   The
fierce whispering of that dark mass of men was very
horrible.

" At last they divided into two parties and moved off.
When they had passed me I rose, weary and hopeless.
The path to the warders' house was dark and silent,
but on each side the bushes rustled slightly.   Presently I
saw a faint thread of light before me.   The chief warder,
followed by his three men, was approaching cautiously.
But he had failed to close his dark lantern properly.
The convicts had seen that faint gleam too.   There was
an awful savage yell, a turmoil on the dark path, shots
fired, blows, groans : and with the sound of smashed
bushes, the shouts of the pursuers and the screams of the
pursued, the man-hunt, the warder-hunt, passed by me
into the interior of the island.   I was alone.   And I
assure you, monsieur, I was indifferent to everything.
After standing still for a while, I walked on along the
path till I kicked something hard.   I stooped and picked
up a warder's revolver.   I felt with my fingers that it was
loaded in five chambers.   In the gusts of wind I heard
the convicts calling to each other far away, and then a
roll of thunder would cover the soughing and rustling of
the trees.   Suddenly, a big light ran across my path
very low along the ground.   And it showed a woman's
skirt with the edge of an apron.

" I knew that the person who carried it must be the
wife of the head warder.   They had forgotten all about
her, it seems.   A shot rang out in the interior of the island,
and she cried out to herself as she ran.   She passed on.

I followed, and presently I saw her again. She was pulling at the cord of the big bell which hangs at the end of the landing-pier, with one hand, and with the other she was swinging the heavy lantern to and fro. This is the agreed signal for the *Ile Royale* should assistance be required at night. The wind carried the sound away from our island and the light she swung was hidden on the shore side by the few trees that grow near the warders' house.

"I came up quite close to her from behind. She went on without stopping, without looking aside, as though she had been all alone on the island. A brave woman, monsieur. I put the revolver inside the breast of my blue blouse and waited. A flash of lightning and a clap of thunder destroyed both the sound and the light of the signal for an instant, but she never faltered, pulling at the cord and swinging the lantern as regularly as a machine. She was a comely woman of thirty—no more. I thought to myself, 'All that's no good on a night like this.' And I made up my mind that if a body of my fellow-convicts came down to the pier—which was sure to happen soon—I would shoot her through the head before I shot myself. I knew the ' comrades ' well. This idea of mine gave me quite an interest in life, monsieur ; and at once, instead of remaining stupidly exposed on the pier, I retreated a little way and crouched behind a bush. I did not intend to let myself be pounced upon unawares and be prevented perhaps from rendering a supreme service to at least one human creature before I died myself.

"But we must believe the signal was seen, for the galley from *Ile Royale* came over in an astonishingly short time. The woman kept right on till the light of her lantern flashed upon the officer in command and the bayonets of the soldiers in the boat. Then she sat down and began to cry.

"She didn't need me any more. I did not budge. Some soldiers were only in their shirt-sleeves, others without boots, just as the call to arms had found them. They passed by my bush at the double. The galley had

been sent away for more ; and the woman sat all alone
crying at the end of the pier, with the lantern standing
on the ground near her.

"Then suddenly I saw in the light at the end of the
pier the red pantaloons of two more men. I was overcome with astonishment. They too started off at a
run. Their tunics flapped unbuttoned and they were
bare-headed. One of them panted out to the other,
'Straight on, straight on ! '

"Where on earth did they spring from, I wondered.
Slowly I walked down the short pier. I saw the
woman's form shaken by sobs and heard her moaning
more and more distinctly, ' Oh, my man ! my poor man !
my poor man ! ' I stole on quietly. She could neither
hear nor see anything. She had thrown her apron over
her head and was rocking herself to and fro in her grief.
But I remarked a small boat fastened to the end of the
pier.

"Those two men—they looked [like *sous officiers*—
must have come in it, after being too late, I suppose, for
the galley. It is incredible that they should have thus
broken the regulations from a sense of duty. And it
was a stupid thing to do. I could not believe my eyes in
the very moment I was stepping into that boat.

"I pulled along the shore slowly. A black cloud
hung over the *Iles de Salut*. I heard firing, shouts.
Another hunt had begun—the convict-hunt. The oars
were too long to pull comfortably. I managed them
with difficulty, though the boat herself was light. But
when I got round to the other side of the island the
squall broke in rain and wind. I was unable to make
head against it. I let the boat drift ashore and secured
her.

"I knew the spot. There was a tumbledown old hovel
standing near the water. Cowering in there, I heard
through the noises of the wind and the falling downpour
some people tearing through the bushes. They came
out on the strand. Soldiers perhaps. A flash of
lightning threw everything near me into violent relief.
Two convicts !

"And directly an amazed voice exclaimed, 'It's a miracle!' It was the voice of Simon, otherwise Biscuit.

"And another voice growled, 'What's a miracle?'

"'Why, there's a boat lying here!'

"'You must be mad, Simon! But there is, after all, . . . A boat.'

"They seemed awed into complete silence. The other man was Mafile. He spoke again, cautiously.

"'It is fastened up. There must be somebody here.'

"'I spoke to them from within the hovel: 'I am here.'

"They came in then, and soon gave me to understand that the boat was theirs, not mine. 'There are two of us,' said Mafile, 'against you alone.'

"I got out into the open to keep clear of them for fear of getting a treacherous blow on the head. I could have shot them both where they stood. But I said nothing. I kept down the laughter rising in my throat. I made myself very humble and begged to be allowed to go. They consulted in low tones about my fate, while with my hand on the revolver in the bosom of my blouse I had their lives in my power. I let them live. I meant them to pull that boat. I represented to them with abject humility that I understood the managment of a boat, and that, being three to pull, we could get a rest in turns. That decided them at last. It was time. A little more and I would have gone into screaming fits at the drollness of it."

At this point his excitement broke out. He jumped off the bench and gesticulated. The great shadows of his arms darting over roof and walls made the shed appear too small to contain his agitation.

"I deny nothing," he burst out. "I was elated, monsieur. I tasted a sort of felicity. But I kept very quiet. I took my turn at pulling all through the night. We made for the open sea, putting our trust in a passing ship. It was a foolhardy action. I persuaded them to it. When the sun rose the immensity of water was calm, and the *Iles de Salut* appeared only like dark specks from the top of each swell. I was steering then.

Mafile, who was pulling bow, let out an oath and said, 'We must rest.'

"The time to laugh had come at last. And I took my fill of it, I can tell you. I held my sides and rolled in my seat they had such startled faces. 'What's got into him, the animal?' cries Mafile.

"And Simon, who was nearest to me, says over his shoulder to him, 'Devil take me if I don't think he's gone mad!'

"Then I produced the revolver. Aha! In a moment they both got the stoniest eyes you can imagine. Ha, ha! They were frightened. But they pulled. Oh, yes, they pulled all day, sometimes looking wild and sometimes looking faint. I lost nothing of it because I had to keep my eyes on them all the time, or else—crack!—they would have been on top of me in a second. I rested my revolver hand on my knee all ready and steered with the other. Their faces began to blister. Sky and sea seemed on fire round us and the sea steamed in the sun. The boat made a sizzling sound as she went through the water. Sometimes Mafile foamed at the mouth and sometimes he groaned. But he pulled. He dared not stop. His eyes became blood-shot all over, and he had bitten his lower lip to pieces. Simon was as hoarse as a crow.

"'Comrade——' he begins.

"'There are no comrades here. I am your *patron*.

"'*Patron*, then,' he says, 'in the name of humanity let us rest.'

"I let them. There was a little rainwater washing about the bottom of the boat. I permitted them to snatch some of it in the hollow of their palms. But as I gave the command '*En route*' I caught them exchanging significant glances. They thought I would have to go to sleep sometime! Aha! But I did not want to go to sleep. I was more awake than ever. It is they who went to sleep as they pulled, tumbling off the thwarts head over heels suddenly, one after another. I let them lie. All the stars were out. It was a quiet world. The sun rose, Another day. *Allez! En route!*

"They pulled badly. Their eyes rolled about and their tongues hung out. In the middle of the forenoon Mafile croaks out : 'Let us make a rush at him, Simon. I would just as soon be shot at once as to die of thirst, hunger, and fatigue at the oar.'

"But while he spoke he pulled ; and Simon kept on pulling too. It made me smile. Ah! They loved their life, these two, in this evil world of theirs, just as I used to love my life, too, before they spoiled it for me with their phrases. I let them go on to the point of exhaustion, and only then I pointed out at the sails of a ship on the horizon.

"Aha! You should have seen them revive and buckle to their work! For I kept them at it to pull right across that ship's path. They were changed. The sort of pity I had felt then left me. They looked more like themselves every minute. They looked at me with the glances I remembered so well. They were happy. They smiled.

"'Well,' says Simon, ' the energy of that youngster has saved our lives. If he hadn't made us, we could never have pulled so far out into the track of ships. Comrade, I forgive you. I admire you.'

"And Mafile growls from forward : 'We owe you a famous debt of gratitude, comrade. You are cut out for a chief.'

"Comrade! Monsieur! Ah, what a good word! And they, such men as these two, had made it accursed. I looked at them. I remembered their lies, their promises, their menaces, and all my days of misery. Why could they not have left me alone after I came out of prison ? I looked at them and thought that while they lived I could never be free. Never. Neither I nor others like me with warm hearts and weak heads. For I know I have not a strong head, monsieur. A black rage came upon me—the rage of extreme intoxication—but not against the injustice of society. Oh, no !

"' I must be free ! ' I cried, furiously.

"' *Vive la liberté !* ' yells that ruffian Mafile. ' *Mort aux bourgeois* who send us to Cayenne ! They shall soon know that we are free.'

" The sky, the sea, the whole horizon, seemed to turn red, blood red all round the boat. My temples were beating so loud that I wondered they did not hear. How is it that they did not ? How is it that they did not understand ?

" I heard Simon ask, ' Have we not pulled far enough out now ? '

" ' Yes. Far enough,' I said. I was sorry for him ; it was the other I hated. He hauled in his oar with a loud sigh, and as he was raising his hand to wipe his forehead with the air of a man who has done his work, I pulled the trigger of my revolver and shot him like this off the knee, right through the heart.

" He tumbled down, with his head hanging over the side of the boat. I did not give him a second glance. The other cried out piercingly. Only one shriek of horror. Then all was still.

" He slipped off the thwart on to his knees and raised his clasped hands before his face in an attitude of supplication. ' Mercy,' he whispered, faintly. ' Mercy for me ! —comrade.'

" ' Ah, comrade,' I said, in a low tone. ' Yes, comrade, of course. Well, then, shout *Vive l'anarchie.*'

" He flung up his arms, his face up to the sky and his mouth wide open in a great yell of despair. ' *Vive l'anarchie ! Vive——*'

" He collapsed all in a heap, with a bullet through his head.

" I flung them both overboard. I threw away the revolver, too. Then I sat down quietly. I was free at last ! At last. I did not even look towards the ship ; I did not care ; indeed, I think I must have gone to sleep, becaue all of a sudden there were shouts and I found the ship almost on top of me. They hauled me on board and secured the boat astern. They were all blacks, except the captain, who was a mulatto. He alone knew a few words of French. I could not find out where they were going nor who they were. They gave me something to eat every day ; but I did not like the way they used to discuss me in their language. Perhaps they were deliberating about throwing me overboard in order to keep possession of the boat. How do I know ? As we were passing this island I asked whether it was inhabited. I understood from the mulatto that there was a house on it. A farm, I fancied, they meant. So I asked them to put me ashore on the beach and keep the boat for their trouble. This, I imagine, was just what they wanted. The rest you know."

After pronouncing these words he lost suddenly all control over himself. He paced to and fro rapidly, till at last he broke into a run ; his arms went like a windmill and his ejaculations became very much like raving. The burden of them was that he " denied nothing, nothing ! " I could only let him go on, and sat out of his way, repeating, " *Calmez vous, calmez vous,*" at intervals, till his agitation exhausted itself.

I must confess, too, that I remained there long after he had crawled under his mosquito-net. He had entreated me not to leave him ; so, as one sits up with a nervous child, I sat up with him—in the name of humanity—till he fell asleep.

On the whole, my idea is that he was much more of an anarchist than he confessed to me or to himself ; and that, the special features of his case apart, he was very much like many other anarchists. Warm heart and weak head—that is the word of the riddle ; and it is a fact that the bitterest contradictions and the deadliest conflicts of the world are carried on in every individual breast capable of feeling and passion.

From personal inquiry I can vouch that the story of the convict mutiny was in every particular as stated by him.

When I got back to Horta from Cayenne and saw the " anarchist " again, he did not look well. He was more worn, still more frail, and very livid indeed under the grimy smudges of his calling. Evidently the meat of the company's main herd (in its unconcentrated form) did not agree with him at all.

It was on the Pontoon in Horta that we met; and I tried to induce him to leave the launch moored where she was and follow me to Europe there and then. It would have been delightful to think of the excellent manager's surprise and disgust at the poor fellow's escape. But he refused with unconquerable obstinacy.

"Surely you don't mean to live always here!" I cried. He shook his head.

"I shall die here," he said. Then added moodily, "Away from them."

Sometimes I think of him lying open-eyed on his horseman's gear in the low shed full of tools and scraps of iron—the anarchist slave of the Marañon estate, waiting with resignation for that sleep which "fled" from him, as he used to say, in such an unaccountable manner.

THE DUEL

I

NAPOLEON I., whose career had the quality of a duel against the whole of Europe, disliked duelling between the officers of his army. The great military emperor was not a swashbuckler, and had little respect for tradition.

Nevertheless, a story of duelling, which became a legend in the army, runs through the epic of imperial wars. To the surprise and admiration of their fellows, two officers, like insane artists trying to gild refined gold or paint the lily, pursued a private contest through the years of universal carnage. They were officers of cavalry, and their connection with the high-spirited but fanciful animal which carries men into battle seems particularly appropriate. It would be difficult to imagine for heroes of this legend two officers of infantry of the line, for example, whose fantasy is tamed by much walking exercise, and whose valour necessarily must be of a more plodding kind. As to gunners or engineers, whose heads are kept cool on a diet of mathematics, it is simply unthinkable.

The names of the two officers were Feraud and D'Hubert, and they were both lieutenants in a regiment of hussars, but not in the same regiment.

Feraud was doing regimental work, but Lieut. D'Hubert had the good fortune to be attached to the person of the general commanding the division, as *officier d'ordonnance*. It was in Strasbourg, and in this agreable and important garrison they were enjoying greatly a short interval of peace. They were enjoying it, though both intensely war-like, because it was a sword-sharpening, fire-lock-cleaning peace, dear to a military heart and undamaging to military prestige, inasmuch that no one believed in its sincerity or duration.

Under those historical circumstances, so favourable to the proper appreciation of military leisure, Lieut. D'Hubert, one fine afternoon, made his way along a quiet street of a cheerful suburb towards Lieut. Feraud's quarters, which were in a private house with a garden at the back, belonging to an old maiden lady.

His knock at the door was answered instantly by a young maid in Alsatian costume. Her fresh complexion and her long eyelashes, lowered demurely at the sight of the tall officer, caused Lieut. D'Hubert, who was accessible to esthetic impressions, to relax the cold, severe gravity of his face. At the same time he observed that the girl had over her arm a pair of hussars breeches, blue with a red stripe.

" Lieut. Feraud in ? " he inquired benevolently.

" Oh, no, sir ! He went out at six this morning."

The pretty maid tried to close the door. Lieut. D'Hubert stepped into the anteroom, jingling his spurs.

" Come, my dear ! You don't mean to say he has not been home since six o'clock this morning ? "

Saying these words, Lieut. D'Hubert opened without ceremony the door of a room so comfortable and neatly ordered that only from internal evidence in the shape of boots, uniforms, and military accoutrements did he acquire the conviction that it was Lieut. Feraud's room. And he saw also that Lieut. Feraud was not at home. The truthful maid had followed him, and raised her candid eyes to his face.

"H'm!" said Lieut. D'Hubert, greatly disappointed, for he had already visited all the haunts where a lieut-tenant of hussars could be found of a fine afternoon. " So he's out ? And do you happen to know, my dear, why he went out at six this morning ? "

" No," she answered readily. " He came home late

last night, and snored. I heard him when I got up at five. Then he dressed himself in his oldest uniform and went out. Service, I suppose."

"Service? Not a bit of it!" cried Lieut. D'Hubert. "Learn, my angel, that he went out thus early to fight a duel with a civilian."

She heard this news without a quiver of her dark eyelashes. It was very obvious that the actions of Lieut. Feraud were generally above criticism. She only looked up for a moment in mute surprise, and Lieut. D'Hubert concluded from this absence of emotion that she must have seen Lieut. Feraud since that morning. He looked around the room.

"Come!" he insisted, with confidential familiarity. "He's perhaps somewhere in the house now?"

She shook her head.

"So much the worse for him!" continued Lieut. D'Hubert, in a tone of anxious conviction. "But he has been home this morning."

This time the pretty maid nodded slightly.

"He has!" cried Lieut. D'Hubert. "And went out again? What for? Couldn't he keep quietly indoors! What a lunatic! My dear girl——"

Lieut. D'Hubert's natural kindness of disposition and strong sense of comradeship helped his powers of observation. He changed his tone to a most insinuating softness, and, gazing at the hussars breeches hanging over the arm of the girl, he appealed to the interest she took in Lieut. Feraud's comfort and happiness. He was pressing and persuasive. He used his eyes, which were kind and fine, with excellent effect. His anxiety to get hold at once of Lieut. Feraud, for Lieut. Feraud's own good, seemed so genuine that at last it overcame the girl's unwillingness to speak. Unluckily she had not much to tell. Lieut. Feraud had returned home shortly before ten, had walked straight into his room, and had thrown himself on his bed to resume his slumbers. She had heard him snore rather louder than before far into the afternoon. Then he got up, put on his best uniform, and went out. That was all she knew

She raised her eyes, and Lieut. D'Hubert stared into them incredulously.

"It's incredible. Gone parading the town in his best uniform! My dear child, don't you know he ran that civilian through this morning? Clean through, as you spit a hare."

The pretty maid heard the gruesome intelligence without any signs of distress. But she pressed her lips together thoughtfully.

"He isn't parading the town," she remarked in a low tone. "Far from it."

"The civilian's family is making an awful row," continued Lieut. D'Hubert, pursuing his train of thought. "And the general is very angry. It's one of the best families in the town. Feraud ought to have kept close at least——"

"What will the general do to him?" inquired the girl anxiously.

"He won't have his head cut off, to be sure," grumbled Lieut. D'Hubert. "His conduct is positively indecent. He's making no end of trouble for himself by this sort of bravado."

"But he isn't parading the town," the maid insisted in a shy murmur.

"Why, yes! Now I think of it, I haven't seen him anywhere about. What on earth has he done with himself?"

"He's gone to pay a call," suggested the maid, after a moment of silence.

Lieut. D'Hubert started.

"A call! Do you mean a call on a lady? The cheek of the man! And how do you know this, my dear?"

Without concealing her woman's scorn for the denseness of the masculine mind, the pretty maid reminded him that Lieut. Feraud had arrayed himself in his best uniform before going out. He had also put on his newest dolman, she added, in a tone as if this conversation were getting on her nerves, and turned away brusquely.

Lieut. D'Hubert, without questioning the accuracy of the deduction, did not see that it advanced him much on his official quest. For his quest after Lieut. Feraud had an official character. He did not know any of the women this fellow, who had run a man through in the morning, was likely to visit in the afternoon. The two young men knew each other but slightly. He bit his gloved finger in perplexity.

"Call!" he exclaimed. "Call on the devil!"

The girl, with her back to him, and folding the hussars breeches on a chair, protested with a vexed little laugh:

"Oh dear, no! On Madame de Lionne."

Lieut. D'Hubert whistled softly. Madame de Lionne was the wife of a high official who had a well-known *salon* and some pretensions to sensibility and elegance. The husband was a civilian, and old; but the society of the *salon* was young and military. Lieut. D'Hubert had whistled, not because the idea of pursuing Lieut. Feraud into that very *salon* was disagreeable to him, but because, having arrived in Strasbourg only lately, he had not had the time as yet to get an introduction to Madame de Lionne. And what was that swashbuckler Feraud doing there, he wondered. He did not seem the sort of man who——

"Are you certain of what you say?" asked Lieut. D'Hubert.

The girl was perfectly certain. Without turning round to look at him, she explained that the coachman of their next door neighbours knew the *maître-d'hotel* of Madame de Lionne. In this way she had her information. And she was perfectly certain. In giving this assurance she sighed. Lieut. Feraud called there nearly every afternoon, she added.

"Ah, bah!" exclaimed D'Hubert ironically. His opinion of Madame de Lionne went down several degrees. Lieut. Feraud did not seem to him specially worthy of attention on the part of a woman with a reputation for sensibility and elegance. But there was no saying. At bottom they were all alike—very practical rather than idealistic. Lieut. D'Hubert, however, did not allow his mind to dwell on these considerations.

"By thunder!" he reflected aloud. "The general

goes there sometimes. If he happens to find the fellow making eyes at the lady there will be the devil to pay ! Our general is not a very accommodating person, I can tell you."

"Go quickly, then ! Don't stand here now I've told you where he is ! " cried the girl, colouring to the eyes.

"Thanks, my dear ! I don't know what I would have done without you."

After manifesting his gratitude in an aggressive way, which at first was repulsed violently, and then submitted to with a sudden and still more repellent indifference, Lieut. D'Hubert took his departure.

He clanked and jingled along the streets with a martial swagger. To run a comrade to earth in a drawing-room where he was not known did not trouble him in the least. A uniform is a passport. His position as *officier d'ordonnance* of the general added to his assurance. Moreover, now that he knew where to find Lieut. Feraud, he had no option. It was a service matter.

Madame de Lionne's house had an excellent appearance. A man in livery, opening the door of a large drawing-room with a waxed floor, shouted his name and stood aside to let him pass. It was a reception day. The ladies wore big hats surcharged with a profusion of feathers; their bodies sheathed in clinging white gowns from the armpits to the tips of the low satin shoes, looked sylph-like and cool in a great display of bare necks and arms. The men who talked with them, on the contrary, were arrayed heavily in multi-coloured garments with collars up to their ears and thick sashes round their waists. Lieut. D'Hubert made his unabashed way across the room, and, bowing low before a sylph-like form reclining on a couch, offered his apologies for this intrusion, which nothing could excuse but the extreme urgency of the service order he had to communicate to his comrade Feraud. He proposed to himself to return presently in a more regular manner and beg forgiveness for interrupting the interesting conversation . . .

A bare arm was extended towards him with gracious nonchalance even before he had finished speaking. He pressed the hand respectfully to his lips, and made the mental remark that it was bony. Madame de Lionne was a blonde, with too fine a skin and a long face.

"*C'est ça!*" she said, with an ethereal smile, disclosing a set of large teeth. "Come this evening to plead for your forgiveness."

"I will not fail, madame."

Meantime Lieut. Feraud, splendid in his new dolman and the extremely polished boots of his calling, sat on a chair within the foot of a couch, one hand resting on his thigh, the other twirling his moustache to a point. At a significant glance from D'Hubert he rose without alacrity and followed him into the recess of a window.

"What is it you want with me?" he asked, with astonishing indifference. Lieut. D'Hubert could not imagine that in the innocence of his heart and simplicity of his conscience Lieut. Feraud took a view of his duel in which neither remorse nor yet a rational apprehension of consequences had any place. Though he had no clear recollection how the quarrel had originated (it was begun in an establishment where beer and wine are drunk late at night), he had not the slightest doubt of being himself the outraged party. He had had two experienced friends for his seconds. Everything had been done according to the rules governing that sort of adventures. And a duel is obviously fought for the purpose of some one being at least hurt, if not killed outright. The civilian got hurt. That also was in order. Lieut. Feraud was perfectly tranquil; but Lieut. D'Hubert took it for affectation, and spoke with a certain vivacity.

"I am directed by the general to give you the order to go at once to your quarters, and remain there under close arrest."

It was now the turn of Lieut. Feraud to be astonished. "What the devil are you telling me there?" he murmured faintly, and fell into such profound wonder that he could only follow mechanically the motions of Lieut. D'Hubert. The two officers, one tall, with an interesting face and a moustache the colour of ripe corn, the other, short and sturdy, with a hooked nose and a thick crop of black curly hair, approached the mistress of the house to take their leave. Madame de Lionne, a woman of eclectic taste, smiled upon these armed young men with impartial sensibility and an equal share of interest. Madame de Lionne took her delight in the infinite variety of human species. All the other eyes in the drawing-room followed the departing officers; and when they had gone out one or two men who had already heard of the duel, imparted the information to the sylph-like ladies, who received it with faint shrieks of humane concern.

Meantime the two hussars walked side by side, Lieut. Féraud trying to master the hidden reason of things which in this instance eluded the grasp of his intellect; Lieut. D'Hubert feeling annoyed at the part he had to play, because the general's instructions were that he should see personally that Lieut, Feraud carried out his orders to the letter, and at once.

"The chief seems to know this animal," he thought, eyeing his companion, whose round face, the round eyes and even the twisted up jet black little moustache seemed animated by a mental exasperation against the incomprehensible. And louder he observed rather reproachfully, "The general is in a devilish fury with you!"

Lieut. Feraud stopped short on the edge of the pavement, and cried in the accents of unmistakable sincerity, "What on earth for?" The innocence of the fiery Gascon soul was depicted in the manner in which he seized his head in both hands as if to prevent it bursting with perplexity.

"For the duel," said Lieut. D'Hubert curtly. He was annoyed greatly by this sort of perverse fooling.

"The duel! The . . ."

Lieut. Feraud passed from one paroxysm of astonishment into another. He dropped his hands and walked on slowly, trying to reconcile this information with the state of his own feelings. It was impossible. He burst out indignantly, "Was I to let that sauerkraut-eating civilian wipe his boots on the uniform of the 7th Hussars ? "

Lieut. D'Hubert could not remain altogether unmoved by that simple sentiment. This little fellow was a lunatic, he thought to himself, but there was something in what he said.

"Of course, I don't know how far you were justified," he began soothingly. "And the general himself may not be exactly informed. Those people have been deafening him with their lamentations."

"Ah ! the general is not exactly informed," mumbled Lieut. Feraud, walking faster and faster as his choler at the injustice of his fate began to rise. "He is not exactly . . . And he orders me under close arrest, with God knows what afterwards ! "

"Don't excite yourself like this," remonstrated the other. "Your adversary's people are very influential, you know, and it looks bad enough on the face of it. The general had to take notice of their complaint at once. I don't think he means to be over-severe with you. It's the best thing for you to be kept out of sight for a while."

"I am very much obliged to the general," muttered Lieut. Feraud through his teeth. "And perhaps you would say I ought to be grateful to you too for the trouble you have taken to hunt me up in the drawing-room of a lady who——"

"Frankly," interrupted Lieut. D'Hubert, with an innocent laugh, "I think you ought to be. I had no end of trouble to find out where you were. It wasn't exactly the place for you to disport yourself in under the circumstances. If the general had caught you there making eyes at the goddess of the temple . . . oh, my word ! . . . He hates to be bothered with complaints against his officers, you know. And it looked uncommonly like sheer bravado."

The two officers had arrived now at the street door of Lieut. Feraud's lodgings. The latter turned towards his companion. "Lieutenant D'Hubert," he said, "I have something to say to you, which can't be said very well in the street.   You can't refuse to come up."

The pretty maid had opened the door. Lieut. Feraud brushed past her brusquely, and she raised her scared and questioning eyes to Lieut. D'Hubert, who could do nothing but shrug his shoulders slightly as he followed with marked reluctance.

In his room Lieut. Feraud unhooked the clasp, flung his new dolman on the bed, and, folding his arms across his chest, turned to the other hussar.

"Do you imagine I am a man to submit tamely to injustice ? " he inquired, in a boisterous voice.

"Oh, do be reasonable !" remonstrated Lieut. D'Hubert.

"I am reasonable !   I am perfectly reasonable ! " retorted the other with ominous restraint.   "I can't call the general to account for his behaviour, but you are going to answer me for yours."

"I can't listen to this nonsense," murmured Lieut. D'Hubert, making a slightly contemptuous grimace.

"You call this nonsense ?   It seems to me a perfectly plain statement.   Unless you don't understand French."

"What on earth do you mean ? "

"I mean," screamed suddenly Lieut. Feraud, "to cut off your ears to teach you to disturb me with the general's orders when I am talking to a lady ! "

A profound silence followed this mad declaration ; and through the open window Lieut. D'Hubert heard the little birds singing sanely in the garden.   He said, preserving his calm, "Why ! if you take that tone, of course I shall hold myself at your disposition whenever you are at liberty to attend to this affair ; but I don't think you will cut my ears off."

"I am going to attend to it at once," declared Lieut. Feraud, with extreme truculence.   "If you are thinking of displaying your airs and graces to-night in Madame de Lionne's salon you are very much mistaken."

"Really ! " said Lieut. D'Hubert, who was beginning to feel irritated, "you are an impracticable sort of fellow. The general's orders to me were to put you under arrest, not to carve you into small pieces.   Good-morning ! " And turning his back on the little Gascon, who, always sober in his potations, was as though born intoxicated with the sunshine of his vine-ripening country, the Northman, who could drink hard on occasion, but was born sober under the watery skies of Picardy, made for the door. Hearing, however, the unmistakable sound behind his back of a sword drawn from the scabbard, he had no option but to stop.

"Devil take this mad southerner!" he thought, spinning round and surveying with composure the warlike posture of Lieut. Feraud, with a bare sword in his hand.

"At once!—at once!" stuttered Feraud, beside himself.

"You had my answer," said the other, keeping his temper very well.

At first he had been only vexed, and somewhat amused; but now his face got clouded. He was asking himself seriously how he could manage to get away. It was impossible to run from a man with a sword, and as to fighting him, it seemed completely out of the question. He waited awhile, then said exactly what was in his heart.

"Drop this! I won't fight with you. I won't be made ridiculous."

"Ah, you won't?" hissed the Gascon. "I suppose you prefer to be made infamous. Do you hear what I say? . . . Infamous! Infamous! Infamous!" he shrieked, rising and falling on his toes and getting very red in the face.

Lieut. D'Hubert on the contrary became very pale at the sound of the unsavoury word for a moment, then flushed pink to the roots of his fair hair. "But you can't go out to fight; you are under arrest, you lunatic!" he objected, with angry scorn.

"There's the garden: it's big enough to lay out your long carcass in," spluttered the other, with such ardour that somehow the anger of the cooler man subsided.

"This is perfectly absurd," he said, glad enough to think he had found a way out of it for the moment. "We shall never get any of our comrades to serve as seconds. It's preposterous."

"Seconds! Damn the seconds! We don't want any seconds. Don't you worry about any seconds. I shall send word to your friends to come and bury you when I am done. And if you want any witnesses, I'll send word to the old girl to put her head out of a window at the back. Stay! There's the gardener. He'll do. He's as deaf as a post, but he has two eyes in his head. Come along! I will teach you, my staff officer, that the carrying about of a general's orders is not always child's play."

While thus discoursing he had unbuckled his empty scabbard. He sent it flying under the bed, and, lowering the point of the sword, brushed past the perplexed Lieut. D'Hubert, exclaimimg, "Follow me!" Directly he had flung open the door a faint shriek was heard, and the pretty maid, who had been listening at the keyhole, staggered away, putting the backs of her hand over her eyes. Feraud did not seem to see her, but she ran after him and seized his left arm. He shook her off, and then she rushed towards Lieut. D'Hubert and clawed at the sleeve of his uniform.

"Wretched man!" she sobbed, "Is this what you wanted to find him for?"

"Let me go," entreated Lieut. D'Hubert, trying to disengage himself gently. "It's like being in a madhouse," he protested, with exasperation. "Do let me go. I won't do him any harm."

A fiendish laugh from Lieut. Feraud commented that assurance. "Come along!" he shouted, with a stamp of his foot.

And Lieut. D'Hubert did follow. He could do nothing else. Yet in vindication of his sanity it must be recorded that as he passed through the ante-room the notion of opening the street door and bolting out presented itself to this brave youth, only of course to be instantly dismissed, for he felt sure that the other would pursue him without shame or compunction. And the prospect of an officer of hussars being chased along the street by another officer of hussars with a naked sword could not be for a moment entertained. Therefore he followed into the garden. Behind them the girl tottered out too. With ashy lips and wild scared eyes, she surrendered herself to a dreadful curiosity. She had also the notion of rushing if need be between Lieut. Feraud and death.

The deaf gardener, utterly unconscious of approaching footsteps, went on watering his flowers till Lieut. Feraud thumped him on the back. Beholding suddenly an enraged man flourishing a big sabre, the old chap trembling in all his limbs dropped the watering-pot. At once Lieut. Feraud kicked it away with great animosity, and, seizing the gardener by the throat, backed him against a tree. He held him there, shouting in his ear, "Stay here, and look on! You understand? You've got to look on! Don't dare budge from the spot!"

Lieut. D'Hubert came slowly down the walk, unclasping his dolman with unconcealed disgust. Even then, with his hand already on the hilt of his sword, he hesitated to draw till a roar "En garde, fichtre. What do you think you came here for?" and the rush of his adversary forced him to put himself as quickly as possible in a posture of defence.

The clash of arms filled that prim garden, which hitherto had known no more warlike sound than the click of clipping shears; and presently the upper part of an old lady's body was projected out of a window upstairs. She tossed her arms above her white cap, scolding in a cracked voice. The gardener remained glued to the tree, his toothless mouth open in idiotic astonishment, and a little farther up the path the pretty girl, as if spellbound to a small grass plot, ran a few steps this way and that wringing her hands and muttering crazily. She did not rush between the combatants: the onslaughts of Lieut. Feraud were so fierce that her heart failed her. Lieut. D'Hubert, his faculties concentrated upon defence, needed all his skill and science of the sword to stop the rushes of his adversary. Twice already he had to break ground. It bothered him to feel his foothold made insecure by the round, dry gravel of the path rolling under the hard soles of his boots.

This was most unsuitable ground, he thought, keeping
a watchful, narrowed gaze, shaded by long eye-lashes,
upon the fiery stare of his thick-set adversary. This
absurd affair would ruin his reputation of a sensible,
well-behaved, promising officer. It would damage at
any rate his immediate prospects, and lose him the
good-will of his general. These worldly preoccupations
were no doubt misplaced in view of the solemnity of
the moment. A duel, whether regarded as a ceremony
in the cult of honour, or even when reduced in its moral
essence to a form of manly sport, demands a perfect
singleness of intention, a homicidal austerity of mood.
On the other hand this vivid concern for his future had
not a bad effect inasmuch as it began to rouse the anger
of Lieut. D'Hubert. Some seventy seconds had elapsed
since they had crossed blades, and Lieut. D'Hubert had
to break ground again in order to avoid impaling his reckless adversary like a beetle for a cabinet of specimens.
The result was that misapprehending the motive, Lieut.
Feraud with a triumphant sort of snarl pressed his
attack.

"This enraged animal will have me against the wall
directly," thought Lieut. D'Hubert. He imagined himself much closer to the house than he was, and he dared
not turn his head; it seemed to him he was keeping
his adversary off with his eyes rather more than with
his point. Lieut. Feraud crouched and bounded with a
fierce tigerish agility fit to trouble the stoutest heart.
But what was more appalling than the fury of a wild
beast, accomplishing in all innocence of heart a natural
function, was the fixity of savage purpose man alone is
capable of displaying. Lieut. D'Hubert in the midst of
his worldly preoccupations perceived it at last. It was
an absurd and damaging affair to be drawn into, but
whatever silly intention the fellow had started with it
was clear enough that by this time he meant to kill—
nothing less. He meant it with an intensity of will
utterly beyond the inferior faculties of a tiger.

As is the case with constitutionally brave men, the
full view of the danger interested Lieut. D'Hubert. And

directly he got properly interested, the length of his arm and the coolness of his head told in his favour. It was the turn of Lieut. Feraud to recoil, with a bloodcurdling grunt of baffled rage. He made a swift feint, and then rushed straight forward.

"Ah! you would, would you?" Lieut. D'Hubert exclaimed mentally. The combat had lasted nearly two minutes, time enough for any man to get embittered, apart from the merits of the quarrel. And all at once it was over. Trying to close breast to breast under his adversary's guard Lieut. Feraud received a slash on his shortened arm. He did not feel it in the least, but it checked his rush, and his feet slipping on the gravel he fell backwards with great violence. The shock jarred his boiling brain into the perfect quietude of insensibility. Simultaneously with his fall the pretty servant-girl shrieked; but the old maiden lady at the window ceased her scolding, and began to cross herself piously.

Beholding his adversary stretched out perfectly still, his face to the sky, Lieut. D'Hubert thought he had killed him outright. The impression of having slashed hard enough to cut his man clean in two abode with him for a while in an exaggerated memory of the right good will he had put into the blow. He dropped on his knees hastily by the side of the prostrate body. Discovering that not even the arm was severed, a slight sense of disappointment mingled with the feeling of relief. The fellow deserved the worst. But truly he did not want the death of that sinner. The affair was ugly enough as it stood, and Lieut. D'Hubert addressed himself at once to the task of stopping the bleeding. In this task it was his fate to be ridiculously impeded by the pretty maid. Rending the air with screams of horror, she attacked him from behind and, twining her fingers in his hair, tugged back at his head. Why she should choose to hinder him at this precise moment he could not in the least understand. He did not try. It was all like a very wicked and harassing dream. Twice to save himself from being pulled over he had to rise and fling her off. He did this stoically, without a word, kneeling down again at once to go on with his work. But the third time, his work being done, he seized her and held her arms pinned to her body. Her cap was half off, her face was red, her eyes blazed with crazy boldness. He looked mildly into them while she called him a wretch, a traitor and a murderer many times in succession. This did not annoy him so much as the conviction that she had managed to scratch his face abundantly. Ridicule would be added to the scandal of the story. He imagined the adorned tale making its way through the garrison of the town, through the whole army on the frontier, with every possible distortion of motive and sentiment and circumstance, spreading a doubt upon the sanity of his conduct and the distinction of his taste even to the very ears of his honourable family. It was all very well for that fellow Feraud, who had no connections, no family to speak of, and no quality but courage, which, anyhow, was a matter of course, and possessed by every single trooper in the whole mass of French cavalry. Still holding down the arms of the girl in a strong grip, Lieut. D'Hubert glanced over his shoulder. Lieut. Feraud had opened his eyes. He did not move. Like a man just waking from a deep sleep he stared without any expression at the evening sky.

Lieut. D'Hubert's urgent shouts to the old gardener produced no effect—not so much as to make him shut his toothless mouth. Then he remembered that the man was stone deaf. All that time the girl struggled, not with maidenly coyness, but like a pretty dumb fury, kicking his shins now and then. He continued to hold her as if in a vice, his instinct telling him that were he to let her go she would fly at his eyes. But he was greatly humiliated by his position. At last she gave up; she was more exhausted than appeased, he feared. Nevertheless, he attempted to get out of this wicked dream by way of negotiation.

"Listen to me," he said, as calmly as he could. "Will you promise to run for a surgeon if I let you go?"

With real affliction he heard her declare that she would do nothing of the kind. On the contrary, her sobbed out intention was to remain in the garden, and fight tooth and nail for the protection of the vanquished man. This was shocking.

"My dear child!" he cried in despair, "is it possible that you think me capable of murdering a wounded adversary? Is it. . . . Be quiet, you little wild cat, you!"

They struggled. A thick, drowsy voice said behind him, "What are you after with that girl?"

Lieut. Feraud had raised himself on his good arm. He was looking sleepily at his other arm, at the mess of blood on his uniform, at a small red pool on the ground, at his sabre lying a foot away on the path. Then he laid himself down gently again to think it all out, as far as a thundering headache would permit of mental operations.

Lieut. D'Hubert released the girl, who crouched at once by the side of the other lieutenant. The shades of night were falling on the little trim garden with this touching group, whence proceeded low murmurs of sorrow and compassion, with other feeble sounds of a different character, as if an imperfectly awake invalid were trying to swear. Lieut. D'Hubert went away.

He passed theough the silent house, and congratulated himself upon the dusk concealing his gory hands and scratched face from the passers-by. But this story could by no means be concealed. He dreaded the discredit and ridicule above everything, and was painfully aware of sneaking through the back streets in the manner of a murderer. Presently the sounds of a flute coming out of the open window of a lighted upstairs room in a modest house interrupted his dismal reflections. It was being played with a persevering virtuosity, and through the *fioritures* of the tune one could hear the regular thumping of the foot beating time on the floor.

Lieut. D'Hubert shouted a name, which was that of an army surgeon whom he knew fairly well. The

11

sounds of the flute ceased, and the musician appeared at the window, his instrument still in his hand, peering into the street.

"Who calls? You, D'Hubert? What brings you this way?"

He did not like to be disturbed at the hour when he was playing the flute. He was a man whose hair had turned grey already in the thankless task of tying up wounds on battlefields where others reaped advancement and glory.

"I want you to go at once and see Feraud. You know Lieut. Feraud? He lives down the second street. It's but a step from here."

"What's the matter with him?"

"Wounded."

"Are you sure?"

"Sure!" cried D'Hubert. "I come from there."

"That's amusing," said the elderly surgeon. Amusing was his favourite word; but the expression of his face when he pronounced it never corresponded. He was a stolid man. "Come in," he added. "I'll get ready in a moment."

"Thanks! I will. I want to wash my hands in your room."

Lieut. D'Hubert found the surgeon occupied in unscrewing his flute, and packing the pieces methodically in a case. He turned his head.

"Water there—in the corner. Your hands do want washing."

"I've stopped the bleeding," said Lieut. D'Hubert. "But you had better make haste. It's rather more than ten minutes ago, you know."

The surgeon did not hurry his movements.

"What's the matter? Dressing came off? That's amusing. I've been at work in the hospital all day, but I've been told this morning by somebody that he had come off without a scratch."

"Not the same duel, probably," growled moodily Lieut. D'Hubert, wiping his hands on a coarse towel.

"Not the same. . . . What? Another. It would

take the very devil to make me go out twice in one day." The surgeon looked narrowly at Lieut. D'Hubert. "How did you come by that scratched face? Both sides too— and symmetrical. It's amusing."

"Very!" snarled Lieut. D'Hubert. "And you will find his slashed arm amusing too. It will keep both of you amused for quite a long time."

The doctor was mystified and impressed by the brusque bitterness of Lieut. D'Hubert's tone. They left the house together, and in the street he was still more mystified by his conduct.

"Aren't you coming with me?" he asked.

"No," said Lieut. D'Hubert. "You can find the house by yourself. The front door will be standing open very likely."

"All right. Where's his room?"

"Ground floor. But you had better go right through and look in the garden first."

This astonishing piece of information made the surgeon go off without further parley. Lieut. D'Hubert regained his quarters nursing a hot and uneasy indignation. He dreaded the chaff of his comrades almost as much as the anger of his superiors. The truth was confoundedly grotesque and embarrassing, even putting aside the irregularity of the combat itself, which made it come abominably near a criminal offence. Like all men without much imagination, a faculty which helps the processes of reflective thought, Lieut. D'Hubert became frightfully harassed by the obvious aspects of his predicament. He was certainly glad that he had not killed Lieut. Feraud outside all rules, and without the regular witnesses proper to such a transaction. Uncommonly glad. At the same time he felt as though he would have liked to wring his neck for him without ceremony.

He was still under the sway of these contradictory sentiments when the surgeon amateur of the flute came to see him. More than three days had elapsed. Lieut. D'Hubert was no longer *officier d'ordonnance* to the general commanding the division. He had been sent back to his regiment. And he was resuming his connection with the soldiers' military family by being shut up in close confinement, not at his own quarters in town but in a room in the barracks. Owing to the gravity of the incident, he was forbidden to see anyone. He did not know what had happened, and what was being said, or what was being thought. The arrival of the surgeon was a most unexpected thing to the worried captive. The amateur of the flute began by explaining that he was there only by special favour of the colonel.

"I represented to him that it would be only fair to let you have some authentic news of your adversary," he continued. "You'll be glad to hear he's getting better fast."

Lieut. D'Hubert's face exhibited no conventional signs of gladness. He continued to walk the floor of the dusty bare room.

"Take this chair, doctor," he mumbled.

The doctor sat down.

"This affair is variously appreciated—in town and in the army. In fact, the diversity of opinions is amusing."

"Is it," mumbled Lieut. D'Hubert, tramping steadily from wall to wall. But within himself he marvelled that there could be two opinions on the matter. The surgeon continued.

"Of course, as the real facts are not known——"

"I should have thought," interrupted D'Hubert, "that the fellow would have put you in possession of facts."

"He said something," admitted the other, "the first time I saw him. And, by the bye, I did find him in the garden. The thump on the back of his head had made him a little incoherent then. Afterwards he was rather reticent than otherwise."

"Didn't think he would have the grace to be ashamed," mumbled D'Hubert, resuming his pacing, while the doctor murmured, "It's very amusing. Ashamed! Shame was not exactly his frame of mind. However, you may look at the matter otherwise."

"What are you talking about? What matter?" asked D'Hubert, with a sidelong look at the heavy-faced, grey-haired figure seated on a wooden chair.

"Whatever it is," said the surgeon a little impatiently. "I don't want to pronounce any opinion on your conduct——

"By heavens, you had better not!" burst out D'Hubert.

"There!—there! Don't be so quick in flourishing the sword. It doesn't pay in the long run. Understand once for all that I would not carve any of you youngsters except with the tools of my trade. But my advice is good. If you go on like this you will make for yourself an ugly reputation."

"Go on like what?" demanded Lieut. D'Hubert, stopping short, quite startled. "I!—I!—make for myself a reputation. . . . What do you imagine?"

"I told you I don't wish to judge of the rights and wrongs of this incident. It's not my business. Nevertheless——"

"What on earth has he been telling you?" interrupted Lieut. D'Hubert, in a sort of awed scare.

"I told you already, that at first, when I picked him up in the garden, he was incoherent. Afterwards he was naturally reticent. But I gather at least that he could not help himself."

"He couldn't?" shouted Lieut. D'Hubert in a great voice. Then, lowering his tone impressively, "And what about me? Could I help myself?"

The surgeon stood up. His thoughts were running upon the flute, his constant companion with a consoling voice. In the vicinity of field ambulances, after twenty-four hours' hard work, he had been known to trouble with its sweet sounds the horrible stillness of battlefields, given over to silence and the dead. The solacing hour of his daily life was approaching, and in peace time he held on to the minutes as a miser to his hoard.

"Of course!—of course!" he said perfunctorily. "You would think so. It's amusing. However, being perfectly neutral and friendly to you both, I have consented to deliver his message to you. Say that I am humouring an invalid if you like. He wants you to

know that this affair is by no means at an end. He
intends to send you his seconds directly he has regained
his strength—providing, of course, the army is not in the
field at that time."

"He intends, does he? Why, certainly," sputtered
Lieut. D'Hubert in a passion.

The secret of his exasperation was not apparent to
the visitor; but this passion confirmed the surgeon in
the belief which was gaining ground outside that some
very serious difference had risen between these two
young men, something serious enough to wear an air of
mystery, some fact of the utmost gravity. To settle
their urgent difference about that fact, those two young
men had risked being broken and disgraced at the outset
almost of their career. The surgeon feared that the forth-
coming inquiry would fail to satisfy the public curiosity.
They would not take the public into their confidence as
to that something which had passed between them of a
nature so outrageous as to make them face a charge of
murder—neither more nor less. But what could it be?

The surgeon was not very curious by temperament;
but that question haunting his mind caused him twice
that evening to hold the instrument off his lips and sit
silent for a whole minute—right in the middle of a tune
—trying to form a plausible conjecture.

II

HE succeeded in this object no better than the rest
of the garrison and the whole of society. The two
young officers, of no especial consequence till then,
became distinguished by the universal curiosity as to
the origin of their quarrel. Madame de Lionne's *salon*
was the centre of ingenious surmises; that lady herself
was for a time assailed by inquiries as being the last
person known to have spoken to these unhappy and
reckless young men before they went out together
from her house to a savage encounter with swords,
at dusk, in a private garden. She protested she had

not observed anything unusual in their demeanour. Lieut. Feraud had been visibly annoyed at being called away. That was natural enough ; no man likes to be disturbed in a conversation with a lady famed for her elegance and sensibility. But in truth the subject bored Madame de Lionne, since her personality could by no stretch of reckless gossip be connected with this affair. And it irritated her to hear it advanced that there might have been some woman in the case. This irritation arose, not from her elegance or sensibility, but from a more instinctive side of her nature. It became so great at last that she peremptorily forbade the subject to be mentioned under her roof. Near her couch the prohibition was obeyed, but farther off in the *salon* the pall of the imposed silence continued to be lifted more or less. A personage with a long, pale face, resembling the countenance of a sheep, opined, shaking his head, that it was a quarrel of long standing envenomed by time. It was objected to him that the men themselves were too young for such a theory. They belonged also to different and distant parts of France. There were other physical impossibilities, too. A sub-commissary of the Intendance, an agreeable and cultivated bachelor in kerseymere breeches, Hessian boots, and a blue coat embroidered with silver lace, who affected to believe in the transmigration of souls, suggested that the two men met perhaps in some previous existence. The feud was in the forgotten past. It might have been something quite inconceivable in the present state of their being ; but their souls remembered the animosity, and mani-fested an instinctive antagonism. He developed this theme jocularly. Yet the affair was so absurd from the worldly, the military, the honourable, or the prudential point of view, that this weird explanation seemed rather more reasonable than any other.

The two officers had confided nothing definite to any one. Humiliation at having been worsted arms in hand, and an uneasy feeling of having been involved in a scrape by the injustice of fate, kept Lieut. Feraud savagely dumb. He mistrusted the sympathy of mankind. That would, of course, go to that dandified staff officer. Lying in bed, he raved aloud to the pretty maid who administered to his needs with devotion, and listened to his horrible imprecations with alarm. That Lieut. D'Hubert should be made to "pay for it," seemed to her just and natural. Her principal care was that Lieut. Feraud should not excite himself. He appeared so wholly admirable and fascinating to the humility of her heart that her only concern was to see him get well quickly, even if it were only to resume his visits to Madame de Lionne's *salon*.

Lieut. D'Hubert kept silent for the immediate reason that there was no one, except a stupid young soldier servant, to speak to. Further, he was aware that the episode, so grave professionally, had its comic side. When reflecting upon it, he still felt that he would like to wring Lieut. Feraud's neck for him. But this formula was figurative rather than precise, and expressed more a state of mind than an actual physical impulse. At the same time, there was in that young man a feeling of comradeship and kindness which made him unwilling to make the position of Lieut. Feraud worse than it was. He did not want to talk at large about this wretched affair. At the inquiry he would have, of course, to speak the truth in self-defence. This prospect vexed him.

But no inquiry took place. The army took the field instead. Lieut. D'Hubert, liberated without remark, took up his regimental duties ; and Lieut. Feraud, his arm just out of the sling, rode unquestioned with his squadron to complete his convalescence in the smoke of battlefields and the fresh air of night bivouacs. This bracing treatment turned out so well, that at the first rumour of an armistice being signed he could turn without misgivings to the thoughts of his private warfare.

This time it was to be regular warfare. He sent two friends to Lieut. D'Hubert, whose regiment was stationed only a few miles away. Those friends had asked no questions of their principal. "I owe him one, that pretty staff officer," he had said grimly, and they went away quite contentedly on their mission. Lieut. D'Hubert had no difficulty in finding two friends equally discreet and devoted to their principal. "There's a crazy fellow to whom I must give a lesson," he had declared curtly ; and they asked for no better reasons.

On these grounds an encounter with duelling-swords was arranged one early morning in a convenient field. At the third set-to Lieut. D'Hubert found himself lying on his back on the dewy grass with a hole in his side. A serene sun rising over a landscape of meadows and woods hung on his left. A surgeon—not the flute player, but another—was bending over him, feeling around the wound.

"Narrow squeak. But it will be nothing," he pronounced.

Lieut. D'Hubert heard these words with pleasure. One of his seconds, sitting on the wet grass, and sustaining his head on his lap, said, "The fortune of war, *mon pauvre vieux*. What will you have? You had better make it up like two good fellows. Do!"

"You don't know what you ask," murmured Lieut. D'Hubert, in a feeble voice. "However, if he . . ."

In another part of the meadow the seconds of Lieut. Feraud were urging him to go over and shake hands with his adversary.

"You have paid him off now—*que diable*. It's the proper thing to do. This D'Hubert is a decent fellow."

"I know the decency of these generals' pets," muttered Lieut. Feraud through his teeth, and the sombre expression of his face discouraged further efforts at reconciliation. The seconds, bowing from a distance, took their men off the field. In the afternoon Lieut. D'Hubert, very popular as a good comrade uniting great bravery with a frank and equable temper, had many visitors. It was remarked that Lieut. Feraud did not, as is customary, show himself much abroad to receive the felicitations of his friends. They would not have failed him, because he too was liked for the exuberance of his southern nature and the simplicity of his char-

acter. In all the places where officers were in the habit
of assembling at the end of the day the duel of the
morning was talked over from every point of view.
Though Lieut. D'Hubert had got worsted this time, his
sword play was commended. No one could deny that
it was very close, very scientific. It was even
whispered that if he got touched it was because he
wished to spare his adversary. But by many the
vigour and dash of Lieut. Feraud's attack were pronounced irresistible.

The merits of the two officers as combatants were
frankly discussed ; but their attitude to each other after
the duel was criticized lightly and with caution. It
was irreconcilable, and that was to be regretted.
But after all they knew best what the care of their
honour dictated. It was not a matter for their comrades
to pry into over-much. As to the origin of the quarrel,
the general impression was that it dated from the time
they were holding garrison in Strasbourg. The musical
surgeon shook his head at that. It went much farther
back, he thought.

"Why, of course ! You must know the whole
story," cried several voices, eager with curiosity.
"What was it ? "

He raised his eyes from his glass deliberately. "Even
if I knew ever so well, you can't expect me to tell you
since both the principals choose to say nothing."

He got up and went out, leaving the sense of mystery
behind him. He could not stay any longer, because
the witching hour of flute playing was drawing near.

After he had gone a very young officer observed
solemnly, "Obviously ! His lips are sealed."

Nobody questioned the high correctness of that
remark. Somehow it added to the impressiveness of the
affair. Several older officers of both regiments,
prompted by nothing but sheer kindness and love of
harmony, proposed to form a Court of Honour, to
which the two young men would leave the task of their
reconciliation. Unfortunately they began by approaching Lieut. Feraud, on the assumption that, having just

scored heavily, he would be found placable and disposed to moderation.

The reasoning was sound enough. Nevertheless, the move turned out unfortunate. In that relaxation of moral fibre, which is brought about by the ease of soothed vanity, Lieut. Feraud had condescended in the secret of his heart to review the case, and even had come to doubt not the justice of his cause, but the absolute sagacity of his conduct. This being so, he was disinclined to talk about it. The suggestion of the regimental wise men put him in a difficult position. He was disgusted at it, and this disgust, by a paradoxical logic, reawakened his animosity against Lieut. D'Hubert. Was he to be pestered with this fellow for ever—the fellow who had an infernal knack of getting round people somehow ? And yet it was difficult to refuse point blank that mediation sanctioned by the code of honour.

He met the difficulty by an attitude of grim reserve. He twisted his moustache and used vague words. His case was perfectly clear. He was not ashamed to state it before a proper Court of Honour, neither was he afraid to defend it on the ground. He did not see any reason to jump at the suggestion before ascertaining how his adversary was likely to take it.

Later in the day, his exasperation growing upon him, he was heard in a public place saying sardonically, " that it would be the very luckiest thing for Lieut. D'Hubert, because the next time of meeting he need not hope to get off with the mere trifle of three weeks in bed."

This boastful phrase might have been prompted by the most profound Machiavellism. Southern natures often hide, under the outward impulsiveness of action and speech, a certain amount of astuteness.

Lieut. Feraud, mistrusting the justice of men, by no means desired a Court of Honour ; and the above words, according so well with his temperament, had also the merit of serving his turn. Whether meant so or not, they found their way in less than four-and-twenty hours into Lieut. D'Hubert's bedroom. In consequence Lieut. D'Hubert, sitting propped up with pillows, received the overtures made to him next day by the statement that the affair was of a nature which could not bear discussion.

The pale face of the wounded officer, his weak voice, which he had yet to use cautiously, and the courteous dignity of his tone had a great effect on his hearers. Reported outside all this did more for deepening the mystery than the vapourings of Lieut. Feraud. This last was greatly relieved at the issue. He began to enjoy the state of general wonder, and was pleased to add to it by assuming an attitude of fierce discretion.

The colonel of Lieut. D'Hubert's regiment was a grey-haired, weather-beaten warrior, who took a simple view of his responsibilities. "I can't," he said to himself, "let the best of my subalterns get damaged like this for nothing. I must get to the bottom of this affair privately. He must speak out if the devil were in it. The colonel should be more than a father to these youngsters." And indeed he loved all his men with as much affection as a father of a large family can feel for every individual member of it. If human beings by an oversight of providence came into the world as mere civilians, they were born again into a regiment as infants are born into a family, and it was that military birth alone which counted.

At the sight of Lieut. D'Hubert standing before him very bleached and hollow-eyed the heart of the old warrior felt a pang of genuine compassion. All his affection for the regiment—that body of men which he held in his hand to launch forward and draw back, who ministered to his pride and commanded all his thoughts—seemed centred for a moment on the person of the most promising subaltern. He cleared his throat in a threatening manner, and frowned terribly. "You must understand," he began, "that I don't care a rap for the life of a single man in the regiment. I would send the eight hundred and forty-three of you men and horses galloping into the pit of perdition with no more compunction than I would kill a fly!"

"Yes, Colonel. You would be riding at our head," said Lieut. D'Hubert with a wan smile.

The colonel, who felt the need of being very diplomatic, fairly roared at this. "I want you to know, Lieut. D'Hubert, that I could stand aside and see you all riding to Hades if need be. I am a man to do even that if the good of the service and my duty to my country required it from me. But that's unthinkable, so don't you even hint at such a thing." He glared awfully, but his tone softened. "There's some milk yet about that moustache of yours, my boy. You don't know what a man like me is capable of. I would hide behind a haystack if . . . Don't grin at me, sir ! How dare you ? If this were not a private conversation I would . . . Look here ! I am responsible for the proper expenditure of lives under my command for the glory of our country and honour of the regiment. Do you understand that ? Well, then, what the devil do you mean by letting yourself be spitted like this by that fellow of the 7th Hussars ? It's simply disgraceful ! "

Lieut. D'Hubert felt vexed beyond measure. His shoulders moved slightly. He made no other answer. He could not ignore his responsibility.

The colonel veiled his glance and lowered his voice still more. "It's deplorable ! " he murmured. And again he changed his tone. "Come ! " he went on persuasively, but with that note of authority which dwells in the throat of a good leader of men, " this affair must be settled. I desire to be told plainly what it is all about. I demand, as your best friend, to know."

The compelling power of authority, the persuasive influence of kindness, affected powerfully a man just risen from a bed of sickness. Lieut. D'Hubert's hand, which grasped the knob of a stick, trembled slightly. But his northern temperament, sentimental yet cautious, and clear-sighted, too, in its idealistic way, checked his impulse to make a clean breast of the whole deadly absurdity. According to the precept of transcendental wisdom, he turned his tongue seven times in his mouth before he spoke. He made then only a speech of thanks.

The colonel listened, interested at first, then looked mystified. At last he frowned. " You hesitate ?—*mil'le tonnerres!* Haven't I told you that I will condescend to argue with you—as a friend ? "

" Yes, Colonel ! " answered Lieut. D'Hubert gently. " But I am afraid that after you have heard me out as a friend you will take action as my superior officer."

The attentive colonel snapped his jaws. " Well, what of that ? " he said frankly. " Is it so damnably disgraceful ? "

" It is not," negatived Lieut. D'Hubert, in a faint but firm voice.

" Of course, I shall act for the good of the service. Nothing can prevent me doing that. What do you think I want to be told for ? "

" I know it is not from idle curiosity," protested Lieut. D'Hubert. " I know you will act wisely. But what about the good fame of the regiment ? "

" It cannot be affected by any youthful folly of a lieutenant," said the colonel severely.

" No. It cannot be. But it can be by evil tongues. It will be said that a lieutenant of the 4th Hussars, afraid of meeting his adversary, is hiding behind his colonel. And that would be worse than hiding behind a haystack —for the good of the service. I cannot afford to do that, Colonel."

" Nobody would dare to say anything of the kind," began the colonel very fiercely, but ended the phrase on an uncertain note. The bravery of Lieut. D'Hubert was well known. But the colonel was well aware that the duelling courage, the single combat courage, is rightly or wrongly supposed to be courage of a special sort. And it was eminently necessary that an officer of his regiment should possess every kind of courage—and prove it, too. The colonel stuck out his lower lip, and looked far away with a peculiar glazed stare. This was the expression of his perplexity—an expression practically unknown to his regiment ; for perplexity is a sentiment which is incompatible with the rank of colonel of cavalry. The colonel himself was overcome by the unpleasant novelty of the sensation. As he was not accustomed to think except on professional matters connected with the welfare of men and horses, and the proper use thereof on the field of glory, his intellectual efforts degenerated into mere mental repetitions of profane language. "*Mille tonnerres!* . . . *Sacré nom de nom* . . ." he thought.

Lieut. D'Hubert coughed painfully, and added in a weary voice. "There will be plenty of evil tongues to say that I've been cowed. And I am sure you will not expect me to pass that over. I may find myself suddenly with a dozen duels on my hands instead of this one affair."

The direct simplicity of this argument came home to the colonel's understanding. He looked at his subordinate fixedly. "Sit down, Lieutenant!" he said gruffly. "This is the very devil of a . . . Sit down!"

"*Mon Colonel*," D'Hubert began again, "I am not afraid of evil tongues. There's a way of silencing them. But there's my peace of mind, too. I wouldn't be able to shake off the notion that I've ruined a brother officer. Whatever action you take, it is bound to go farther. The inquiry has been dropped—let it rest now. It would have been absolutely fatal to Feraud."

"Hey! What! Did he behave so badly?"

"Yes. It was pretty bad," muttered Lieut. D'Hubert. Being still very weak, he felt a disposition to cry.

As the other man did not belong to his own regiment, the colonel had no difficulty in believing this. He began to pace up and down the room. He was a good chief, a man capable of discreet sympathy. But he was human in other ways too, and this became apparent because he was not capable of artifice.

"The very devil, Lieutenant," he blurted out, in the innocence of his heart, "is that I have declared my intention to get to the bottom of this affair. And when a colonel says something . . . you see . . ."

Lieut. D'Hubert broke in earnestly. "Let me entreat you, Colonel, to be satisfied with taking my word of honour that I was put into a damnable position where I had no option ; I had no choice whatever, consistent with my dignity as a man and an officer. . . . After all, Colonel, this fact is the very bottom of this affair. Here you've got it. The rest is mere detail. . . ."

The colonel stopped short. The reputation of Lieut. D'Hubert for good sense and good temper weighed in the balance. A cool head, a warm heart, open as the day. Always correct in his behaviour. One had to trust him. The colonel repressed manfully an immense curiosity. "H'm ! You affirm that as a man and an officer. . . . No option ? Eh ? "

" As an officer—an officer of the 4th Hussars, too," insisted Lieut. D'Hubert, " I had not. And that is the bottom of the affair, Colonel."

" Yes. But still I don't see why, to one's colonel. . . . A colonel is a father—*que diable !* "

Lieut. D'Hubert ought not to have been allowed out as yet. He was becoming aware of his physical insufficiency with humiliation and despair. But the morbid obstinacy of an invalid possessed him, and at the same time he felt with dismay his eyes filling with water. This trouble seemed too big to handle. A tear fell down the thin, pale cheek of Lieut. D'Hubert.

The colonel turned his back on him hastily. You could have heard a pin drop. " This is some silly woman story—is it not ? "

Saying these words the chief spun round to seize the truth which is not a beautiful shape living in a well, but a shy bird best caught by stratagem. This was the last move of the colonel's diplomacy. He saw the truth shining unmistakably in the gesture of Lieut. D'Hubert raising his weak arms and his eyes to heaven in supreme protest.

" Not a woman affair—eh ? " growled the colonel, staring hard. " I don't ask you who or where. All I want to know is whether there is a woman in it ? "

Lieut. D'Hubert's arms dropped, and his weak voice was pathetically broken.

" Nothing of the kind, *mon Colonel.*"

" On your honour ? " insisted the old warrior,

"On my honour."

"Very well," said the Colonel thoughtfully, and bit his lip. The arguments of Lieut. D'Hubert, helped by his liking for the man, had convinced him. On the other hand, it was highly improper that his intervention, of which he had made no secret, should produce no visible effect. He kept Lieut. D'Hubert a few minutes longer, and dismissed him kindly.

"Take a few days more in bed, Lieutenant. What the devil does the surgeon mean by reporting you fit for duty ? "

On coming out of the colonel's quarters, Lieut. D'Hubert said nothing to the friend who was waiting outside to take him home. He said nothing to anybody. Lieut. D'Hubert made no confidences. But on the evening of that day the colonel, strolling under the elms growing near his quarters, in the company of his second in command, opened his lips.

"I've got to the bottom of this affair," he remarked.

The lieut.-colonel, a dry, brown chip of a man with a short side-whiskers, pricked up his ears at that without letting a sign of curiosity escape him.

"It's no trifle," added the colonel oracularly. The other waited for a long while before he murmured.—

"Indeed, sir !"

"No trifle," repeated the colonel, looking straight before him. "I've however forbidden D'Hubert either to send to or receive a challenge from Feraud for the next twelve months."

He had imagined this prohibition to save the prestige a colonel should have. The result of it was to give an official seal to the mystery surrounding this deadly quarrel. Lieut. D'Hubert repelled by an impassive silence all attempts to worm the truth out of him. Lieut. Feraud, secretly uneasy at first, regained his assurance as time went on. He disguised his ignorance of the meaning of the imposed truce by slight sardonic laughs, as though he were amused by what he intended to keep to himself. "But what will you do ? " his chums used to ask him. He contented himself by replying "*Qui*

12

vivra verra" with a little truculent air.   And everybody admired his discretion.

Before the end of the truce Lieut. D'Hubert got his troop.   The promotion was well earned, but somehow no one seemed to expect the event.   When Lieut. Feraud heard of it at a gathering of officers, he muttered through his teeth, " Is that so ? " At once he unhooked his sabre from a peg near the door, buckled it on carefully, and left the company without another word.   He walked home with measured steps, struck a light with his flint and steel, and lit his tallow candle.   Then snatching an unlucky glass tumbler off the mantelpiece he dashed it violently on the floor.

Now that D'Hubert was an officer of superior rank there could be no question of a duel.   Neither of them could send or receive a challenge without rendering himself amenable to a court-martial.   It was not to be thought of.   Lieut. Feraud, who for many days now had experienced no real desire to meet Lieut. D'Hubert arms in hand, chafed again at the systematic injustice of fate. " Does he think he will escape me in that way ? " he thought indignantly.   He saw in this promotion an intrigue, a conspiracy, a cowardly manœuvre.   That colonel knew what he was doing.   He had hastened to recommend his favourite for a step.   It was outrageous that a man should be able to avoid the consequences of his acts in such a dark and tortuous manner.

Of a happy-go-lucky disposition, of a temperament more pugnacious than military, Lieut. Feraud had been content to give and receive blows for sheer love of armed strife, and without much thought of advancement ; but now an urgent desire to get on sprang up in his breast.   This fighter by vocation resolved in his mind to seize showy occasions and to court the favourable opinion of his chiefs like a mere worldling.   He knew he was as brave as any one, and never doubted his personal charm.   Nevertheless, neither the bravery nor the charm seemed to work very swiftly.   Lieut. Feraud's engaging, careless truculence of a *beau sabreur* underwent a change.   He began to make bitter allusions to

" clever fellows who stick at nothing to get on." The army was full of them, he would say ; you had only to look round. But all the time he had in view one person only, his adversary, D'Hubert. Once he confided to an appreciative friend. "You see, I don't know how to fawn on the right sort of people. It isn't in my character."

He did not get his step till a week after Austerlitz. The Light Cavalry of the Grand Army had its hands very full of interesting work for a little while. Directly the pressure of professional occupation had been eased Captain Feraud took measures to arrange a meeting without loss of time. "I know my bird," he observed grimly. "If I don't look sharp he will take care to get himself promoted over the heads of a dozen better men than himself. He's got the knack for that sort of thing."

This duel was fought in Silesia. If not fought to a finish, it was, at any rate, fought to a standstill. The weapon was the cavalry sabre, and the skill, the science, the vigour, and the determination displayed by the adversaries compelled the admiration of the beholders. It became the subject of talk on both shores of the Danube, and as far as the garrisons of Gratz and Laybach. They crossed blades seven times. Both had many cuts which bled profusely. Both refused to have the combat stopped, time after time, with what appeared the most deadly animosity. This appearance was caused on the part of Captain D'Hubert by a rational desire to be done once for all with this worry ; on the part of Captain Feraud by a tremendous exaltation of his pugnacious instincts and the incitement of wounded vanity. At last, dishevelled, their shirts in rags, covered with gore and hardly able to stand, they were led away forcibly by their marvelling and horrified seconds. Later on, besieged by comrades avid of details, these gentlemen declared that they could not have allowed that sort of hacking to go on indefinitely. Asked whether the quarrel was settled this time, they gave it out as their conviction that it was a difference which could only be settled by one of the parties remaining lifeless on the ground. The sensation spread from army corps to army corps, and penetrated at last to the smallest detachments of the troops cantoned between the Rhine and the Save. In the cafés in Vienna it was generally estimated, from details to hand, that the adversaries would be able to meet again in three weeks' time on the outside. Something really transcendent in the way of duelling was expected.

These expectations were brought to naught by the necessities of the service which separated the two officers. No official notice had been taken of their quarrel. It was now the property of the army, and not to be meddled with lightly. But the story of the duel, or rather their duelling propensities, must have stood somewhat in the way of their advancement, because they were still captains when they came together again during the war with Prussia. Detached north after Jena, with the army commanded by Marshal Bernadotte, Prince of Ponte Corvo, they entered Lübeck together.

It was only after the occupation of that town that Captain Feraud found leisure to consider his future conduct in view of the fact that Captain D'Hubert had been given the position of third aide-de-camp to the marshal. He considered it a great part of a night, and in the morning summoned two sympathetic friends.

"I've been thinking it over calmly," he said, gazing at them with blood-shot, tired eyes. "I see that I must get rid of that intriguing personage. Here he's managed to sneak on to the personal staff of the marshal. It's a direct provocation to me. I can't tolerate a situation in which I am exposed any day to receive an order through him. And God knows what order, too! That sort of thing has happened once before— and that's once too often. He understands this perfectly, never fear. I can't tell you any more. Now you know what it is you have to do."

This encounter took place outside the town of Lübeck, on very open ground, selected with special care in deference to the general sentiment of the cavalry division belonging to the army corps, that this time the two officers should meet on horseback. After all, this duel was a cavalry affair, and to persist in fighting on foot would look like a slight on one's own arm of the service. The seconds, startled by the unusual nature of the suggestion, hastened to refer to their principals. Captain Feraud jumped at it with alacrity. For some obscure reason, depending, no doubt, on his psychology, he imagined himself invincible on horseback. All alone within the four walls of his room he rubbed his hands and muttered triumphantly, "Aha! my pretty staff officer, I've got you now."

Captain D'Hubert on his side, after staring hard for a considerable time at his friends shrugged his shoulders slightly. This affair had hopelessly and unreasonably complicated his existence for him. One absurdity or less in the development did not matter—all absurdity was distasteful to him; but, urbane as ever, he produced a faintly ironic smile, and said in his calm voice, "It certainly will do away to some extent with the monotony of the thing."

When left alone, he sat down at a table and took his head into his hands. He had not spared himself of late and the marshal had been working all his aides-de-camp particularly hard. The last three weeks of campaigning in horrible weather had affected his health. When over-tired he suffered from a stitch in his wounded side, and that uncomfortable sensation always depressed him. "It's that brute's doing, too," he thought bitterly.

The day before he had received a letter from home, announcing that his only sister was going to be married. He reflected that from the time she was nineteen and he twenty-six, when he went away to garrison life in Strasbourg, he had had but two short glimpses of her. They had been great friends and confidants; and now she was going to be given away to a man whom he did not know —a very worthy fellow no doubt, but not half good enough for her. He would never see his old Léonie again. She had a capable little head, and plenty of

tact ; she would know how to manage the fellow, to be
sure. He was easy in his mind about her happiness,
but he felt ousted from the first place in her thoughts,
which had been his ever since the girl could speak. A
melancholy regret of the days of his childhood settled
upon Captain D'Hubert, third aide-de-camp to the
Prince of Ponte Corvo.

He threw aside the letter of congratulation he had
begun to write as in duty bound, but without enthusiasm.
He took a fresh piece of paper, and traced on it the
words : "This is my last will and testament." Looking
at these words he gave himself up to unpleasant reflection ; a presentiment that he would never see the scenes
of his childhood weighed down the equable spirits of
Captain D'Hubert. He jumped up, pushing his chair
back, yawned elaborately in sign that he didn't care
anything for presentiments, and throwing himself on the
bed went to sleep. During the night he shivered from
time to time without waking up. In the morning he
rode out of town between his two seconds, talking of
indifferent things, and looking right and left with
apparent detachment into the heavy morning mists
shrouding the flat green fields bordered by hedges. He
leaped a ditch, and saw the forms of many mounted men
moving in the fog. "We are to fight before a gallery, it
seems," he muttered to himself bitterly.

His seconds were rather concerned at the state of
the atmosphere, but presently a pale, sickly sun struggled
out of the low vapours, and Captain D'Hubert made
out, in the distance, three horsemen riding a little apart
from the others. It was Captain Feraud and his
seconds. He drew his sabre, and assured himself that
it was properly fastened to his wrist. And now the
seconds, who had been standing in close group with
the heads of their horses together, separated at an easy
canter, leaving a large, clear field between him and his
adversary. Captain D'Hubert looked at the pale sun, at
the dismal fields, and the imbecility of the impending
fight filled him with desolation. From a distant part of
the field a stentorian voice shouted commands at proper

intervals : *Au pas—Au trot—Charrrgez!* . . . Presentiments of death don't come to a man for nothing, he thought at the very moment he put spurs to his horse.

And therefore he was more than surprised when, at the very first set-to, Captain Feraud laid himself open to a cut over the forehead, which blinding him with blood, ended the combat almost before it had fairly begun. It was impossible to go on. Captain D'Hubert, leaving his enemy swearing horribly and reeling in the saddle between his two appalled friends, leaped the ditch again into the road and trotted home with his two seconds, who seemed rather awestruck at the speedy issue of that encounter. In the evening Captain D'Hubert finished the congratulatory letter on his sister's marriage.

He finished it late. It was a long letter. Captain D'Hubert gave reigns to his fancy. He told his sister that he would feel rather lonely after this great change in her life ; but then the day would come for him too to get married. In fact, he was thinking already of the time when there would be no one left to fight with in Europe and the epoch of wars would be over. "I expect then," he wrote, "to be within measurable distance of a marshal's bâton, and you will be an experienced married woman. You shall look out a wife for me. I will be, probably, bald by then, and a little *blasé.* I shall require a young girl, pretty of course, and with a large fortune, which should help me to close my glorious career in the splendour befitting my exalted rank." He ended with the information that he had just given a lesson to a worrying, quarrelsome fellow who imagined he had a grievance against him. "But if you, in the depth of your province," he continued, "ever hear it said that your brother is of a quarrelsome disposition, don't you believe it on any account. There is no saying what gossip from the army may reach your innocent ears. Whatever you hear you may rest assured that your ever-loving brother is not a duellist." Then Captain D'Hubert crumpled up the blank sheet of paper headed with the words "This is my last will and testament," and threw it in the fire with a great laugh at himself. He didn't care a snap for what that lunatic could do. He had suddenly acquired the conviction that his adversary was utterly powerless to affect his life in any sort of way ; except, perhaps, in the way of putting special excitement into delightful, gay intervals between the campaigns.

From this on there were, however, to be no peaceful intervals in the career of Captain D'Hubert. He saw the fields of Eylau and Friedland, marched and countermarched in the snow, in the mud, in the dust of Polish plains, picking up distinction and advancenent on all the roads of North-eastern Europe. Meantime Captain Feraud, despatched southwards with his regiment, made unsatisfactory war in Spain. It was only when the preparations for the Russian campaign began that he was ordered north again. He left the country of mantillas and oranges without regret.

The first signs of a not unbecoming baldness added to the lofty aspect of Colonel D'Hubert'a forehead. This feature was no longer white and smooth as in the days of his youth ; the kindly open glance of his blue eyes had grown a little hard as if from much peering through the smoke of battles. The ebony crop on Colonel Feraud's head, coarse and crinkly like a cap of horsehair, showed many silver threads about the temples. A detestable warfare of ambushes and inglorious surprises had not improved his temper. The beak-like curve of his nose was unpleasantly set off by a deep fold on each side of his mouth. The round orbits of his eyes radiated wrinkles. More than ever he recalled an irritable and staring bird—something like a cross between a sparrow and an owl. He was still extremely outspoken in his dislike of " intriguing fellows." He seized every opportunity to state that he did not pick up his rank in the ante-rooms of marshals. The unlucky persons, civil or military, who, with an intention of being pleasant begged Colonel Feraud to tell them how he came by that very apparent scar on the forehead, were astonished to find themselves snubbed in various ways, some of which were simply rude and others mysteriously sardonic. Young officers were warned kindly by their more experienced comrades not to stare openly at the colonel's scar. But indeed an officer need have been very young in his profession not to have heard the legendary tale of that duel originating in a mysterious, unforgivable offence.

III

THE retreat from Moscow submerged all private feelings in a sea of disaster and misery. Colonels without regiments, D'Hubert and Feraud carried the musket in the ranks of the so-called sacred battalion—a battalion recruited from officers of all arms who had no longer any troops to lead.

In that battalion promoted colonels did duty as sergeants; the generals captained the companies; a marshal of France, Prince of the Empire, commanded the whole. All had provided themselves with muskets picked up on the road, and with cartridges taken from the dead. In the general destruction of the bonds of discipline and duty holding together the companies, the battalions, the regiments, the brigades, and divisions of an armed host, this body of men put its pride in preserving some semblance of order and formation. The only stragglers were those who fell out to give up to the frost their exhausted souls. They plodded on, and their passage did not disturb the mortal silence of the plains, shining with the livid light of snows under a sky the colour of ashes. Whirlwinds ran along the fields, broke against the dark column, enveloped it in a turmoil of flying icicles, and subsided, disclosing it creeping on its tragic way without the swing and rhythm of the military pace. It struggled onwards, the men exchanging neither words nor looks; whole ranks marched touching elbows day after day, and never raising their eyes from the ground, as if lost in despairing reflections. In the dumb, black forests of pines the crackling of overloaded

branches was the only sound they heard. Often from
daybreak to dusk no one spoke in the whole column.
It was like a *macabre* march of struggling corpses
towards a distant grave. Only an alarm of Cossacks
could restore to their eyes a semblance of martial resolution. The battalion faced about and deployed, or formed
square under the endless fluttering of snowflakes. A cloud
of horsemen with fur caps on their heads, levelled long
lances, and yelled "Hurrah! Hurrah!" around their
menacing immobility whence, with muffled detonations,
hundreds of dark red flames darted through the air thick
with falling snow. In a very few moments the horsemen
would disappear, as if carried off yelling in the gale, and
the sacred battalion standing still, alone in the blizzard,
heard only the howling of the wind, whose blasts
searched their very hearts. Then, with a cry or two of
Vive l'Empereur! it would resume its march, leaving
behind a few lifeless bodies lying huddled up, tiny black
specks on the white immensity of the snows.

Though often marching in the ranks, or skirmishing
in the woods side by side, the two officers ignored each
other; this not so much from inimical intention as from
a very real indifference. All their store of moral energy
was expended in resisting the terrific enmity of nature
and the crushing sense of irretrievable disaster. To the
last they counted among the most active, the least
demoralized of the battalion; their vigorous vitality
invested them both with the appearance of an heroic
pair in the eyes of their comrades. And they never
exchanged more than a casual word or two, except one
day, when skirmishing in front of the battalion against
a worrying attack of cavalry, they found themselves cut
off in the woods by a small party of Cossacks. A score
of fur-capped, hairy horsemen rode to and fro, brandish-
ing their lances in ominous silence; but the two officers
had no mind to lay down their arms, and Colonel
Feraud suddenly spoke up in a hoarse, growling voice,
bringing his firelock to the shoulder. "You take the
nearest brute, Colonel D'Hubert; I'll settle the next
one. I am a better shot than you are."

Colonel D'Hubert nodded over his levelled musket. Their shoulders were pressed against the trunk of a large tree; on their front enormous snowdrifts protected them from a direct charge. Two carefully aimed shots rang out in the frosty air, two Cossacks reeled in their saddles. The rest, not thinking the game good enough, closed round their wounded comrades and galloped away out of range. The two officers managed to rejoin their battalion halted for the night. During that afternoon they had leaned upon each other more than once, and towards the end, Colonel D'Hubert, whose long legs gave him an advantage in walking through soft snow, peremptorily took the musket of Colonel Feraud from him and carried it on his shoulder, using his own as a staff.

On the outskirts of a village half buried in the snow an old wooden barn burned with a clear and an immense flame. The sacred battalion of skeletons, muffled in rags, crowded greedily the windward side, stretching hundreds of numbed, bony hands to the blaze. Nobody had noted their approach. Before entering the circle of light playing on the sunken, glassy-eyed, starved faces Colonel D'Hubert spoke in his turn.

"Here's your musket, Colonel Feraud. I can walk better than you."

Colonel Feraud nodded, and pushed on towards the warmth of the fierce flames. Colonel D'Hubert was more deliberate, but not the less bent on getting a place in the front rank. Those they shouldered aside tried to greet with a faint cheer the reappearance of the two indomitable companions in activity and endurance. Those manly qualities had never perhaps received a higher tribute than this feeble acclamation.

This is the faithful record of speeches exchanged during the retreat from Moscow by Colonels Feraud and D'Hubert. Colonel Feraud's taciturnity was the outcome of concentrated rage. Short, hairy, black faced with layers of grime and the thick sprouting of a wiry beard, a frost-bitten hand wrapped up in filthy rags carried in a sling, he accused fate of unparalleled per-

fidy towards the sublime Man of Destiny. Colonel
D'Hubert, his long moustaches pendent in icicles on
each side of his cracked blue lips, his eyelids inflamed
with the glare of snows, the principal part of his costume
consisting of a sheepskin coat looted with difficulty
from the frozen corpse of a camp follower found in an
abandoned cart, took a more thoughtful view of events.
His regularly handsome features, now reduced to mere
bony lines and fleshless hollows, looked out of a woman's
black velvet hood, over which was rammed forcibly a
cocked hat picked up under the wheels of an empty
army fourgon, which must have contained at one time
some general officer's luggage. The sheepskin coat
being short for a man of his inches ended very high up,
and the skin of his legs, blue with the cold, showed
through the tatters of his nether garments. This under
the circumstances provoked neither jeers nor pity. No
one cared how the next man felt or looked. Colonel
D'Hubert himself, hardened to exposure, suffered mainly
in his self-respect from the lamentable indecency of
his costume. A thoughtless person may think that with
a whole host of inanimate bodies bestrewing the path
of retreat there could not have been much difficulty
in supplying the deficiency. But to loot a pair of
breeches from a frozen corpse is not so easy as it may
appear to a mere theorist. It requires time and labour.
You must remain behind while your companions march
on. Colonel D'Hubert had his scruples as to falling
out. Once he had stepped aside he could not be sure
of ever rejoining his battalion ; and the ghastly intimacy
of a wrestling match with the frozen dead opposing the
unyielding rigidity of iron to your violence was repugnant
to the delicacy of his feelings. Luckily, one day, grub-
bing in a mound of snow between the huts of a village in
the hope of finding there a frozen potato or some vege-
table garbage he could put between his long and shaky
teeth, Colonel D'Hubert uncovered a couple of mats of
the sort Russian peasants use to line the sides of their
carts with. These, beaten free of frozen snow, bent about
his elegant person and fastened solidly round his waist,

made a bellshaped nether garment, a sort of stiff petticoat which rendered Colonel D'Hubert a perfectly decent, but a much more noticeable figure than before.

Thus accoutred, he continued to retreat, never doubting of his personal escape, but full of other misgivings. The early buoyancy of his belief in the future was destroyed. If the road of glory led through such unforeseen passages, he asked himself—for he was reflective—whether the guide was altogether trustworthy. It was a patriotic sadness, not unmingled with some personal concern, and quite unlike the unreasoning indignation against men and things nursed by Colonel Feraud. Recruiting his strength in a little German town for three weeks, Colonel D'Hubert was surprised to discover within himself a love of repose. His returning vigour was strangely pacific in its aspirations. He meditated silently upon this bizarre change of mood. No doubt many of his brother officers of field rank went through the same moral experience. But these were not the times to talk of it. In one of his letters home Colonel D'Hubert wrote, " All your plans, my dear Léonie, for marrying me to the charming girl you have discovered in your neighbourhood, seem farther off than ever. Peace is not yet. Europe wants another lesson. It will be a hard task for us, but it shall be done, because the Emperor is invincible."

Thus wrote Colonel D'Hubert from Pomerania to his married sister Léonie, settled in the south of France. And so far the sentiments expressed would not have been disowned by Colonel Feraud, who wrote no letters to anybody, whose father had been in life an illiterate blacksmith, who had no sister or brother, and whom no one desired ardently to pair off for a life of peace with a charming young girl. But Colonel D'Hubert's letter contained also some philosophical generalities upon the uncertainty of all personal hopes, when bound up entirely with the prestigious fortune of one incomparably great it is true, yet still remaining but a man in his greatness. This view would have appeared rank heresy to Colonel Feraud. Some melancholy forebodings of a military

kind, expressed cautiously, would have been pronounced
as nothing short of high treason by Colonel Feraud. But
Léonie, the sister of Colonel D'Hubert, read them with
profound satisfaction, and, folding the letter thoughtfully, remarked to herself that "Armand was likely to
prove eventually a sensible fellow." Since her marriage
into a Southern family she had become a convinced
believer in the return of the legitimate king. Hopeful
and anxious she offered prayers night and morning, and
burnt candles in churches for the safety and prosperity
of her brother.

She had every reason to suppose that her prayers
were heard. Colonel D'Hubert passed through Lutzen,
Bautzen and Leipsic, losing no limb, and acquiring
additional reputation. Adapting his conduct to the
need of that desperate time, he had never voiced his
misgivings. He concealed them under a cheerful
courtesy of such pleasant character that people were
inclined to ask themselves with wonder whether Colonel
D'Hubert was aware of any disasters. Not only his
manners, but even his glances remained untroubled.
The steady amenity of his blue eyes disconcerted all
grumblers, and made despair itself pause.

This bearing was remarked favourably by the Emperor himself ; for Colonel D'Hubert, attached now to
the Major-General's staff, came on several occasions
under the imperial eye. But it exasperated the higher
strung nature of Colonel Feraud. Passing through Mag-
deburg on service, this last allowed himself, while seated
gloomily at dinner with the *Commandant de Place*, to
say of his life-long adversary : "This man does not love
the Emperor," and his words were received by the other
guests in profound silence. Colonel Feraud, troubled in
his conscience at the atrocity of the aspersion, felt the
need to back it up by a good argument. "I ought to
know him," he cried, adding some oaths. "One studies
one's adversary. I have met him on the ground half a
dozen times, as all the army knows. What more do you
want ? If that isn't opportunity enough for any fool to
size up his man, may the devil take me if I can tell what

is." And he looked around the table obstinate and sombre.

Later on in Paris, while extremely busy reorganising his regiment, Colonel Feraud learned that Colonel D'Hubert had been made a general. He glared at his informant incredulously, then folded his arms and turned away muttering, " Nothing surprises me on the part of that man."

And aloud he added, speaking over his shoulder, " You would oblige me greatly by telling General D'Hubert at the first opportunity that his advancement saves him for a time from a pretty hot encounter. I was only waiting for him to turn up here."

The other officer remonstrated.

" Could you think of it, Colonel Feraud, at this time, when every life should be consecrated to the glory and safety of France ? "

But the strain of unhappiness caused by military reverses had spoiled Colonel Feraud's character. Like many other men, he was rendered wicked by misfortune.

" I cannot consider General D'Hubert's existence of any account either for the glory or safety of France," he snapped viciously. " You don't pretend, perhaps, to know him better than I do—I who have met him half a dozen times on the ground—do you ? "

His interlocutor, a young man, was silenced. Colonel Feraud walked up and down the room.

" This is not the time to mince matters," he said. " I can't believe that that man ever loved the Emperor. He picked up his general's stars under the boots of Marshal Berthier. Very well. I'll get mine in another fashion, and then we shall settle this business which has been dragging on too long."

General D'Hubert, informed indirectly of Colonel Feraud's attitude, made a gesture as if to put aside an importunate person. His thoughts were solicited by graver cares. He had had no time to go and see his family. His sister, whose royalist hopes were rising higher every day, though proud of her brother regretted his recent advancement in a measure, because it put on him a prominent mark of the usurper's favour, which later on could have an adverse influence upon his career. He wrote to her that no one but an inveterate enemy could say he had got his promotion by favour. As to his career, he assured her that he looked no farther forward into the future than the next battlefield.

Beginning the campaign of France in this dogged spirit, General D'Hubert was wounded on the second day of the battle under Laon. While being carried off the field he heard that Colonel Feraud, promoted this moment to general, had been sent to replace him at the head of his brigade. He cursed his luck impulsively, not being able at the first glance to discern all the advantages of a nasty wound. And yet it was by this heroic method that Providence was shaping his future. Travelling slowly south to his sister's country home, under the care of a trusty old servant, General D'Hubert was spared the humiliating contacts and the perplexities of conduct which assailed the men of Napoleonic empire at the moment of its downfall. Lying in his bed, with the windows of his room open wide to the sunshine of Provence, he perceived the undisguised aspect of the blessing conveyed by that jagged fragment of a Prussian shell, which, killing his horse and ripping open his thigh, saved him from an active conflict with his conscience. After the last fourteen years spent sword in hand in the saddle, and with the sense of his duty done to the very end, General D'Hubert found resignation an easy virtue. His sister was delighted with his reasonableness. " I leave myself altogether in your hands, my dear Léonie," he had said to her.

He was still laid up when, the credit of his brother-in-law's family being exerted on his behalf, he received from the royal government not only the confirmation of his rank, but the assurance of being retained on the active list. To this was added an unlimited convalescent leave. The unfavourable opinion entertained of him in Bonapartist circles, though it rested on nothing more solid than the unsupported pronouncement of General Feraud, was directly responsible for General D'Hubert's retention on the active list. As to General Feraud, his rank was confirmed too. It was more than he dared to expect; but Marshal Soult, then Minister of War to the restored king, was partial to officers who had served in Spain. Only not even the marshal's protection could secure for him active employment. He remained irreconcilable, idle, and sinister. He sought in obscure restaurants the company of other half-pay officers who cherished dingy, but glorious old tricolour cockades in their breast-pockets, and buttoned with the forbidden eagle buttons their shabby uniforms, declaring themselves too poor to afford the expense of the prescribed change.

The triumphant return from Elba, a historical fact as marvellous and incredible as the exploits of some mythological demi-god, found General D'Hubert still quite unable to sit a horse. Neither could he walk very well. These disabilities, which Madame Léonie accounted most lucky, helped to keep her brother out of all possible mischief. His frame of mind at that time, she noted with dismay, became very far from reasonable. This general officer, still menaced by the loss of a limb, was discovered one night in the stables at the château by a groom, who, seeing a light, raised an alarm of thieves. His crutch was lying half-buried in the straw of the litter, and the general was hopping on one leg in a loose box around a snorting horse he was trying to saddle. Such were the effects of imperial magic upon a calm temperament and a pondered mind. Beset in the light of stable lanterns, by the tears, entreaties, indignation, remonstrances and reproaches of his family, he got out of the difficult situation by fainting away there and then in the arms of his nearest relatives, and was carried off to bed. Before he got out of it again, the second reign of Napoleon, the Hundred Days of feverish agitation and supreme effort, passed away like a terrifying dream. The tragic year 1815, begun in the trouble and unrest of consciences, was ending in vengeful proscriptions.

How General Feraud escaped the clutches of the Special Commission and the last offices of a firing squad he never knew himself. It was partly due to the subordinate position he was assigned during the Hundred Days. The Emperor had never given him active command, but had kept him busy at the cavalry depôt in Paris, mounting and despatching hastily drilled troopers into the field. Considering this task as unworthy of his abilities, he had discharged it with no offensively noticeable zeal; but for the greater part he was saved from the excesses of royalist reaction by the interference of General D'Hubert.

This last, still on convalescent leave, but able now to travel, had been despatched by his sister to Paris to present himself to his legitimate sovereign. As no one in the capital could possibly know anything of the episode in the stable he was received there with distinction. Military to the very bottom of his soul, the prospect of rising in his profession consoled him from finding himself the butt of Bonapartist malevolence, which pursued him with a persistence he could not account for. All the rancour of that embittered and persecuted party pointed to him as the man who had *never* loved the Emperor—a sort of monster essentially worse than a mere betrayer.

General D'Hubert shrugged his shoulders without anger at this ferocious prejudice. Rejected by his old friends, and mistrusting profoundly the advances of Royalist society, the young and handsome general (he was barely forty) adopted a manner of cold, punctilious courtesy, which at the merest shadow of an intended slight passed easily into harsh haughtiness. Thus prepared, General D'Hubert went about his affairs in Paris feeling inwardly very happy with the peculiar uplifting happiness of a man very much in love. The charming girl looked out by his sister had come upon the scene, and had conquered him in the thorough manner in which a young girl by merely existing in his sight can make a man of forty her own. They were going to be married as soon as General D'Hubert had obtained his official nomination to a promised command.

One afternoon, sitting on the *terrasse* of the *Café*

Tortoni, General D'Hubert learned from the conversation
of two strangers occupying a table near his own, that
General Feraud, included in the batch of superior officers
arrested after the second return of the king, was in
danger of passing before the Special Commission. Living all his spare moments, as is frequently the case
with expectant lovers, a day in advance of reality, and in
a state of bestarred hallucination, it required nothing less
than the name of his perpetual antagonist pronounced
in a loud voice to call the youngest of Napoleon's generals
away from the mental contemplation of his betrothed.
He looked round. The strangers wore civilian clothes.
Lean and weather-beaten, lolling back in their chairs,
they scowled at people with moody and defiant abstrac-
tion from under their hats pulled low over their eyes.
It was not difficult to recognize them for two of the
compulsorily retired officers of the Old Guard. As
from bravado or carelessness they chose to speak in loud
tones, General D'Hubert, who saw no reason why he
should change his seat, heard every word. They did not
seem to be the personal friends of General Feraud.
His name came up amongst others. Hearing it repeated,
General D'Hubert's tender anticipations of a domestic
future adorned with a woman's grace were traversed
by the harsh regret of his warlike past, of that one
long, intoxicating clash of arms, unique in the magnitude of its glory and disaster—the marvellous work
and the special possession of his own generation. He
felt an irrational tenderness towards his old adversary
and appreciated emotionally the murderous absurdity
their encounter had introduced into his life. It was like
an additional pinch of spice in a hot dish. He remembered the flavour with sudden melancholy. He would
never taste it again. It was all over. "I fancy it
was being left lying in the garden that had exasperated
him so against me from the first," he thought indul-
gently.

The two strangers at the next table had fallen silent
after the third mention of General Feraud's name. Presently the elder of the two, speaking again in a bitter

tone, affirmed that General Feraud's account was settled. And why ? Simply because he was not like some big- wigs who loved only themselves. The Royalists knew they could never make anything of him. He loved *The Other* too well.

The Other was the Man of St. Helena. The two officers nodded and touched glasses before they drank to an impossible return. Then the same who had spoken before, remarked with a sardonic laugh, " His adversary showed more cleverness."

" What adversary ? " asked the younger, as if puzzled.

" Don't you know ? They were two hussars. At each promotion they fought a duel. Haven't you heard of the duel going on ever since 1801 ? "

The other had heard of the duel, of course. Now he understood the allusion. General Baron D'Hubert would be able now to enjoy his fat king's favour in peace.

" Much good may it do to him," mumbled the elder. " They were both brave men. I never saw this D'Hubert —a sort of intriguing dandy, I am told. But I can well believe what I've heard Feraud say of him—that he *never* loved the Emperor."

They rose and went away.

General D'Hubert experienced the horror of a som- nambulist who wakes up from a complacent dream of activity to find himself walking on a quagmire. A profound disgust of the ground on which he was making his way overcame him. Even the image of the charm- ing girl was swept from his view in the flood of moral distress. Everything he had ever been or hoped to be would taste of bitter ignominy unless he could manage to save General Feraud from the fate which threatened so many braves. Under the impulse of this almost morbid need to attend to the safety of his adversary, General D'Hubert worked so well with hands and feet (as the French saying is), that in less than twenty-four hours he found means of obtaining an extraordinary private audience from the Minister of Police.

General Baron D'Hubert was shown in suddenly

without preliminaries. In the dusk of the Minister's cabinet, behind the forms of writing-desk, chairs and tables, between two bunches of wax candles blazing in sconces, he beheld a figure in a gorgeous coat posturing before a tall mirror. The old *conventionnel* Fouché, Senator of the Empire, traitor to every man, to every principle and motive of human conduct, Duke of Otranto, and the wily artizan of the second Restoration, was trying the fit of a court suit in which his young and accomplished *fiancée* had declared her intention to have his portrait painted on porcelain. It was a caprice, a charming fancy which the first Minister of Police of the second Restoration was anxious to gratify. For that man, often compared in wiliness of conduct to a fox, but whose ethical side could be worthily symbolized by nothing less emphatic than a skunk, was as much possessed by his love as General D'Hubert himself.

Startled to be discovered thus by the blunder of a servant, he met this little vexation with the characteristic impudence which had served his turn so well in the endless intrigues of his self-seeking career. Without altering his attitude a hair's-breadth, one leg in a silk stocking advanced, his head twisted over his left shoulder, he called out calmly, "This way, General. Pray approach. Well ? I am all attention."

While General D'Hubert, ill at ease as if one of his own little weaknesses had been exposed, presented his request as shortly as possible, the Duke of Otranto went on feeling the fit of his collar, settling the lapels before the glass, and buckling his back in an effort to behold the set of the gold embroidered coat-skirts behind. His still face, his attentive eyes, could not have expressed a more complete interest in those matters if he had been alone.

"Exclude from the operations of the Special Court a certain Feraud, Gabriel Florian, General of brigade of the promotion of 1814 ? " he repeated, in a slightly wondering tone, and then turned away from the glass. "Why exclude *him* precisely ? "

"I am surprised that your Excellency, so competent

in the evaluation of men of his time, should have thought
worth while to have that name put down on the list."

"A rabid Bonapartist!"

"So is every grenadier and every trooper of the army,
as your Excellency well knows. And the individuality
of General Feraud can have no more weight than that
of any casual grenadier. He is a man of no mental
grasp, of no capacity whatever. It is inconceivable
that he should ever have any influence."

"He has a well-hung tongue, though," interjected
Fouché.

"Noisy, I admit, but not dangerous."

"I will not dispute with you. I know next to nothing
of him. Hardly his name, in fact."

"And yet your Excellency has the presidency of the
Commission charged by the king to point out those who
were to be tried," said General D'Hubert, with an
emphasis which did not miss the minister's ear.

"Yes, General," he said, walking away into the dark
part of the vast room, and throwing himself into a deep
arm-chair that swallowed him up, all but the soft gleam of
gold embroideries and the pallid patch of the face—
"yes, General. Take this chair there."

General D'Hubert sat down.

"Yes, General," continued the arch-master in the
arts of intrigue and betrayals, whose duplicity, as if at
times intolerable to his self-knowledge, found relief in
bursts of comical openness. "I did hurry on the formation of the proscribing Commission, and I took its presidency. And do you know why? Simply from fear
that if I did not take it quickly into my hands my own
name would head the list of the proscribed. Such are
the times in which we live. But I am minister of the
king yet, and I ask you plainly why I should take the
name of this obscure Feraud off the list? You wonder
how his name got there! Is it possible that you should
know men so little? My dear General, at the very
first sitting of the Commission names poured on us like
rain off the roof of the Tuileries. Names! We had our
choice of thousands. How do you know that the name

of this Feraud, whose life or death don't matter to France, does not keep out some other name ? "

The voice out of the arm-chair stopped. Opposite General D'Hubert sat still, shadowy and silent. Only his sabre clinked slightly. The voice in the arm-chair began again. "And we must try to satisfy the exigencies of the Allied Sovereigns, too. The Prince de Talleyrand told me only yesterday that Nesselrode had informed him officially of His Majesty the Emperor Alexander's dissatisfaction at the small number of examples the Government of the king intends to make—especially amongst military men. I tell you this confidentially."

"Upon my word!" broke out General D'Hubert, speaking through his teeth, "if your Excellency deigns to favour me with any more confidential information I don't know what I will do. It's enough to break one's sword over one's knee, and fling the pieces . . ."

"What government you imagined yourself to be serving ?" interrupted the minister sharply.

After a short pause the crestfallen voice of General D'Hubert answered, "The Government of France."

"That's paying your conscience off with mere words, General. The truth is that you are serving a government of returned exiles, of men who have been without country for twenty years. Of men also who have just got over a very bad and humiliating fright. . . . Have no illusions on that score."

The Duke of Otranto ceased. He had relieved himself, and had attained his object of stripping some self-respect off that man who had inconveniently discovered him posturing in a gold-embroidered court costume before a mirror. But they were a hot-headed lot in the army; it occurred to him that it would be inconvenient if a well-disposed general officer, received in audience on the recommendation of one of the Princes, were to do something rashly scandalous directly after a private interview with the minister. In a changed tone he put a question to the point. "Your relation—this Feraud ?"

"No. No relation at all."

"Intimate friend ?"

"Intimate . . . yes. There is between us an intimate connexion of a nature which makes it a point of
honour with me to try . . ."

The minister rang a bell without waiting for the end
of the phrase. When the servant had gone out, after
bringing in a pair of heavy silver candelabra for the
writing-desk, the Duke of Otranto rose, his breast glistening all over with gold in the strong light, and taking a
piece of paper out of a drawer, held it in his hand osten-
tatiously while he said with persuasive gentleness, "You
must not speak of breaking your sword across your
knee, General. Perhaps you would never get another.
The Emperor will not return this time. . . . *Diable
d'homme!* There was just a moment, here in Paris, soon
after Waterloo, when he frightened me. It looked as
though he were ready to begin all over again. Luckily
one never does begin all over again, really. You must
not think of breaking your sword, General."

General D'Hubert, looking on the ground, moved
slightly his hand in a hopeless gesture of renunciation.
The Minister of Police turned his eyes away from him,
and scanned deliberately the paper he had been holding
up all the time.

"There are only twenty general officers selected to
be made an example of. Twenty. A round number.
And let's see, Feraud. . . . Ah, he's there. Gabriel
Florian. *Parfaitement.* That's your man. Well, there
will be only nineteen examples made now."

General D'Hubert stood up feeling as though he
had gone through an infectious illness. "I must beg
your Excellency to keep my interference a profound
secret. I attach the greatest importance to his never
learning . . ."

"Who is going to inform him, I should like to know?"
said Fouché, raising his eyes curiously to General
D'Hubert's tense, set face. "Take one of these pens,
and run it through the name yourself. This is the only
list in existence. If you are careful to take up enough
ink no one will be able to tell what was the name struck
out. But, *par exemple*, I am not responsible for what

Clarke will do with him afterwards. If he persists in being rabid he will be ordered by the Minister of War to reside in some provincial town under the supervision of the police."

A few days later General D'Hubert was saying to his sister, after the first greetings had been got over, "Ah, my dear Léonie! it seemed to me I couldn't get away from Paris quick enough."

"Effect of love," she suggested, with a malicious smile.

"And horror," added General D'Hubert, with profound seriousness. "I have nearly died there of . . . of nausea."

His face was contracted with disgust. And as his sister looked at him attentively, he continued, "I have had to see Fouché. I have had an audience. I have been in his cabinet. There remains with one, who had the misfortune to breathe the air of the same room with that man, a sense of diminished dignity, an uneasy feeling of being not so clean, after all, as one hoped one was. . . . But you can't understand."

She nodded quickly several times. She understood very well on the contrary. She knew her brother thoroughly, and liked him as he was. Moreover, the scorn and loathing of mankind were the lot of the *Jacobin* Fouché, who, exploiting for his own advantage every weakness, every virtue, every generous illusion of mankind, made dupes of his whole generation, and died obscurely as Duke of Otranto.

"My dear Armand," she said compassionately, "what could you want from that man?"

"Nothing less than a life," answered General D'Hubert. "And I've got it. It had to be done. But I feel yet as if I could never forgive the necessity to the man I had to save."

General Feraud, totally unable (as in the case with most of us) to comprehend what was happening to him, received the Minister of War's order to proceed at once to a small town of Central France with feelings whose natural expression consisted in a fierce rolling of the eye and savage grinding of the teeth. The passing away of the state of war, the only condition of society he had ever known, the horrible view of a world at peace, frightened him. He went away to his little town firmly convinced that this could not last. There he was informed of his retirement from the army, and that his pension (calculated on the scale of a colonel's rank) was made dependent on the correctness of his conduct, and on the good reports of the police. No longer in the army ! He felt suddenly strange to the earth, like a disembodied spirit. It was impossible to exist. But at first he reacted from sheer incredulity. This could not be. He waited for thunder, earthquakes, natural cataclysms ; but nothing happened. The leaden weight of an irremediable idleness descended upon General Feraud, who having no resources within himself sank into a state of awe-inspiring hebetude. He haunted the streets of the little town, gazing before him with lack-lustre eyes, disregarding the hats raised on his passage ; and people, nudging each other as he went by, whispered, "That's poor General Feraud. His heart is broken. Behold how he loved the Emperor."

The other living wreckage of Napoleonic tempest clustered round General Feraud with infinite respect. He, himself, imagined his soul to be crushed by grief. He suffered from quickly succeeding impulses to weep, to howl, to bite his fists till blood came, to spend days on his bed with his head thrust under the pillow ; but these arose from sheer ennui, from the anguish of an immense, indescribable, inconceivable boredom. His mental inability to grasp the hopeless nature of his case as a whole saved him from suicide. He never even thought of it once. He thought of nothing. But his appetite abandoned him, and the difficulty he experienced to express the overwhelming nature of his feelings (the most furious swearing could do no justice to it) induced gradually a habit of silence—a sort of death to a southern temperament.

Great, therefore, was the sensation amongst the *anciens militaires* frequenting a certain little café full of flies, when one stuffy afternoon "that poor General Feraud" let out suddenly a volley of formidable curses.

He had been sitting quietly in his own privileged corner looking through the Paris gazettes with just as much interest as a condemned man on the eve of execution could be expected to show in the news of the day. A cluster of martial, bronzed faces, amongst which there was one lacking an eye, and another the tip of a nose frost-bitten in Russia, surrounded him anxiously.

"What's the matter, General?"

General Feraud sat erect, holding the folded newspaper at arm's length in order to make out the small print better. He read to himself, over again, fragments of the intelligence which had caused, what may be called, his resurrection.

"*We are informed that General D'Hubert, till now on sick leave in the south, is to be called to the command of the 5th Cavalry brigade in . . .*"

He dropped the paper stonily. . . . "Called to the command" . . . and suddenly gave his forehead a mighty slap. "I had almost forgotten him," he muttered, in a conscience-stricken tone.

A deep-chested veteran shouted across the café. "Some new villainy of the Government, General?"

"The villainies of these scoundrels," thundered General Feraud, "are innumerable. One more one less!" . . . He lowered his tone. "But I will set good order to one of them at least."

He looked all round the faces. "There's a pomaded, curled staff-officer, the darling of some of the marshals who sold their father for a handful of English gold. He will find out presently that I am alive yet," he declared, in a dogmatic tone. "However, this is a private affair. An old affair of honour. Bah! Our honour does not matter. Here we are driven off with a split ear like a lot of cast troop horses—good only for a knacker's yard. But it would be like striking a blow for the Emperor. . . . Messieurs, I shall require the assistance of two of you."

Every man moved forward. General Feraud, deeply

touched by this demonstration, called with visible emotion upon the one-eyed veteran cuirassier and the officer of the Chasseurs à Cheval who had left the tip of his nose in Russia. He excused his choice to the others.

"A cavalry affair this—you know."

He was answered with a varied chorus of " *Parfaitement, mon Général. . . . C'est juste. . . . Parbleu, c'est connu. . . .*" Everybody was satisfied. The three left the café together, followed by cries of " *Bonne chance.*"

Outside they linked arms, the general in the middle. The three rusty cocked hats worn *en bataille* with a sinister forward slant barred the narrow street nearly right across. The overheated little town of grey stones and red tiles was drowsing away its provincial afternoon under a blue sky. The loud blows of a cooper hooping a cask reverberated regularly between the houses. The general dragged his left foot a little in the shade of the walls.

"This damned winter of 1813 has got into my bones for good. Never mind. We must take pistols, that's all. A little lumbago. We must have pistols. He's game for my bag. My eyes are as keen as ever. You should have seen me in Russia picking off the dodging Cossacks with a beastly old infantry musket. I have a natural gift for firearms."

In this strain General Feraud ran on, holding up his head, with owlish eyes and rapacious beak. A mere fighter all his life, a cavalry man, a *sabreur*, he conceived war with the utmost simplicity, as, in the main, a massed lot of personal contests, a sort of gregarious duelling. And here he had in hand a war of his own. He revived. The shadow of peace passed away from him like the shadow of death. It was the marvellous resurrection of the named Feraud, Gabriel Florian, *engagé volontaire* of 1793, General of 1814, buried without ceremony by means of a service order signed by the War Minister of the Second Restoration.

IV

No man succeeds in everything he undertakes. In that sense we are all failures. The great point is not to fail in ordering and sustaining the effort of our life. In this matter vanity is what leads us astray. It hurries us into situations from which we must come out damaged; whereas pride is our safeguard, by the reserve it imposes on the choice of our endeavour as much as by the virtue of its sustaining power.

General D'Hubert was proud and reserved. He had not been damaged by his casual love affairs, successful or otherwise. In his war-scarred body his heart at forty remained unscratched. Entering with reserve into his sister's matrimonial plans, he had felt himself falling irremediably in love as one falls off a roof. He was too proud to be frightened. Indeed, the sensation was too delightful to be alarming.

The inexperience of a man of forty is a much more serious thing than the inexperience of a youth of twenty, for it is not helped out by the rashness of hot blood. The girl was mysterious, as young girls are by the mere effect of their guarded ingenuity; and to him the mysteriousness of that young girl appeared exceptional and fascinating. But there was nothing mysterious about the arrangements of the match which Madame Léonie had promoted. There was nothing peculiar either. It was a very appropriate match, commending itself extremely to the young lady's mother (the father was dead) and tolerable to the young lady's uncle—an old *émigré* lately returned from Germany, and pervading, cane in hand, a lean ghost of the *ancien régime*, the garden walks of the young lady's ancestral home.

General D'Hubert was not the man to be satisfied merely with the woman and the fortune—when it came to the point. His pride (and pride aims always at true success) would be satisfied with nothing short of love. But as true pride excludes vanity, he could not imagine any reason why this mysterious creature with deep and brilliant eyes of a violet colour should have any feeling for him warmer than indifference. The young lady (her name was Adèle) baffled every attempt at a clear understanding on that point. It is true that the attempts were clumsy and made timidly, because by then General D'Hubert had become acutely aware of the number of his years, of his wounds, of his many moral imperfections, of his secret unworthiness—and had incidentally learned by experience the meaning of the word funk. As far as he could make out she seemed to imply that, with an unbounded confidence in her mother's affection and sagacity, she felt no unsurmountable dislike for the person of General D'Hubert ; and that this was quite sufficient for a well-brought-up young lady to begin married life upon. This view hurt and tormented the pride of General D'Hubert. And yet he asked himself with a sort of sweet despair, what more could he expect ? She had a quiet and luminous forehead. Her violet eyes laughed while the lines of her lips and chin remained composed in admirable gravity. All this was set off by such a glorious mass of fair hair, by a complexion so marvellous, by such a grace of expression, that General D'Hubert really never found the opportunity to examine with sufficient detachment the lofty exigencies of his pride. In fact he became shy of that line of inquiry since it had led once or twice to a crisis of solitary passion in which it was borne upon him that he loved her enough to kill her rather than lose her. From such passages, not unknown to men of forty, he would come out broken, exhausted, remorseful, a little dismayed. He derived, however, considerable comfort from the quietist practice of sitting now and then half the night by an open window and meditating upon the wonder of her existence, like a believer lost in the mystic contemplation of his faith.

It must not be supposed that all these variations of his inward state were made manifest to the world. General D'Hubert found no difficulty in appearing wreathed in smiles. Because, in fact, he was very happy. He followed the established rules of his condition, sending over flowers (from his sister's garden and hot-houses) early every morning, and a little later following himself to lunch with his intended, her mother, and her *émigré* uncle. The middle of the day was spent in strolling or sitting in the shade. A watchful deference, trembling on the verge of tenderness was the note of their intercourse on his side—with a playful turn of the phrase concealing the profound trouble of his whole being caused by her inaccessible nearness. Late in the afternoon General D'Hubert walked home between the fields of vines, sometimes intensely miserable, sometimes supremely happy, sometimes pensively sad ; but always feeling a special intensity of existence, that elation common to artists, poets, and lovers—to men haunted by a great passion, a noble thought, or a new vision of plastic beauty.

The outward world at that time did not exist with any special distinctness for General D'Hubert. One evening, however, crossing a ridge from which he could see both houses, General D'Hubert became aware of two figures far down the road. The day had been divine. The festal decoration of the inflamed sky lent a gentle glow to the sober tints of the southern land. The grey rocks, the brown fields, the purple, undulating distances harmonised in luminous accord, exhaled already the scents of the evening. The two figures down the road presented themselves like two rigid and wooden silhouettes all black on the ribbon of white dust. General D'Hubert made out the long, straight military *capotes* buttoned closely right up to the black stocks, the cocked hats, the lean, carven brown countenances—old soldiers —*vieilles moustaches* ! The taller of the two had a black patch over one eye ; the other's hard, dry countenance presented some bizarre, disquieting peculiarity, which on nearer approach proved to be the absence of the tip of the nose. Lifting their hands with one movement, to salute the slightly lame civilian walking with a thick stick, they inquired for the house where the General Baron D'Hubert lived, and what was the best way to get speech with him quietly.

"If you think this quiet enough," said General

D'Hubert, looking round at the vine-fields, framed in purple lines, and dominated by the nest of grey and drab walls of a village clustering around the top of a conical hill, so that the blunt church tower seemed but the shape of a crowning rock—"if you think this spot quiet enough, you can speak to him at once. And I beg you, comrades, to speak openly, with perfect confidence."

They stepped back at this, and raised again their hands to their hats with marked ceremoniousness. Then the one with the chipped nose, speaking for both, remarked that the matter was confidential enough, and to be arranged discreetly. Their general quarters were established in that village over there, where the infernal clodhoppers—damn their false, Royalist hearts!—looked remarkably cross-eyed at three unassuming military men. For the present he should only ask for the name of General D'Hubert's friends.

"What friends?" said the astonished General D'Hubert, completely off the track. "I am staying with my brother-in-law over there."

"Well, he will do for one," said the chipped veteran.

"We're the friends of General Feraud," interjected the other, who had kept silent till then, only glowering with his one eye at the man who had *never* loved the Emperor. That was something to look at. For even the gold-laced Judases who had sold him to the English, the marshals and princes, had loved him at some time or other. But this man had *never* loved the Emperor. General Feraud had said so distinctly.

General D'Hubert felt an inward blow in his chest. For an infinitesimal fraction of a second it was as if the spinning of the earth had become perceptible with an awful, slight rustle in the eternal stillness of space. But this noise of blood in his ears passed off at once. Involuntarily he murmured, "Feraud! I had forgotten his existence."

"He's existing at present, very uncomfortably, it is true, in the infamous inn of that nest of savages up there," said the one-eyed cuirassier drily. "We arrived in your parts an hour ago on post horses. He's awaiting our return with impatience. There is hurry, you know. The General has broken the ministerial order to obtain from you the satisfaction he's entitled to by the laws of honour, and naturally he's anxious to have it all over before the *gendarmerie* gets on his scent."

The other elucidated the idea a little further. "Get back on the quiet—you understand ? Phitt. No one the wiser. We have broken out, too. Your friend the king would be glad to cut off our scurvy pittances at the first chance. It's a risk. But honour before everything."

General D'Hubert had recovered his powers of speech. "So you come here like this along this road to invite me to a throat-cutting match with that—that . . ." A laughing sort of rage took possession of him. "Ha ! ha ! ha ! ha ! "

His fists on his hips, he roared without restraint, while they stood before him lank and straight, as though they had been shot up with a snap through a trapdoor in the ground. Only four-and-twenty months ago the masters of Europe, they had already the air of antique ghosts, they seemed less substantial in their faded coats than their own narrow shadows falling so black across the white road : the military and grotesque shadows of twenty years of war and conquests. They had an outlandish appearance of two imperturbable bonzes of the religion of the sword. And General D'Hubert, also one of the ex-masters of Europe, laughed at these serious phantoms standing in his way.

Said one, indicating the laughing General with a jerk of the head. "A merry companion, that."

"There are some of us that haven't smiled from the day *The Other* went away," remarked his comrade.

A violent impulse to set upon and beat those unsubstantial wraiths to the ground frightened General D'Hubert. He ceased laughing suddenly. His desire now was to get rid of them, to get them away from his sight quickly before he lost control of himself. He wondered at the fury he felt rising in his breast. But

14

he had no time to look into that peculiarity just then.

"I understand your wish to be done with me as quickly as possible. Don't let us waste time in empty ceremonies. Do you see that wood there at the foot of that slope. Yes, the wood of pines. Let us meet there to-morrow at sunrise. I will bring with me my sword or my pistols, or both if you like."

The seconds of General Feraud looked at each other.

"Pistols, General," said the cuirassier.

"So be it. Au revoir—to-morrow morning. Till then let me advise you to keep close if you don't want the *gendarmerie* making inquiries about you before it gets dark. Strangers are rare in this part of the country."

They saluted in silence. General D'Hubert, turning his back on their retreating forms, stood still in the middle of the road for a long time, biting his lower lip and looking on the ground. Then he began to walk straight before him, thus retracing his steps till he found himself before the park gate of his intended's house. Dusk had fallen. Motionless he stared through the bars at the front of the house, gleaming clear beyond the thickets and trees. Footsteps scrunched on the gravel, and presently a tall stooping shape emerged from the lateral alley following the inner side of the park wall.

Le Chevalier de Valmassigue, uncle of the adorable Adèle, ex-brigadier in the army of the Princes, bookbinder in Altona, afterwards shoemaker (with a great reputation for elegance in the fit of ladies' shoes) in another small German town, wore silk stockings on his lean shanks, low shoes with silver buckles, a brocaded waistcoat. A long-skirted coat *à la française* covered loosely his thin, bowed back. A small three-cornered hat rested on a lot of powdered hair, tied in a queue.

"*Monsieur le Chevalier,*" called General D'Hubert softly.

"What? You here again, *mon ami*? Have you forgotten something?"

"By heavens! that's just it. I have forgotten something. I am come to tell you of it. No—outside. Behind this wall. It's too ghastly a thing to be let in at all where she lives."

The Chevalier came out at once with that benevolent resignation some old people display towards the fugue of youth. Older by a quarter of a century than General D'Hubert, he looked upon him in the secret of his heart as a rather troublesome youngster in love. He had heard his enigmatical words very well, but attached no undue importance to what a mere man of forty so hard hit was likely to do or say. The turn of mind of the generation of Frenchmen grown up during the years of his exile was almost unintelligible to him. Their sentiments appeared to him unduly violent, lacking fineness and measure, their language needlessly exaggerated. He joined calmly the General on the road, and they made a few steps in silence, the General trying to master his agitation, and get proper control of his voice.

"It is perfectly true; I forgot something. I forgot till half an hour ago that I had an urgent affair of honour on my hands. It's incredible, but it is so!"

All was still for a moment. Then in the profound evening silence of the countryside the clear, aged voice of the Chevalier was heard trembling slightly. "Monsieur! That's an indignity."

It was his first thought. The girl born during his exile, the posthumous daughter of his poor brother murdered by a band of Jacobins, had grown since his return very dear to his old heart, which had been starving on mere memories of affection for so many years. "It is an inconceivable thing, I say! A man settles such affairs before he thinks of asking for a young girl's hand. Why! If you had forgotten for ten days longer, you would have been married before your memory returned to you. In my time men did not forget such things—nor yet what is due to the feelings of an innocent young woman. If I did not respect them myself, I would qualify your conduct in a way which you would not like."

General D'Hubert relieved himself frankly by a

groan. "Don't let that consideration prevent you. You run no risk of offending her mortally."

But the old man paid no attention to this lover's nonsense. It's doubtful whether he even heard. What is it?" he asked. "What's the nature of . . . ?"

"Call it a youthful folly, *Monsieur le Chevalier*. An inconceivable incredible result of . . ." He stopped short. "He will never believe the story," he thought. "He will only think I am taking him for a fool, and get offended," General D'Hubert spoke up again. "Yes, originating in youthful folly, it has become . . ."

The Chevalier interrupted. "Well, then it must be arranged."

"Arranged?"

"Yes, no matter at what cost to your *amour propre*. You should have remembered you were engaged. You forgot that too, I suppose. And then you go and forget your quarrel. It's the most hopeless exhibition of levity I ever heard of."

"Good heavens, Monsieur! You don't imagine I have been picking up this quarrel last time I was in Paris, or anything of the sort, do you?"

"Eh! What matters the precise date of your insane conduct," exclaimed the Chevalier testily. "The principal thing is to arrange it."

Noticing General D'Hubert getting restive and trying to place a word, the old *émigré* raised his hand, and added with dignity, "I've been a soldier too. I would never dare suggest a doubtful step to the man whose name my niece is to bear. I tell you that *entre galants hommes* an affair can always be arranged."

"But, *saperlotte, Monsieur le Chevalier*, it's fifteen or sixteen years ago. I was a lieutenant of hussars then."

The old Chevalier seemed confounded by the vehemently despairing tone of this information. "You were a lieutenant of hussars sixteen years ago," he mumbled in a dazed manner.

"Why, yes! You did not suppose I was made a general in my cradle like a royal prince."

In the deepening purple twilight of the fields spread

with vine leaves, backed by a low band of sombre crimson in the west, the voice of the old ex-officer in the army of the Princes sounded collected, punctiliously civil.

"Do I dream ? Is this a pleasantry ? Or am I to understand that you have been hatching an affair of honour for sixteen years ? "

" It has clung to me for that length of time. That is my precise meaning. The quarrel itself is not to be explained easily. We met on the ground several times during that time, of course."

" What manners ! What horrible perversion of man-liness ! Nothing can account for such inhumanity but the sanguinary madness of the Revolution which has tainted a whole generation," mused the returned *émigré* in a low tone. " Who's your adversary ? " he asked a little louder.

" My adversary ? His name is Feraud."

Shadowy in his *triorne* and old-fashioned clothes, like a bowed, thin ghost of the *ancien régime*, the Che-valier voiced a ghostly memory. " I can remember the feud about little Sophie Derval, between Monsieur de Brissac, Captain in the Bodyguards, and d'Anjorrant (not the pock-marked one, the other—the Beau d'Anjor-rant, as they called him). They met three times in eighteen months in a most gallant manner. It was the fault of that little Sophie too, who *would* keep on play-ing . . ."

"This is nothing of the kind," interrupted General D'Hubert. He laughed a little sardonically. "Not at all so simple," he added. "Nor yet half so reasonable," he finished inaudibly between his teeth, and ground them with rage.

After this sound nothing troubled the silence for a long time till the Chevalier asked, without animation, " What is he—this Feraud ? "

" Lieutenant of hussars, too—I mean, he's a general. A Gascon. Son of a blacksmith, I believe."

"There ! I thought so. That Bonaparte had a special predilection for the *canaille*. I don't mean this

for you, D'Hubert.   You are one of us, though you have
served this usurper, who . . ."

"Let's leave him out of this," broke in General
D'Hubert.

The Chevalier shrugged his peaked shoulders.   "Feraud of sorts.   Offspring of a blacksmith and some
village troll.   See what comes of mixing yourself up
with that sort of people."

"You have made shoes yourself, Chevalier."

"Yes.   But I am not the son of a shoemaker.   Neither
are you, Monsieur D'Hubert.   You and I have something
that your Bonaparte's princes, dukes, and marshals have
not, because there's no power on earth that could give it
to them," retorted the *émigré*, with the rising animation
of a man who has got hold of a hopeful argument.
"Those people don't exist—all these Ferauds.   Feraud !
What is Feraud ?   A *va-nu-pieds* disguised into a general
by a Corsican adventurer masquerading as an emperor.
There is no earthly reason for a D'Hubert to *s'encanailler*
by a duel with a person of that sort.   You can make
your excuses to him perfectly well.   And if the *manant*
takes into his head to decline them, you may simply
refuse to meet him."

"You say I may do that ? "

"I do.   With the clearest conscience."

"*Monsieur le Chevalier* !   To what do you think you
have returned from your emigration ? "

This was said in such a startling tone that the old
man raised sharply his bowed head, glimmering silvery
white under the points of the little *tricorne*.   For a time
he made no sound.

"God knows !" he said at last, pointing with a slow
and grave gesture at a tall, roadside cross mounted on a
block of stone, and stretching its arms of forged iron all
black against the darkening red band in the sky—"God
knows !   If it were not for this emblem, which I remember seeing on this spot as a child, I would wonder to what
we who had remained faithful to God and our king have
returned.   The very voices of the people have changed."

"Yes, it is a changed France," said General D'Hubert.

He seemed to have regained his calm. His tone was slightly ironic. " Therefore I cannot take your advice. Besides, how is one to refuse to be bitten by a dog that means to bite ? It's impracticable. Take my word for it—Feraud isn't a man to be stayed by apologies or refusals. But there are other ways. I could, for instance, send a messenger with a word to the brigadier of the *gendarmerie* in Senlac. He and his two friends are liable to arrest on my simple order. It would make some talk in the army, both the organised and the disbanded—especially the disbanded. All *canaille* ! All once upon a time the companions in arms of Armand D'Hubert. But what need a D'Hubert care what people that don't exist may think. Or, better still, I might get my brother-in-law to send for the mayor of the village and give him a hint. No more would be needed to get the three ' brigands ' set upon with flails and pitchforks and hunted into some nice, deep, wet ditch— and nobody the wiser ! It has been done only ten miles from here to three poor devils of the disbanded Red Lancers of the Guard going to their homes. What says your conscience, *Chevalier* ? Can a D'Hubert do that thing to three men who do not exist ? "

A few stars had come out on the blue obscurity, clear as crystal, of the sky. The dry, thin voice of the Chevalier spoke harshly. " Why are you telling me all this ? "

The General seized the withered old hand with a strong grip. " Because I owe you my fullest confidence. Who could tell Adèle but you ? You understand why I dare not trust my brother-in-law nor yet my own sister. *Chevalier* ! I have been so near doing these things that I tremble yet. You don't know how terrible this duel appears to me. And there's no escape from it."

He murmured after a pause, " It's a fatality," dropped the Chevalier's passive hand, and said in his ordinary conversational voice, " I shall have to go without seconds. If it is my lot to remain on the ground, you at least will know all that can be made known of this affair."

The shadowy ghost of the *ancien régime* seemed to
have become more bowed during the conversation.
" How am I to keep an indifferent face this evening
before these two women," he groaned. "General! I
find it very difficult to forgive you."

General D'Hubert made no answer.

" Is your cause good, at least ? "

" I am innocent."

This time he seized the Chevalier's ghostly arm
above the elbow, and gave it a mighty squeeze. " I
must kill him ! " he hissed, and opening his hand strode
away down the road.

The delicate attentions of his adoring sister had
secured for the General perfect liberty of movement in
the house where he was a guest. He had even his own
entrance through a small door in one corner of the
orangery. Thus he was not exposed that evening to
the necessity of dissembling his agitation before the
calm ignorance of the other inmates. He was glad of it.
It seemed to him that if he had to open his lips he would
break out into horrible and aimless imprecations, start
breaking furniture, smashing china and glass. From the
moment he opened the private door, and while ascending
the twenty-eight steps of a winding staircase, giving
access to the corridor on which his room opened, he went
through a horrible and humiliating scene in which an
infuriated madman with bloodshot eyes and a foaming
mouth played inconceivable havoc with everything
inanimate that may be found in a well-appointed dining-
room. When he opened the door of his apartment the
fit was over, and his bodily fatigue was so great that he
had to catch at the backs of the chairs while crossing the
room to reach a low and broad divan on which he let
himself fall heavily. His moral prostration was still
greater. That brutality of feeling which he had known
only when charging the enemy, sabre in hand, amazed
this man of forty, who did not recognize in it the instinctive fury of his menaced passion. But in his mental and
bodily exhaustion this passion got cleared, distilled,
refined into a sentiment of melancholy despair at having,

perhaps, to die before he had taught this beautiful girl to love him.

That night, General D'Hubert stretched out on his back with his hands over his eyes, or lying on his breast with his face buried in a cushion, made the full pilgrimage of emotions. Nauseating disgust at the absurdity of the situation, doubt of his own fitness to conduct his existence, and mistrust of his best sentiments (for what the devil did he want to go to Fouché for?)—he knew them all in turn. "I am an idiot, neither more nor less," he thought—"A sensitive idiot. Because I overheard two men talking in a café. . . . I am an idiot afraid of lies—whereas in life it is only the truth that matters."

Several times he got up and, walking in his socks in order not to be heard by anybody downstairs, drank all the water he could find in the dark. And he tasted the torments of jealousy, too. She would marry somebody else. His very soul writhed. The tenacity of that Feraud, the awful persistence of that imbecile brute, came to him with the tremendous force of a relentless destiny. General D'Hubert trembled as he put down the empty water ewer. "He will have me," he thought. General D'Hubert was tasting every emotion that life has to give. He had in his dry mouth the faint sickly flavour of fear, not the excusable fear before a young girl's candid and amused glance, but the fear of death and the honourable man's fear of cowardice.

But if true courage consists in going out to meet an odious danger from which our body, soul and heart recoil together, General D'Hubert had the opportunity to practise it for the first time in his life. He had charged exultingly at batteries and at infantry squares, and ridden with messages through a hail of bullets without thinking anything about it. His business now was to sneak out unheard, at break of day, to an obscure and revolting death. General D'Hubert never hesitated. He carried two pistols in a leather bag which he slung over his shoulder. Before he had crossed the garden his mouth was dry again. He picked two oranges. It was only after shutting the gate after him that he felt a slight faintness.

He staggered on, disregarding it, and after going a few yards regained the command of his legs. In the colourless and pellucid dawn the wood of pines detached its columns of trunks and its dark green canopy very clearly against the rocks of the grey hillside. He kept his eyes fixed on it steadily, and sucked at an orange as he walked. That temperamental good-humoured coolness in the face of danger which had made him an officer liked by his men and appreciated by his superiors was gradually asserting itself. It was like going into battle. Arriving at the edge of the wood he sat down on a boulder, holding the other orange in his hand, and reproached himself for coming so ridiculously early on the ground. Before very long, however, he heard the swishing of bushes, footsteps on the hard ground, and the sounds of a disjointed, loud conversation. A voice somewhere behind him said boastfully, " He's game for my bag."

He thought to himself, " Here they are. What's this about game ? Are they talking of me ? " And becoming aware of the other orange in his hand, he thought further, " These are very good oranges. Léonie's own tree. I may just as well eat this orange now instead of flinging it away."

Emerging from a wilderness of rocks and bushes, General Feraud and his seconds discovered General D'Hubert engaged in peeling the orange. They stood still, waiting till he looked up. Then the seconds raised their hats, while General Feraud, putting his hands behind his back, walked aside a little way.

" I am compelled to ask one of you, messieurs, to act for me. I have brought no friends. Will you ? "

The one-eyed cuirassier said judicially, " That cannot be refused."

The other veteran remarked, " It's awkward all the same."

" Owing to the state of the people's minds in this

part of the country there was no one I could trust safely with the object of your presence here," explained General D'Hubert, urbanely.

They saluted, looked round, and remarked both together :

" Poor ground."

" It's unfit."

" Why bother about ground, measurements, and so on. Let us simplify matters. Load the two pairs of pistols. I will take those of General Feraud, and let him take mine. Or, better still, let us take a mixed pair. One of each pair. Then let us go into the wood and shoot at sight, while you remain outside. We did not come here for ceremonies, but for war—war to the death. Any ground is good enough for that. If I fall, you must leave me where I lie and clear out. It wouldn't be healthy for you to be found hanging about here after that."

It appeared after a short parley that General Feraud was willing to accept these conditions. While the seconds were loading the pistols, he could be heard whistling, and was seen to rub his hands with perfect contentment. He flung off his coat briskly, and General D'Hubert took off his own and folded it carefully on a stone.

" Suppose you take your principal to the other side of the wood and let him enter exactly in ten minutes from now," suggested General D'Hubert calmly, but feeling as if he were giving directions for his own execution. This, however, was his last moment of weakness. " Wait. Let us compare watches first."

He pulled out his own. The officer with the chipped nose went over to borrow the watch of General Feraud. They bent their heads over them for a time.

" That's it. At four minutes to six by yours. Seven to by mine."

It was the cuirassier who remained by the side of General D'Hubert, keeping his one eye fixed immovably on the white face of the watch he held in the palm of his hand. He opened his mouth, waiting for the beat of the last second long before he snapped out the word, "*Avancez.*"

General D'Hubert moved on, passing from the glaring sunshine of the Provençal morning into the cool and aromatic shade of the pines. The ground was clear between the reddish trunks, whose multitude, leaning at slightly different angles, confused his eye at first. It was like going into battle. The commanding quality of confidence in himself woke up in his breast. He was all to his affair. The problem was how to kill the adversary. Nothing short of that would free him from this imbecile nightmare. "It's no use wounding that brute," thought General D'Hubert. He was known as a resourceful officer. His comrades years ago used also to call him The Strategist. And it was a fact that he could think in the presence of the enemy. Whereas Feraud had always been a mere fighter—but a dead shot, unluckily.

"I must draw his fire at the greatest possible range," said General D'Hubert to himself.

At that moment he saw something white moving far off between the trees—the shirt of his adversary. He stepped out at once between the trunks, exposing himself freely; then, quick as lightning, leaped back. It had been a risky move but it succeeded in its object. Almost simultaneously with the pop of a shot a small piece of bark chipped off by the bullet stung his ear painfully.

General Feraud, with one shot expended, was getting cautious. Peeping round the tree, General D'Hubert could not see him at all. This ignorance of the foe's whereabouts carried with it a sense of insecurity. General H'Hubert felt himself abominably exposed on his flank and rear. Again something white fluttered in his sight. Ha! The enemy was still on his front, then. He had feared a turning movement. But apparently General Feraud was not thinking of it. General D'Hubert saw him pass without special haste from one tree to another in the straight line of approach. With great firmness of mind General D'Hubert stayed his hand. Too far yet. He knew he was no marksman. His must be a waiting game—to kill.

Wishing to take advantage of the greater thickness of the trunk, he sank down to the ground. Extended at full length, head on to his enemy, he had his person completely protected. Exposing himself would not do now, because the other was too near by this time. A conviction that Feraud would presently do something rash was like balm to General D'Hubert's soul. But to keep his chin raised off the ground was irksome, and not much use either. He peeped round, exposing a fraction of his head with dread, but really with little risk. His enemy, as a matter of fact, did not expect to see anything of him so far down as that. General D'Hubert caught a fleeting view of General Feraud shifting trees again with deliberate caution. "He despises my shooting," he thought, displaying that insight into the mind of his antagonist which is of such great help in winning battles. He was confirmed in his tactics of immobility. "If I could only watch my rear as well as my front!" he thought anxiously, longing for the impossible.

It required some force of character to lay his pistols down; but, on a sudden impulse, General D'Hubert did this very gently—one on each side of him. In the army he had been looked upon as a bit of a dandy because he used to shave and put on a clean shirt on the days of battle. As a matter of fact he had always been very careful of his personal appearance. In a man of nearly forty, in love with a young and charming girl, this praise-worthy self-respect may run to such little weaknesses as, for instance, being provided with an elegant little leather folding-case containing a small ivory comb, and fitted with a piece of looking-glass on the outside. General D'Hubert, his hands being free, felt in his breeches' pockets for that implement of innocent vanity excusable in the possessor of long silky moustaches. He drew it out, and then with the utmost coolness and promptitude turned himself over on his back. In this new attitude, his head a little raised, holding the little looking-glass just clear of his tree, he squinted into it with his left eye, while the right kept a direct watch on the rear of his position. Thus was proved Napoleon's saying, that "for a French soldier, the word impossible does not exist." He had the right tree nearly filling the field of his little mirror.

"If he moves from behind it," he reflected with satisfaction, "I am bound to see his legs. But in any case he can't come upon me unawares."

And sure enough he saw the boots of General Feraud flash in and out, eclipsing for an instant everything else reflected in the little mirror. He shifted its position accordingly. But having to form his judgment of the change from that indirect view he did not realise that now his feet and a portion of his legs were in plain sight of General Feraud.

General Feraud had been getting gradually impressed by the amazing cleverness with which his enemy was keeping cover. He had spotted the right tree with bloodthirsty precision. He was absolutely certain of it. And yet he had not been able to glimpse as much as the tip of an ear. As he had been looking for it at the height of about five feet ten inches from the ground it was no great wonder—but it seemed very wonderful to General Feraud.

The first view of these feet and legs determined a rush of blood to his head. He literally staggered behind his tree, and had to steady himself against it with his hand. The other was lying on the ground then! On the ground! Perfectly still, too! Exposed! What could it mean? . . . The notion that he had knocked over his adversary at the first shot entered then General Feraud's head. Once there it grew with every second of attentive gazing, overshadowing every other supposition —irresistible, triumphant, ferocious.

"What an ass I was to think I could have missed him," he muttered to himself. "He was exposed *en plein*—the fool!—for quite a couple of seconds."

General Feraud gazed at the motionless limbs, the last vestiges of surprise fading before an unbounded admiration of his own deadly skill with the pistol.

"Turned up his toes! By the god of war, that was a shot!" he exulted mentally. "Got it through the head, no doubt, just where I aimed, staggered behind that tree, rolled over on his back and died."

And he stared! He stared, forgetting to move, almost awed, almost sorry. But for nothing in the world would he have had it undone. Such a shot!— such a shot! Rolled over on his back and died!

For it was this helpless position, lying on the back, that shouted its direct evidence at General Feraud! It never occured to him that it might have been deliberately assumed by a living man. It was inconceivable. It was beyond the range of sane supposition. There was no possibility to guess the reason for it. And it must be said, too, that General D'Hubert's turned-up feet looked thoroughly dead. General Feraud expanded his lungs for a stentorian shout to his seconds, but, from what he felt to be an excessive scrupulousness, refrained for a while.

"I will just go and see first whether he breathes yet," he mumbled to himself, leaving carelessly the shelter of his tree. This move was immediately perceived by the resourceful General D'Hubert. He concluded it to be another shift, but when he lost the boots out of the field of the mirror he became uneasy. General Feraud had only stepped a little out of the line, but his adversary could not possibly have supposed him walking up with perfect unconcern. General D'Hubert, beginning to wonder what had become of the other, was taken unawares so completely that the first warning of danger consisted in the long, early-morning shadow of his enemy falling aslant on his outstretched legs. He had not even heard a footfall on the soft ground between the trees!

It was too much even for his coolness. He jumped up thoughtlessly, leaving the pistols on the ground. The irresistible instinct of an average man (unless totally paralysed by discomfiture) would have been to stoop for his weapons, exposing himself to the risk of being shot down in that position. Instinct, of course, is irreflective. It is its very definition. But it may be an inquiry worth pursuing whether in reflective mankind the mechanical promptings of instinct are not affected

by the customary mode of thought. In his young days,
Armand D'Hubert, the reflective, promising officer, had
emitted the opinion that in warfare one should "never
cast back on the lines of a mistake." This idea, defen-
ded and developed in many discussions, had settled into
one of the stock notions of his brain, had become a part
of his mental individuality. Whether it had gone so
inconceivably deep as to affect the dictates of his instinct,
or simply because, as he himself declared afterwards,
he was "too scared to remember the confounded pistols,"
the fact is that General D'Hubert never attempted to
stoop for them. Instead of going back on his mistake,
he seized the rough trunk with both hands, and swung
himself behind it with such impetuosity that, going
right round in the very flash and report of the pistol-
shot, he reappeared on the other side of the tree face to
face with General Feraud. This last, completely un-
strung by such a show of agility on the part of a dead
man, was trembling yet. A very faint mist of smoke
hung before his face which had an extraordinary aspect,
as if the lower jaw had become unhinged.

"Not missed!" he cracked hoarsely from the depths
of a dry throat.

This sinister sound loosened the spell that had fallen
on General D'Hubert's senses. "Yes, missed—à bout
portant," he heard himself saying, almost before he had
recovered the full command of his faculties. The revulsion of feeling was accompanied by a gust of homicidal
fury, resuming in its violence the accumulated resentment
of a lifetime. For years General D'Hubert had been
exasperated and humiliated by an atrocious absurdity
imposed upon him by this man's savage caprice. Besides, General D'Hubert had been in this last instance too
unwilling to confront death for the reaction of his anguish
not to take the shape of a desire to kill. "And I have
my two shots to fire yet," he added pitilessly.

General Feraud snapped-to his teeth, and his face
assumed an irate, undaunted expression. "Go on!" he
said grimly.

These would have been his last words if General

D'Hubert had been holding the pistols in his hands. But the pistols were lying on the ground at the foot of a pine. General D'Hubert had the second of leisure necessary to remember that he had dreaded death not as a man, but as a lover ; not as a danger, but as a rival ; not as a foe to life, but as an obstacle to marriage. And behold ! there was the rival defeated !—utterly defeated, crushed, done for !

He picked up the weapons mechanically, and, instead of firing them into General Feraud's breast, he gave expression to the thought uppermost in his mind, " You will fight no more duels now."

His tone of leisurely, ineffable satisfaction was too much for General Feraud's stoicism. " Don't dawdle, then, damn you for a cold-blooded staff-coxcomb ! " he roared out suddenly, out of an impassive face held erect on a rigidly still body.

General D'Hubert uncocked the pistols carefully. This proceeding was observed with mixed feelings by the other general. " You missed me twice," the victor said coolly, shifting both pistols to one hand ; " the last time within a foot or so. By every rule of single combat your life belongs to me. That does not mean that I want to take it now."

" I have no use for your forbearance," muttered General Feraud gloomily.

" Allow me to point out that this is no concern of mine," said General D'Hubert, whose every word was dictated by a consummate delicacy of feeling. In anger he could have killed that man, but in cold blood he recoiled from humiliating by a show of generosity this unreasonable being—a fellow-soldier of the *Grande Armée*, a companion in the wonders and terrors of the great military epic. " You don't set up the pretension of dictating to me what I am to do with what's my own."

General Feraud looked startled, and the other continued, " You've forced me on a point of honour to keep my life at your disposal, as it were, for fifteen years. Very well. Now that the matter is decided to my advan-

15

tage, I am going to do what I like with your life on the same principle. You shall keep it at my disposal as long as I choose. Neither more or less. You are on your honour till I say the word."

"I am! But, *sacrebleu!* This is an absurd position for a General of the Empire to be placed in!" cried General Feraud, in accents of profound and dismayed conviction. "It amounts to sitting all the rest of my life with a loaded pistol in a drawer waiting for your word. It's—it's idiotic; I shall be an object of—of—derision."

"Absurd?—idiotic? Do you think so?" queried General D'Hubert with sly gravity. "Perhaps. But I don't see how that can be helped. However, I am not likely to talk at large of this adventure. Nobody need ever know anything about it. Just as no one to this day, I believe, knows the origin of our quarrel. . . . Not a word more," he added hastily. "I can't really discuss this question with a man who, as far as I am concerned, does not exist."

When the two duellists came out into the open, General Feraud walking a little behind, and rather with the air of walking in a trance, the two seconds hurried towards them, each from his station at the edge of the wood. General D'Hubert addressed them, speaking loud and distinctly, "Messieurs, I make it a point of declaring to you solemnly, in the presence of General Feraud, that our difference is at last settled for good. You may inform all the world of that fact."

"A reconciliation, after all!" they exclaimed together.

"Reconciliation? Not that exactly. It is something much more binding. Is it not so, General?"

General Feraud only lowered his head in sign of assent. The two veterans looked at each other. Later in the day, when they found themselves alone out of their moody friend's earshot, the cuirassier remarked suddenly, "Generally speaking, I can see with my one eye as far as most people; but this beats me. He won't say anything."

"In this affair of honour I understand there has been

from first to last always something that no one in the army could quite make out," declared the chasseur with the imperfect nose. "In mystery it began, in mystery it went on, in mystery it is to end, apparently."

General D'Hubert walked home with long, hasty strides, by no means uplifted by a sense of triumph. He had conquered, yet it did not seem to him that he had gained very much by his conquest. The night before he had grudged the risk of his life which appeared to him magnificent, worthy of preservation as an opportunity to win a girl's love. He had known moments when, by a marvellous illusion, this love seemed to be already his, and his threatened life a still more magnificent opportunity of devotion. Now that his life was safe it had suddenly lost its special magnificence. It had acquired instead a specially alarming aspect as a snare for the exposure of unworthiness. As to the marvellous illusion of conquered love that had visited him for a moment in the agitated watches of the night, which might have been his last on earth, he comprehended now its true nature. It had been merely a paroxysm of delirious conceit. Thus to this man, sobered by the victorious issue of a duel, life appeared robbed of its charm, simply because it was no longer menaced.

Approaching the house from the back, through the orchard and the kitchen garden, he could not notice the agitation which reigned in front. He never met a single soul. Only while walking softly along the corridor, he became aware that the house was awake and more noisy than usual. Names of servants were being called out down below in a confused noise of coming and going. With some concern he noticed that the door of his own room stood ajar, though the shutters had not been opened yet. He had hoped that his early excursion would have passed unperceived. He expected to find some servant just gone in ; but the sunshine filtering through the usual cracks enabled him to see lying on the low divan something bulky, which had the appearance of two women clasped in each other's arms. Tearful and desolate murmurs issued mysteriously from that appearance. General D'Hubert pulled open the nearest pair of shutters violently. One of the women then jumped up. It was his sister. She stood for a moment with her hair hanging down and her arms raised straight up above her head, and then flung herself with a stifled cry into his arms. He returned her embrace, trying at the same time to disengage himself from it. The other woman had not risen. She seemed, on the contrary, to cling closer to the divan, hiding her face in the cushions. Her hair was also loose; it was admirably fair. General D'Hubert recognized it with staggering emotion. Mademoiselle de Valmassigue! Adèle! In distress!

He became greatly alarmed, and got rid of his sister's hug definitely. Madame Léonie then extended her shapely bare arm out of her *peignoir*, pointing dramatically at the divan. "This poor, terrified child has rushed here from home, on foot, two miles—running all the way."

"What on earth has happened?" asked General D'Hubert in a low, agitated voice.

But Madame Léonie was speaking loudly. "She rang the great bell at the gate and roused all the household—we were all asleep yet. You may imagine what a terrible shock. . . . Adèle, my dear child, sit up."

General D'Hubert's expression was not that of a man who "imagines" with facility. He did, however, fish out of the chaos of surmises the notion that his prospective mother-in-law had died suddenly, but only to dismiss it at once. He could not conceive the nature of the event or the catastrophe which could induce Mademoiselle de Valmassigue, living in a house full of servants, to bring the news over the fields herself, two miles, running all the way.

"But why are you in this room?" he whispered, full of awe.

"Of course, I ran up to see, and this child . . . I did not notice it . . . she followed me. It's that absurd Chevalier," went on Madame Léonie, looking towards the divan. . . . "Her hair is all come down. You may imagine she did not stop to call her maid to dress it before she started. . . . Adèle, my dear, sit up. . .

He blurted it all out to her at half-past five in the morn-ing. She woke up early and opened her shutters to breathe the fresh air, and saw him sitting collapsed on a garden bench at the end of the great alley. At that hour—you may imagine ! And the evening before he had declared himself indisposed. She hurried on some clothes and flew down to him. One would be anxious for less. He loves her, but not very intelli-gently. He had been up all night, fully dressed, the poor old man, perfectly exhausted. He wasn't in a state to invent a plausible story. . . .   What a confidant you chose there ! My husband was furious. He said, ' We can't interfere now.' So we sat down to wait. It was awful. And this poor child running with her hair loose over here publicly ! She has been seen by some people in the fields. She has roused the whole household too. It's awkward for her. Luckily you are to be married next week. . . .   Adèle, sit up. He has come home on his own legs. . . .   We expected to see you coming on a stretcher, perhaps—what do I know ? Go and see if the carriage is ready. I must take this child home at once. It isn't proper for her to stay here a minute longer."

General D'Hubert did not move. It was as though he had heard nothing. Madame Léonie changed her mind. " I will go and see myself," she cried. " I want also my cloak.—Adèle—" she began, but did not add " sit up." She went out saying, in a very loud and cheerful tone : " I leave the door open."

General D'Hubert made a movement towards the divan, but then Adèle sat up, and that checked him dead. He thought, " I haven't washed this morning. I must look like an old tramp. There's earth on the back of my coat and pine-needles in my hair." It occurred to him that the situation required a good deal of circumspection on his part.

" I am greatly concerned, mademoiselle," he began vaguely, and abandoned that line. She was sitting up on the divan with her cheeks unusually pink and her hair, brilliantly fair, falling all over her shoulders—

which was a very novel sight to the general. He walked away up the room, and looking out of the window for safety said, "I fear you must think I behaved like a madman," in accents of sincere despair. Then he spun round, and noticed that she had followed him with her eyes. They were not cast down on meeting his glance. And the expression of her face was novel to him also. It was, one might have said, reversed. Those eyes looked at him with grave thoughtfulness, while the exquisite lines of her mouth seemed to suggest a restrained smile. This change made her transcendental beauty much less mysterious, much more accessible to a man's comprehension. An amazing ease of mind came to the general—and even some ease of manner. He walked down the room with as much pleasurable excitement as he would have found in walking up to a battery vomiting death, fire, and smoke; then stood looking down with smiling eyes at the girl whose marriage with him (next week) had been so carefully arranged by the wise, the good, the admirable Léonie.

"Ah! mademoiselle," he said, in a tone of courtly regret, "if only I could be certain that you did not come here this morning, two miles, running all the way, merely from affection for your mother!"

He waited for an answer imperturbable but inwardly elated. It came in a demure murmur, eyelashes lowered with fascinating effect. "You must not be *méchant* as well as mad."

And then General D'Hubert made an aggressive movement towards the divan which nothing could check. That piece of furniture was not exactly in the line of the open door. But Madame Léonie, coming back wrapped up in a light cloak and carrying a lace shawl on her arm for Adèle to hide her incriminating hair under, had a swift impression of her brother getting up from his knees.

"Come along, my dear child," she cried from the doorway.

The general now himself again in the fullest sense, showed the readiness of a resourceful cavalry officer and the peremptoriness of a leader of men. "You don't expect her to walk to the carriage," he said indignantly. "She isn't fit. I shall carry her downstairs."

This he did slowly, followed by his awed and respectful sister ; but he rushed back like a whirlwind to wash off all the signs of the night of anguish and the morning of war, and to put on the festive garments of a conqueror before hurrying over to the other house. Had it not been for that, General D'Hubert felt capable of mounting a horse and pursuing his late adversary in order simply to embrace him from excess of happiness. "I owe it all to this stupid brute," he thought. "He has made plain in a morning what might have taken me years to find out—for I am a timid fool. No self-confidence whatever. Perfect coward. And the Chevalier ! Delightful old man ! " General D'Hubert longed to embrace him also.

The Chevalier was in bed. For several days he was very unwell. The men of the Empire and the post-revolution young ladies were too much for him. He got up the day before the wedding, and, being curious by nature, took his niece aside for a quiet talk. He advised her to find out from her husband the true story of the affair of honour, whose claim, so imperative and so persistent, had led her to within an ace of tragedy. "It is right that his wife should be told. And next month or so will be your time to learn from him anything you want to know, my dear child."

Later on, when the married couple came on a visit to the mother of the bride, Madame la Générale D'Hubert communicated to her beloved old uncle the true story she had obtained without any difficulty from her husband.

The Chevalier listened with deep attention to the end, took a pinch of snuff, flicked the grains of tobacco from the frilled front of his shirt, and asked calmly, "And that's all it was ! "

"Yes, uncle," replied Madame la Générale, opening her pretty eyes very wide. "Isn't it funny ? *C'est insensé*—to think what men are capable of ! "

"H'm ! " commented the old *émigré*. "It depends what sort of men. That Bonaparte's soldiers were savages. It is *insensé*. As a wife, my dear, you must believe implicitly what your husband says."

But to Léonie's husband the Chevalier confided his true opinion. "If that's the tale the fellow made up for his wife, and during the honeymoon too, you may depend on it that no one will ever know now the secret of this affair."

Considerably later still, General D'Hubert judged the time come, and the opportunity propitious to write a letter to General Feraud. This letter began by disclaiming all animosity. "I've never," wrote the General Baron D'Hubert, "wished for your death during all the time of our deplorable quarrel. Allow me," he continued, "to give you back in all form your forfeited life. It is proper that we two, who have been partners in so much military glory, should be friendly to each other publicly."

The same letter contained also an item of domestic information. It was in reference to this last that General Feraud answered from a little village on the banks of the Garonne, in the following words:

"If one of your boy's names had been Napoleon—or Joseph—or even Joachim, I could congratulate you on the event with a better heart. As you have thought proper to give him the names of Charles Henri Armand, I am confirmed in my conviction that you *never* loved the Emperor. The thought of that sublime hero chained to a rock in the middle of a savage ocean makes life of so little value that I would receive with positive joy your instructions to blow my brains out. From suicide I consider myself in honour debarred. But I keep a loaded pistol in my drawer."

Madame la Générale D'Hubert lifted up her hands in despair after perusing that answer.

"You see? He *won't* be reconciled," said her husband. "He must never, by any chance, be allowed to guess where the money comes from. It wouldn't do. He couldn't bear it."

"You are a *brave homme*, Armand," said Madame la Générale appreciatively.

"My dear, I had the right to blow his brains out;

but as I didn't, we can't let him starve.   He has lost his
pension and he is utterly incapable of doing anything in
the world for himself. We must take care of him,
secretly, to the end of his days.   Don't I owe him the
most ecstatic moment of my life ? . . .   Ha ! ha ! ha !
Over the fields, two miles, running all the way ! I
couldn't believe my ears ! . . .   But for his stupid
ferocity, it would have taken me years to find you out.
It's extraordinary how in one way or another this man
has managed to fasten himself on my deeper feelings."

IL CONDE

" Vedi Napoli e poi mori."

THE first time we got into conversation was in the
National Museum in Naples, in the rooms on the
ground floor containing the famous collection of bronzes
from Herculaneum and Pompeii : that marvellous legacy
of antique art whose delicate perfection has been preserved for us by the catastrophic fury of a volcano.

He addressed me first, over the celebrated Resting
Hermes which we had been looking at side by side. He
said the right things about that wholly admirable piece.
Nothing profound. His taste was natural rather than
cultivated. He had obviously seen many fine things in
his life and appreciated them : but he had no jargon of
a dilettante or the connoisseur. A hateful tribe. He
spoke like a fairly intelligent man of the world, a perfectly
unaffected gentleman.

We had known each other by sight for some few days
past. Staying in the same hotel—good, but not extrava-
gantly up to date—I had noticed him in the vestibule
going in and out. I judged he was an old and valued
client. The bow of the hotel-keeper was cordial in its
deference, and he acknowledged it with familiar courtesy.
For the servants he was *Il Conde*. There was some
squabble over a man's parasol—yellow silk with white
lining sort of thing—the waiters had discovered abandoned outside the dining-room door. Our gold-laced
door-keeper recognized it and I heard him directing one

of the lift boys to run after *Il Conde* with it.   Perhaps he was the only Count staying in the hotel, or perhaps he had the distinction of being *the* Count *par excellence*, conferred upon him because of his tried fidelity to the house.

Having conversed at the Museo—(and by the by he had expressed his dislike of the busts and statues of Roman emperors in the gallery of marbles : their faces were too vigorous, too pronounced for him)—having conversed already in the morning I did not think I was intruding when in the evening, finding the dining-room very full, I proposed to share his little table.   Judging by the quiet urbanity of his consent he did not think so either.   His smile was very attractive.

He dined in an evening waistcoat and a " smoking " (he called it so) with a black tie.   All this of very good cut, not new—just as these things should be.   He was, morning or evening, very correct in his dress.   I have no doubt that his whole existence had been correct, well ordered and conventional, undisturbed by startling events.   His white hair brushed upwards off a lofty forehead gave him the air of an idealist, of an imaginative man.   His white moustache, heavy but carefully trimmed and arranged, was not unpleasantly tinted a golden yellow in the middle.   The faint scent of some very good perfume, and of good cigars (that last an odour quite remarkable to come upon in Italy) reached me across the table.   It was in his eyes that his age showed most. They were a little weary with creased eyelids.   He must have been sixty or a couple of years more.   And he was communicative.   I would not go so far as to call it garrulous—but distinctly communicative.

He had tried various climates, of Abbazia, of the Riviera, of other places, too, he told me ; but the only one which suited him was the climate of the Gulf of Naples.   The ancient Romans, who, he pointed out to me, were men expert in the art of living, knew very well what they were doing when they built their villas on these shores, in Baiæ, in Vico, in Capri.   They came down to this seaside in search of health, bringing with

them their trains of mimes and flute-players to amuse
their leisure. He thought it extremely probable that the
Romans of the higher classes were specially predisposed
to painful rheumatic affections.

This was the only personal opinion I heard him express.
It was based on no special erudition. He knew no more
of the Romans than an average informed man of the
world is expected to know. He argued from personal
experience. He had suffered himself from a painful and
dangerous rheumatic affection till he found relief in this
particular spot of Southern Europe.

This was three years ago, and ever since he had taken
up his quarters on the shores of the gulf, either in one of
the hotels in Sorrento or hiring a small villa in Capri. He
had a piano, a few books : picked up transient acquaintances of a day, week, or month in the stream of travellers
from all Europe. One can imagine him going out for
his walks in the streets and lanes, becoming known to
beggars, shopkeepers, children, country people ; talking
amiably over the walls to the contadini—and coming
back to his rooms or his villa to sit before the piano,
with his white hair brushed up and his thick orderly
moustache, " to make a little music for myself." And,
of course, for a change there was Naples near by—life,
movement, animation, opera. A little amusement,
as he said, is necessary for health. Mimes and flute-
players, in fact. Only, unlike the magnates of ancient
Rome, he had no affairs of the city to call him away
from these moderate delights. He had no affairs at all.
Probably he had never had any grave affairs to attend to
in his life. It was a kindly existence, with its joys and
sorrows regulated by the course of Nature—marriages,
births, deaths—ruled by the prescribed usages of good
society and protected by the State.

He was a widower ; but in the months of July and
August he ventured to cross the Alps for six weeks on a
visit to his married daughter. He told me her name.
It was that of a very aristocratic family. She had a
castle—in Bohemia, I think. This is as near as I ever
came to ascertaining his nationality. His own name,

strangely enough, he never mentioned. Perhaps he thought I had seen it on the published list. Truth to say, I never looked. At any rate, he was a good European—he spoke four languages to my certain knowledge —and a man of fortune. Not of great fortune, evidently and appropriately. I imagine that to be extremely rich would have appeared to him improper, *outré*— too blatant altogether. And obviously, too, the fortune was not of his making. The making of a fortune cannot be achieved without some roughness. It is a matter of temperament. His nature was too kindly for strife. In the course of conversation he mentioned his estate quite by the way, in reference to that painful and alarming rheumatic affection. One year, staying incautiously beyond the Alps as late as the middle of September, he had been laid up for three months in that lonely country house with no one but his valet and the caretaking couple to attend to him. Because, as he expressed it, he "kept no establishment there." He had only gone for a couple of days to confer with his land agent. He promised himself never to be so imprudent in the future. The first weeks of September would find him on the shores of his beloved gulf.

Sometimes in travelling one comes upon such lonely men, whose only business is to wait for the unavoidable. Deaths and marriages have made a solitude round them, and one really cannot blame their endeavours to make the waiting as easy as possible. As he remarked to me, "At my time of life freedom from physical pain is a very important matter."

It must not be imagined that he was a wearisome hypochondriac. He was really too well-bred to be a nuisance. He had an eye for the small weaknesses of humanity. But it was a good-natured eye. He made a restful, easy, pleasant companion for the hours between dinner and bedtime. We spent three evenings together, and then I had to leave Naples in a hurry to look after a friend who had fallen seriously ill in Taormina. Having nothing to do, *Il Conde* came to see me off at the station. I was somewhat upset, and his idleness was always ready to take a kindly form. He was by no means an indolent man.

He went along the train peering into the carriages for a good seat for me, and then remained talking cheerily from below. He declared he would miss me that evening very much and announced his intention of going after dinner to listen to the band in the public garden, the Villa Nazionale. He would amuse himself by hearing excellent music and looking at the best society. There would be a lot of people, as usual.

I seem to see him yet—his raised face with a friendly smile under the thick moustaches, and his kind, fatigued eyes. As the train began to move, he addressed me in two languages: first in French, saying, " *Bon voyage* "; then, in his very good, somewhat emphatic English, encouragingly, because he could see my concern : " All will—be—well—yet ! "

My friend's illness having taken a decidedly favourable turn, I returned to Naples on the tenth day. I cannot say I had given much thought to *Il Conde* during my absence, but entering the dining-room I looked for him in his habitual place. I had an idea he might have gone back to Sorrento to his piano and his books and his fishing. He was great friends with all the boatmen, and fished a good deal with lines from a boat. But I made out his white head in the crowd of heads, and even from a distance noticed something unusual in his attitude. Instead of sitting erect, gazing all round with alert urbanity, he drooped over his plate. I stood opposite him for some time before he looked up, a little wildly, if such a strong word can be used in connexion with his correct appearance.

" Ah, my dear sir ! Is it you ? " he greeted me. " I hope all is well."

He was very nice about my friend. Indeed, he was always nice, with the niceness of people whose hearts are genuinely humane. But this time it cost him an effort. His attempts at general conversation broke down into dulness. It occurred to me he might have been indisposed. But before I could frame the inquiry he muttered :

"You find me here very sad."

"I am sorry for that," I said. "You haven't had bad news, I hope?"

It was very kind of me to take an interest. No. It was not that. No bad news, thank God. And he became very still as if holding his breath. Then, leaning forward a little, and in an odd tone of awed embarrassment, he took me into his confidence.

"The truth is that I have had a very—a very—how shall I say?—abominable adventure happen to me."

The energy of the epithet was sufficiently startling in that man of moderate feelings and toned-down vocabulary. The word unpleasant I should have thought would have fitted amply the worst experience likely to befall a man of his stamp. And an adventure, too. Incredible! But it is in human nature to believe the worst; and I confess I eyed him stealthily, wondering what he had been up to. In a moment, however, my unworthy suspicions vanished. There was a fundamental refinement of nature about the man which made me dismiss all idea of some more or less disreputable scrape.

"It is very serious. Very serious." He went on nervously. "I will tell you after dinner, if you will allow me."

I expressed my perfect acquiescence by a little bow, nothing more. I wished him to understand that I was not likely to hold him to that offer, if he thought better of it later on. We talked of indifferent things, but with a sense of difficulty quite unlike our former easy, gossipy intercourse. The hand raising a piece of bread to his lips, I noticed, trembled slightly. This symptom, in regard of my reading of the man, was no less than startling.

In the smoking-room he did not hang back at all. Directly we had taken our usual seats he leaned sideways over the arm of his chair and looked straight into my eyes earnestly.

"You remember," he began, "that day you went away? I told you then I would go to the Villa Nazionale to hear some music in the evening."

I remembered. His handsome old face, so fresh for his age, unmarked by any trying experience, appeared haggard for an instant. It was like the passing of a shadow. Returning his steadfast gaze, I took a sip of my black coffee. He was systematically minute in his narrative, simply in order, I think, not to let his excitement get the better of him.

After leaving the railway station, he had an ice, and read the paper in a café. Then he went back to the hotel, dressed for dinner and dined with a good appetite. After dinner he lingered in the hall (there were chairs and tables there) smoking his cigar; talked to the little girl of the Primo Tenore of the San Carlo theatre, and exchanged a few words with that "amiable lady," the wife of the Primo Tenore. There was no performance that evening, and these people were going to the Villa also. They went out of the hotel. Very well.

At the moment of following their example—it was half-past nine already—he remembered he had a rather large sum of money in his pocket-book. He entered, therefore, the office and deposited the greater part of it with the book-keeper of the hotel. This done, he took a carozella and drove to the seashore. He got out of the cab and entered the Villa on foot from the Largo di Vittoria end.

He stared at me very hard. And I understood then how really impressionable he was. Every small fact and event of that evening stood out in his memory as if endowed with mystic significance. If he did not mention to me the colour of the pony which drew the carozella, and the aspect of the man who drove, it was a mere oversight arising from his agitation, which he repressed manfully.

He had then entered the Villa Nazionale from the Largo di Vittoria end. The Villa Nazionale is a public pleasure-ground laid out in grass plots, bushes and flower-beds between the houses of the Riviera di Chiaja and the waters of the bay. Alleys of trees, more or less parallel, stretch its whole length—which is considerable. On the Riviera di Chiaja side the electric tramcars run

16

close to the railings.   Between the garden and the sea is
the fashionable drive, a broad road bordered by a low
wall, beyond which the Mediterranean splashes with
gentle murmurs when the weather is fine.

As life goes on late at night in Naples, the broad
drive was all astir with a brilliant swarm of carriage
lamps moving in pairs, some creeping slowly, others
running rapidly under the thin motionless line of electric
lamps defining the shore.   And a brilliant swarm of
stars hung above the land humming with voices, piled
up with houses, glittering with lights—and over the
silent flat shadows of the sea.

The gardens themselves are not very well lit.   Our
friend went forward in the warm gloom, his eyes fixed
upon a distant luminous region extending nearly across
the whole width of the Villa, as if the air had glowed
there with its own cold, bluish and dazzling light.   This
magic spot, behind the black trunks of trees and masses
of inky foliage, breathed out sweet sounds mingled with
bursts of brassy roar, sudden clashes of metal and grave
vibrating thuds.

As he walked on, all these noises combined together
into a piece of elaborate music whose harmonious phrases
came persuasively through a great disorderly murmur of
voices and shuffling of feet on the gravel of that open
space.   An enormous crowd immersed in the electric
light, as if in a bath of some radiant and tenuous fluid
shed upon their heads by luminous globes, drifted in its
hundreds round the band.   Hundreds more sat on
chairs in more or less concentric circles, receiving unflinch-
ingly the great waves of sonority that ebbed out into the
darkness.   The Count penetrated the throng, drifted
with it in tranquil enjoyment, listening and looking at
the faces.   All people of good society : mothers with
their daughters, parents and children, young men and
young women all talking, smiling, nodding to each other.
Very many pretty faces, and very many pretty toilettes.
There was, of course, a quantity of diverse types :
showy old fellows with white moustaches, fat men, thin
men, officers in uniform ; but what predominated, he

told me, was the South Italian type of young man, with a colourless, clear complexion, red lips, jet-black little moustache and liquid black eyes so wonderfully effective in leering or scowling.

Withdrawing from the throng, the Count shared a little table in front of the café with a young man of just such a type. Our friend had some lemonade. The young man was sitting moodily before an empty glass. He looked up once, and then looked down again. He also tilted his hat forward. Like this—

The Count made the gesture of a man pulling his hat down over his brow, and went on.

"I think to myself : he is sad ; something is wrong with him ; young men have their troubles. I take no notice of him, of course. I pay for my lemonade and go away."

Strolling about in the neighbourhood of the band, the Count thinks he saw twice that young man wandering alone in the crowd. Once their eyes met. It must have been the same young man, but there were so many there of that type that he could not be certain. More-over, he was not very much concerned except in so far that he had been struck by the marked, peevish discontent of that face.

Presently, tired of the feeling of confinement one experiences in a crowd, the Count edged away from the band. An alley, very sombre by contrast, presented itself invitingly with its promise of solitude and coolness. He entered it, walking slowly on till the sound of the orchestra became distinctly deadened. Then he walked back and turned about once more. He did this several times before he noticed that there was somebody occupying one of the benches.

The spot being midway between two lamp-posts the light was faint.

The man lolled back in the corner of the seat, his legs stretched out, his arms folded and his head drooping on his breast, He never stirred, as though he had fallen asleep there, but when the Count passed by next time he had changed his attitude. He sat leaning forward. His elbows were propped on his knees, and his hands were rolling a cigarette. He never looked up from that occupation.

The Count continued his stroll away from the band. He returned slowly, he said. I can imagine him enjoying to the full, but with his usual tranquillity, the balminess of this southern night and the sounds of music softened delightfully by the distance.

Presently, he approached for the third time the man on the garden seat, still leaning forward with his elbows on his knees. It was a dejected pose. In the semi-obscurity of the alley his high shirt collar and his cuffs made small patches of vivid whiteness. The Count said that he had noticed him getting up brusquely as if to walk away, but almost before he was aware of it the man stood before him asking in a low, gentle tone whether the signore would have the kindness to oblige him with a light.

The Count answered this request by a polite " Certainly" and dropped his hands with the intention of exploring both pockets of his trousers for the matches.

" I dropped my hands," he said, " but I never put them in my pockets. I felt a pressure there——"

He put the tip of his finger on a spot close under his breast bone, the very spot of the human body where a Japanese gentleman begins the operation of the Hara-kiri, which is a form of suicide following upon dishonour, upon an intolerable outrage to the delicacy of one's feelings.

" I glance down," the Count continued in an awes-struck voice, " and what do I see ? A knife ! A long knife——"

" You don't mean to say," I exclaimed amazed, "that you have been held up like this in the Villa at half-past ten o'clock, within a stone's throw of a thousand people ! "

He nodded several times, staring at me with all his might.

" The clarionet," he declared solemnly, "was finishing his solo, and I assure you I could hear every note. Then the band crashed *fortissimo*, and that creature rolled its eyes and gnashed its teeth hissing at me with the greatest ferocity, 'Be silent! No noise or——'"

I could not get over my astonishment.

"What sort of knife was it?" I asked stupidly.

"A long blade. A stiletto—perhaps a kitchen knife. A long narrow blade. It gleamed. And his eyes gleamed. His white teeth, too. I could see them. He was very ferocious. I thought to myself: 'If I hit him he will kill me.' How could I fight with him? He had the knife and I had nothing. I am nearly seventy, you know, and that was a young man. I seemed even to recognize him. The moody young man of the café. The young man I met in the crowd. But I could not tell. There are so many like him in this country."

The distress of that moment was reflected in his face. I should think that physically he must have been paralysed by surprise. His thoughts, however, remained extremely active. They ranged over every alarming possibility. The idea of setting up a vigorous shouting for help occurred to him too. But he did nothing of the kind, and the reason why he refrained gave me a good opinion of his mental self-possession. He saw in a flash that nothing prevented the other from shouting, too.

"That young man might in an instant have thrown away his knife and pretended I was the aggressor. Why not? He might have said I attacked him. Why not? It was one incredible story against another! He might have said anything — bring some dishonouring charge against me—what do I know? By his dress he was no common robber. He seemed to belong to the better classes. What could I say? He was an Italian —I am a foreigner. Of course, I have my passport, and there is our consul—but to be arrested, dragged at night to the police office like a criminal."

He shuddered. It was in his character to shrink from scandal, much more than from mere death. And certainly for many people this would have always remained—considering certain peculiarities of Neapolitan

manners—a deucedly queer story. The Count was no
fool. His belief in the respectable placidity of life
having received this rude shock, he thought that now
anything might happen. But also a notion came into
his head that this young man was perhaps merely an
infuriated lunatic.

This was for me the first hint of his attitude towards
this adventure. In his exaggerated delicacy of sentiment he felt that nobody's self-esteem need be affected
by what a madman may choose to do to one. It became
apparent, however, that the Count was to be denied that
consolation. He enlarged upon the abominably savage
way in which that young man rolled his glistening eyes
and gnashed his white teeth. The band was going now
through a slow movement of solemn braying by all
the trombones, with deliberately repeated bangs of the
big drum.

"But what did you do?" I asked greatly excited.

"Nothing," answered the Count. "I let my hands
hang down very still. I told him quietly I did not intend
making a noise. He snarled like a dog, then said in an
ordinary voice:

"'Vostro portofolio,'"

"So I naturally," continued the Count—and from
this point acted the whole thing in pantomine. Holding me with his eyes, he went through all the motions
of reaching into his inside breast pocket, taking out a
pocket-book and handing it over. But that young man,
still bearing steadily on the knife, refused to touch it.

He directed the Count to take the money out himself, received it into his left hand, motioned the pocket-
book to be returned to the pocket, all this being done to
the sweet thrilling of flutes and clarionets sustained by
the emotional drone of the hautboys. And the "young
man," as the Count called him, said: "This seems very
little."

"It was, indeed, only 340 or 360 lire," the Count
pursued. "I had left my money in the hotel, as you
know. I told him this was all I had on me. He shook
his head impatiently and said:

" ' *Vostro orologio.*' "

The Count gave me the dumb show of pulling out his watch, detaching it. But, as it happened, the valuable gold half-chronometer he possessed had been left at a watchmaker's for cleaning. He wore that evening (on a leather guard) the Waterbury fifty-franc thing he used to take with him on his fishing expeditions. Perceiving the nature of this booty, the well-dressed robber made contemptuous clicking sound with his tongue like this, "Tse-Ah!" and waved it away hastily. Then, as the Count was returning the disdained object to his pocket, he demanded with a threateningly increased pressure of the knife on the epigastrum, by way of reminder :

" *Vostri anelli.*"

" One of the rings," went on the Count, " was given me many years ago by my wife ; the other is the signet ring of my father. I said, ' No. *That* you shall not have ! ' "

Here the Count reproduced the gesture corresponding to that declaration by clapping one hand upon the other, and pressing both thus against his chest. It was touching in its resignation. " That you shall not have," he repeated firmly and closed his eyes, fully expecting — I don't know whether I am right in recording that such an unpleasant word had passed his lips—fully expecting to feel himself being—I really hesitate to say—being disembowelled by the push of the long sharp blade resting murderously against the pit of his stomach—the very seat, in all human beings, of anguishing sensations.

Great waves of harmony went on flowing from the band.

Suddenly the Count felt the nightmarish pressure removed from the sensitive spot. He opened his eyes. He was alone. He had heard nothing. It is probable that " the young man " had departed, with light steps, some time before, but the sense of the horrid pressure had lingered even after the knife had gone. A feeling of weakness came over him. He had just time to stagger to the garden seat. He felt as though he had held his breath for a long time. He sat all in a heap panting with the shock of the reaction.

The band was executing with immense bravura, the complicated finale. It ended with a tremendous crash. He heard it unreal and remote, as if his ears had been stopped, and then the hard clapping of a thousand, more or less, pairs of hands, like a sudden hailshower passing away. The profound silence which succeeded recalled him to himself.

A tramcar resembling a long glass box wherein people sat with their heads strongly lighted, ran along swiftly within sixty yards of the spot where he had been robbed, then another rustled by, and yet another going the other way. The audience about the band had broken up, and were entering the alley in small conversing groups. The Count sat up straight and tried to think calmly of what had happened to him. The vileness of it took his breath away again. As far as I can make out he was disgusted with himself. I do not mean to say his behaviour. Indeed, if his pantomimic rendering of it for my information was to be trusted, it was simply perfect. No, it was not that. He was not ashamed. He was shocked at being the selected victim, not of robbery so much as of contempt. His tranquillity had been wantonly desecrated. His life-long, kindly nicety of outlook had been defaced.

Nevertheless, at that stage, before the iron had time to sink deep, he was able to argue himself into comparative equanimity. As his agitation calmed down somewhat, he became aware that he was frightfully hungry. Yes, hungry. The sheer emotion had made him simply ravenous. He left the seat and, after walking for some time, found himself outside the gardens and before an arrested tramcar, without knowing very well how he came there. He got in as if in a dream, by a sort of instinct. Fortunately he found in his trouser pocket a copper to satisfy the conductor. Then the car stopped, and as everybody was getting out he got out too. He recognised the Piazza San Ferdinando, but apparently it did not occur to him to take a cab and drive to the hotel. He remained in distress on the Piazza like a lost dog, thinking vaguely of the best way of getting something to eat at once.

Suddenly he remembered his twenty-franc piece. He explained to me that he had that piece of French gold for something like three years. He used to carry it about with him as a sort of reserve in case of accident. Anybody is liable to have his pocket picked—a quite different thing from a brazen and insulting robbery.

The monumental arch of the Galleria Umberto faced him at the top of a noble flight of stairs. He climbed these without loss of time, and directed his steps towards the Café Umberto. All these tables outside were occupied by a lot of people who were drinking. But as he wanted something to eat, he went inside into the café, which is divided into aisles by square pillars set all round with long looking-glasses. The Count sat down on a red plush bench against one of these pillars, waiting for his risotto. And his mind reverted to his abominable adventure.

He thought of the moody, well-dressed young man, with whom he had exchanged glances in the crowd around the bandstand, and who, he felt confident, was the robber. Would he recognize him again? Doubtless. But he did not want ever to see him again. The best thing was to forget this humiliating episode.

The Count looked round anxiously for the coming of his risotto, and, behold! to the left against the wall—there sat the young man. He was alone at a table, with a bottle of some sort of wine or syrup and a carafe of iced water before him. The smooth olive cheeks, the red lips, the little jet-black moustache turned up gallantly, the fine black eyes a little heavy and shaded by long eyelashes, that peculiar expression of cruel discontent to be seen only in the busts of some Roman emperors—it was he, no doubt at all. But that was a type. The Count looked away hastily. The young officer over there reading a paper was like that, too. Same type. Two young men farther playing draughts also resembled——"

The Count lowered his head with the fear in his heart of being everlastingly haunted by the vision of that young man. He began to eat his risotto. Presently he heard the young man on his left call the waiter in a bad-tempered tone.

At the call, not only his own waiter, but two other idle waiters belonging to a quite different row of tables, rushed towards him with obsequious alacrity, which is not the general characteristic of the waiters in the Café Umberto. The young man muttered something, and one of the waiters walking rapidly to the nearest door called out into the Galleria : "Pasquale! O ! Pasquale !"

Everybody knows Pasquale, the shabby old fellow who, shuffling between the tables, offers for sale cigars, cigarettes, picture postcards and matches to the clients of the café. He is in many respects an engaging scoundrel. The Count saw the grey-haired, unshaven ruffian enter the café, the glass case hanging from his neck by a leather strap, and, at a word from the waiter, make his shuffling way with a sudden spurt to the young man's table. The young man was in need of a cigar with which Pasquale served him fawningly. The old pedlar was going out, when the Count, on a sudden impulse, beckoned to him.

Pasquale approached, the smile of deferential recognition combining oddly with the cynical searching expression of his eyes. Leaning his case on the table, he lifted the glass lid without a word. The Count took a box of cigarettes and urged by a fearful curiosity, asked as casually as he could:

"Tell me, Pasquale, who is that young signore sitting over there ? "

The other bent over his box confidentially.

" That, *Signor Conde*," he said, beginning to rearrange his wares busily and without looking up, " that is a young *Cavaliere* of a very good family from Bari. He studies in the University here, and is the chief, *capo*, of an association of young men—of very nice young men."

He paused, and then, with mingled discretion and pride of knowledge, murmured the explanatory word

"Camorra " and shut down the lid. "A very powerful Camorra," he breathed out. "The professors themselves respect it greatly... *una lira e cinquanti centesimi, Signor Conde.*"

Our friend paid with the gold piece. While Pasquale was making up the change, he observed that the young man, of whom he had heard so much in a few words, was watching the transaction covertly. After the old vagabond had withdrawn with a bow, the Count settled with the waiter and sat still. A numbness, he told me, had come over him.

The young man paid, too, got up and crossed over, apparently for the purpose of looking at himself in the mirror set in the pillar nearest to the Count's seat. He was dressed all in black with a dark green bow tie. The Count looked round, and was startled by meeting a vicious glance out of the corners of the other's eyes. The young *Cavaliere* from Bari (according to Pasquale ; but Pasquale is, of course, an accomplished liar) went on arranging his tie, settling his hat before the glass, and meantime he spoke just loud enough to be heard by the Count. He spoke through his teeth with the most insulting venom of contempt and gazing straight into the mirror.

"Ah ! So you had some gold on you—you old liar —you old *birba*—you *furfante !* But you are not done with me yet."

The fiendishness of his expression vanished like lightning, and he lounged out of the café with a moody, impassive face.

The poor Count, after telling me this last episode, fell back trembling in his chair. His forehead broke into perspiration. There was a wanton insolence in the spirit of this outrage which appalled even me. What it was to the Count's delicacy I won't attempt to guess. I am sure that if he had not been too refined to do such a blatantly vulgar thing as dying from apoplexy in a café, he would have had a fatal stroke there and then. All irony apart, my difficulty was to keep him from seeing the full extent of my commiseration. He shrank from every excessive sentiment, and my commiseration was practically unbounded. It did not surprise me to hear that he had been in bed a week. He had got up to make his arrangements for leaving Southern Italy for good and all.

And the man was convinced that he could not live through a whole year in any other climate!

No argument of mine had any effect. It was not timidity, though he did say to me once : "You do not know what a Camorra is, my dear sir. I am a marked man." He was not afraid of what could be done to him. His delicate conception of his dignity was defiled by a degrading experience. He couldn't stand that. No Japanese gentleman, outraged in his exaggerated sense of honour, could have gone about his preparations for Hara-kiri with greater resolution. To go home really amounted to suicide for the poor Count.

There is a saying of Neapolitan patriotism, intended for the information of foreigners, I presume : "See Naples and then die." *Vedi Napoli e poi mori.* It is a saying of excessive vanity, and everything excessive was abhorrent to the nice moderation of the poor Count. Yet, as I was seeing him off at the railway station, I thought he was behaving with singular fidelity to its conceited spirit. *Vedi Napoli !* . . . He had seen it. He had seen it with startling thoroughness—and now he was going to his grave. He was going to it by the *train de luxe* of the International Sleeping Car Company, *viâ* Trieste and Vienna. As the four long, sombre coaches pulled out of the station I raised my hat with the solemn feeling of paying the last tribute of respect to a funeral *cortège.* . *Il Conde's* profile, much aged already, glided away from me in stony immobility, behind the lighted pane of glass—*Vedi Napoli e poi mori !*

Printed in Great Britain by
Butler & Tanner,
Frome and London

MESSRS. METHUEN'S PUBLICATIONS

This Catalogue contains only a selection of the more important books published by Messrs. Methuen. A complete catalogue of their publications may be obtained on application.

Bain (F. W.)—
A DIGIT OF THE MOON: A Hindoo Love Story. THE DESCENT OF THE SUN: A Cycle of Birth. A HEIFER OF THE DAWN. IN THE GREAT GOD'S HAIR. A DRAUGHT OF THE BLUE. AN ESSENCE OF THE DUSK. AN INCARNATION OF THE SNOW. A MINE OF FAULTS. THE ASHES OF A GOD. BUBBLES OF THE FOAM. A SYRUP OF THE BEES. THE LIVERY OF EVE. THE SUBSTANCE OF A DREAM. *All Fcap. 8vo. 5s. net.* AN ECHO OF THE SPHERES. *Wide Demy. 12s. 6d net.*

Balfour (Graham). THE LIFE OF ROBERT LOUIS STEVENSON. *Fifteenth Edition. In one Volume. Cr. 8vo. Buckram, 7s. 6d. net.*

Belloc (H.)—
PARIS, 8s. 6d. net. HILLS AND THE SEA, 6s. net. ON NOTHING AND KINDRED SUBJECTS, 6s. net. ON EVERYTHING, 6s. net. ON SOMETHING, 6s. net. FIRST AND LAST, 6s. net. THIS AND THAT AND THE OTHER, 6s. net. MARIE ANTOINETTE, 18s. net. THE PYRENEES, 10s. 6d. net.

Bloemfontein (Bishop of). ARA CŒLI: AN ESSAY IN MYSTICAL THEOLOGY. *Seventh Edition. Cr. 8vo. 5s. net.*
FAITH AND EXPERIENCE. *Third Edition. Cr. 8vo. 5s. net.*
THE CULT OF THE PASSING MOMENT. *Fourth Edition. Cr. 8vo. 5s. net.*
THE ENGLISH CHURCH AND REUNION. *Cr. 8vo. 5s. net.*
SCALA MUNDI. *Cr. 8vo. 4s. 6d net.*

Chesterton (G. K.)—
THE BALLAD OF THE WHITE HORSE. ALL THINGS CONSIDERED. TREMENDOUS TRIFLES. ALARMS AND DISCURSIONS. A MISCELLANY OF MEN. *All Fcap. 8vo. 6s. net.* WINE, WATER, AND SONG. *Fcap. 8vo. 1s. 6d. net.* THE USES OF DIVERSITY. 6s. net.

Clutton-Brock (A.). WHAT IS THE KINGDOM OF HEAVEN? *Fourth Edition. Fcap. 8vo. 5s. net.*
ESSAYS ON ART. *Second Edition. Fcap. 8vo. 5s. net.*
ESSAYS ON BOOKS. *Fcap. 8vo. 6s. net.*
MORE ESSAYS ON BOOKS. *Fcap. 8vo. 6s. net.*

Cole (G. D. H.). SOCIAL THEORY. *Cr. 8vo 5s. net.*

Conrad (Joseph). THE MIRROR OF THE SEA: Memories and Impressions. *Fourth Edition. Fcap. 8vo. 6s. net.*

Einstein (A.). RELATIVITY: THE SPECIAL AND THE GENERAL THEORY. Translated by ROBERT W. LAWSON. *Third Edition. Cr. 8vo. 5s. net.*

Eliot (T. S.). THE SACRED WOOD: ESSAYS ON POETRY. *Fcap. 8vo. 6s. net.*

Fyleman (Rose.). FAIRIES AND CHIMNEYS. *Fcap. 8vo. Eighth Edition. 3s. 6d. net.*
THE FAIRY GREEN. *Third Edition. Fcap. 8vo. 3s. 6d. net.*

Gibbins (H. de B.). INDUSTRY IN ENGLAND: HISTORICAL OUTLINES. With Maps and Plans. *Tenth Edition. Demy 8vo. 12s. 6d. net.*
THE INDUSTRIAL HISTORY OF ENGLAND. With 5 Maps and a Plan. *Twenty-seventh Edition. Cr. 8vo. 5s.*

Gibbon (Edward). THE DECLINE AND FALL OF THE ROMAN EMPIRE. Edited, with Notes, Appendices, and Maps, by J. B. BURY. Illustrated. *Seven Volumes. Demy 8vo. Illustrated. Each 12s. 6d. net. Also in Seven Volumes. Cr. 8vo. Each 7s. 6d. net.*

Glover (T. R.). THE CONFLICT OF RELIGIONS IN THE EARLY ROMAN EMPIRE. *Ninth Edition. Demy 8vo. 10s. 6d. net.*
POETS AND PURITANS. *Second Edition. Demy 8vo. 10s. 6d. net.*
FROM PERICLES TO PHILIP. *Third Edition. Demy 8vo. 10s. 6d. net.*
VIRGIL. *Fourth Edition. Demy 8vo. 10s. 6d. net.*
THE CHRISTIAN TRADITION AND ITS VERIFICATION. (The Angus Lecture for 1912.) *Second Edition. Cr. 8vo. 6s. net.*

Grahame (Kenneth). THE WIND IN THE WILLOWS. *Eleventh Edition. Cr. 8vo. 7s. 6d. net.*

Hall (H. R.). THE ANCIENT HISTORY OF THE NEAR EAST FROM THE EARLIEST TIMES TO THE BATTLE OF SALAMIS. Illustrated. *Fifth Edition. Demy 8vo. 21s. net.*

Hawthorne (Nathaniel). THE SCARLET LETTER. With 31 Illustrations in Colour by HUGH THOMSON. *Wide Royal 8vo. 31s. 6d. net.*

Holdsworth (W. S.). A HISTORY OF ENGLISH LAW. *Vols. I., II., III. Each Second Edition. Demy 8vo. Each* 15*s. net.*

Inge (W. R.). CHRISTIAN MYSTICISM. (The Bampton Lectures of 1899.) *Fourth Edition. Cr. 8vo.* 7*s.* 6*d. net.*

Jenks (E.). AN OUTLINE OF ENGLISH LOCAL GOVERNMENT. *Fourth Edition.* Revised by R. C. K. ENSOR. *Cr. 8vo.* 5*s. net.*

A SHORT HISTORY OF ENGLISH LAW: FROM THE EARLIEST TIMES TO THE END OF THE YEAR 1911. *Second Edition, revised. Demy 8vo.* 12*s.* 6*d. net.*

Julian (Lady) of Norwich. REVELATIONS OF DIVINE LOVE. Edited by GRACE WARRACK. *Seventh Edition. Cr. 8vo.* 5*s. net.*

Keats (John). POEMS. Edited, with Introduction and Notes, by E. DE SÉLINCOURT. With a Frontispiece in Photogravure. *Fourth Edition. Demy 8vo.* 12*s.* 6*d. net.*

Kidd (Benjamin). THE SCIENCE OF POWER. *Ninth Edition. Crown 8vo.* 7*s.* 6*d. net.*

SOCIAL EVOLUTION. *Demy 8vo.* 8*s.* 6*d. net.*

Kipling (Rudyard). BARRACK-ROOM BALLADS. *208th Thousand. Cr. 8vo. Buckram,* 7*s.* 6*d. net. Also Fcap. 8vo. Cloth,* 6*s. net; leather,* 7*s.* 6*d. net.*
Also a Service Edition. *Two Volumes. Square fcap. 8vo. Each* 3*s. net.*

THE SEVEN SEAS. *157th Thousand. Cr. 8vo. Buckram,* 7*s.* 6*d. net. Also Fcap. 8vo. Cloth,* 6*s. net; leather,* 7*s.* 6*d. net.*
Also a Service Edition. *Two Volumes. Square fcap. 8vo. Each* 3*s. net.*

THE FIVE NATIONS. *126th Thousand. Cr. 8vo. Buckram,* 7*s.* 6*d. net. Also Fcap. 8vo. Cloth,* 6*s. net; leather,* 7*s.* 6*d. net.*
Also a Service Edition. *Two Volumes. Square fcap. 8vo. Each* 3*s. net.*

DEPARTMENTAL DITTIES. *94th Thousand. Cr. 8vo. Buckram,* 7*s.* 6*d. net. Also Fcap. 8vo. Cloth,* 6*s. net; leather,* 7*s.* 6*d. net.*
Also a Service Edition. *Two Volumes. Square fcap. 8vo. Each* 3*s. net.*

THE YEARS BETWEEN. *Cr. 8vo. Buckram,* 7*s.* 6*d. net. Also on thin paper. Fcap. 8vo. Blue cloth,* 6*s. net; Limp lambskin,* 7*s.* 6*d. net.*
Also a Service Edition. *Two Volumes. Square fcap. 8vo. Each* 3*s. net.*

HYMN BEFORE ACTION. Illuminated. *Fcap. 4to.* 1*s.* 6*d. net.*

RECESSIONAL. Illuminated. *Fcap. 4to.* 1*s.* 6*d. net.*

TWENTY POEMS FROM RUDYARD KIPLING. *360th Thousand. Fcap. 8vo.* 1*s. net.*

Lamb (Charles and Mary). THE COMPLETE WORKS. Edited by E. V. LUCAS. *A New and Revised Edition in Six Volumes. With Frontispieces. Fcap. 8vo. Each* 6*s. net.*
The volumes are :—
I. MISCELLANEOUS PROSE. II. ELIA AND THE LAST ESSAY OF ELIA. III. BOOKS FOR CHILDREN. IV. PLAYS AND POEMS v. and vi. LETTERS.

THE ESSAYS OF ELIA. With an Introduction by E. V. LUCAS, and 28 Illustrations by A. GARTH JONES. *Fcap. 8vo.* 5*s. net.*

Lankester (Sir Ray). SCIENCE FROM AN EASY CHAIR. Illustrated. *Thirteenth Edition. Cr. 8vo.* 7*s.* 6*d. net.*

MORE SCIENCE FROM AN EASY CHAIR. Illustrated. *Third Edition. Cr. 8vo.* 7*s.* 6*d. net.*

DIVERSIONS OF A NATURALIST. Illustrated. *Third Edition. Cr. 8vo.* 7*s.* 6*d. net.*

SECRETS OF EARTH AND SEA. *Cr. 8vo.* 8*s.* 6*d net.*

Lodge (Sir Oliver). MAN AND THE UNIVERSE : A STUDY OF THE INFLUENCE OF THE ADVANCE IN SCIENTIFIC KNOWLEDGE UPON OUR UNDERSTANDING OF CHRISTIANITY. *Ninth Edition. Crown 8vo.* 7*s.* 6*d. net.*

THE SURVIVAL OF MAN : A STUDY IN UNRECOGNISED HUMAN FACULTY. *Seventh Edition. Cr. 8vo.* 7*s.* 6*d. net.*

MODERN PROBLEMS. *Cr. 8vo.* 7*s.* 6*d. net.*

RAYMOND ; OR LIFE AND DEATH. Illustrated. *Twelfth Edition. Demy 8vo.* 15*s. net.*

Lucas (E. V.).
THE LIFE OF CHARLES LAMB, 2 vols., 21*s. net.* A WANDERER IN HOLLAND, 10*s.* 6*d. net.* A WANDERER IN LONDON, 10*s.* 6*d. net.* LONDON REVISITED, 10*s.* 6*d. net.* A WANDERER IN PARIS, 10*s.* 6*d. net and 6*s. net.* A WANDERER IN FLORENCE, 10*s.* 6*d. net.* A WANDERER IN VENICE, 10*s.* 6*d. net.* THE OPEN ROAD : A Little Book for Wayfarers, 6*s.* 6*d. net and 7*s.* 6*d. net.* THE FRIENDLY TOWN : A Little Book for the Urbane, 6*s. net.* FIRESIDE AND SUNSHINE, 6*s. net.* CHARACTER AND COMEDY, 6*s. net.* THE GENTLEST ART : A Choice of Letters by Entertaining Hands, 6*s.* 6*d. net.* THE SECOND POST, 6*s. net.* HER INFINITE VARIETY : A Feminine Portrait Gallery, 6*s. net.* GOOD COMPANY : A Rally of Men, 6*s. net.* ONE DAY AND ANOTHER, 6*s. net.* OLD LAMPS FOR NEW, 6*s. net.* LOITERER'S HARVEST, 6*s. net.* CLOUD AND SILVER, 6*s. net.* A BOSWELL OF BAGHDAD, AND OTHER ESSAYS, 6*s. net.* 'TWIXT EAGLE AND DOVE, 6*s. net.* THE PHANTOM JOURNAL, AND OTHER ESSAYS AND DIVERSIONS, 6*s. net.* SPECIALLY SELECTED : A Choice of Essays, 7*s.* 6*d. net.* THE BRITISH SCHOOL : An Anecdotal Guide to the British Painters and Paintings in the National Gallery, 6*s. net.* TRAVEL NOTES.

McDougall (William). AN INTRODUC-
TION TO SOCIAL PSYCHOLOGY.
Sixteenth Edition. Cr. 8vo. 8s. *net.*
BODY AND MIND: A HISTORY AND A
DEFENCE OF ANIMISM. *Fifth Edition.*
Demy 8vo. 12s. 6d. *net.*

Maeterlinck (Maurice)—
THE BLUE BIRD: A Fairy Play in Six Acts,
6s. *net.* MARY MAGDALENE: A Play in
Three Acts, 5s. *net.* DEATH, 3s. 6d. *net.*
OUR ETERNITY, 6s. *net.* THE UNKNOWN
GUEST, 6s. *net.* POEMS, 5s. *net.* THE
WRACK OF THE STORM, 6s. *net.* THE
MIRACLE OF ST. ANTHONY: A Play in One
Act, 3s. 6d. *net.* THE BURGOMASTER OF
STILEMONDE: A Play in Three Acts, 5s.
net. THE BETROTHAL; or, The Blue Bird
Chooses, 6s. *net.* MOUNTAIN PATHS, 6s.
net. THE STORY OF TYLTYL, 21s. *net.*

Milne (A. A.). THE DAY'S PLAY. THE
HOLIDAY ROUND. ONCE A WEEK. *All
Cr. 8vo.* 7s. *net.* NOT THAT IT MATTERS.
Fcap 8vo. 6s. *net.* IF I MAY. *Fcap. 8vo.*
6s. *net.*

Oxenham (John)—
BEES IN AMBER; A Little Book of Thought-
ful Verse. ALL'S WELL: A Collection of
War Poems. THE KING'S HIGH WAY. THE
VISION SPLENDID. THE FIERY CROSS.
HIGH ALTARS: The Record of a Visit to
the Battlefields of France and Flanders.
HEARTS COURAGEOUS. ALL CLEAR!
WINDS OF THE DAWN. *All Small Pott
8vo. Paper,* 1s. 3d. *net; cloth boards,* 2s.
net. GENTLEMEN—THE KING, 2s. *net.*

Petrie (W. M. Flinders). A HISTORY
OF EGYPT. Illustrated. *Six Volumes.*
Cr. 8vo. Each 9s. *net.*
VOL. I. FROM THE IST TO THE XVITH
DYNASTY. *Ninth Edition.* (10s. 6d. *net.*)
VOL. II. THE XVIITH AND XVIIITH
DYNASTIES. *Sixth Edition.*
VOL. III. XIXTH TO XXXTH DYNASTIES.
Second Edition.
VOL. IV. EGYPT UNDER THE PTOLEMAIC
DYNASTY. J. P. MAHAFFY. *Second Edition.*
VOL. V. EGYPT UNDER ROMAN RULE. J. G.
MILNE. *Second Edition.*
VOL. VI. EGYPT IN THE MIDDLE AGES.
STANLEY LANE POOLE. *Second Edition.*
SYRIA AND EGYPT, FROM THE TELL
EL AMARNA LETTERS. *Cr. 8vo.*
5s. *net.*
EGYPTIAN TALES. Translated from the
Papyri. First Series, IVth to XIIth Dynasty.
Illustrated. *Third Edition. Cr. 8vo.*
5s. *net.*
EGYPTIAN TALES. Translated from the
Papyri. Second Series, XVIIITH to XIXTH
Dynasty. Illustrated. *Second Edition.*
Cr. 8vo. 5s. *net.*

Pollard (A. F.). A SHORT HISTORY
OF THE GREAT WAR. With 19 Maps.
Second Edition. Cr. 8vo. 10s. 6d. *net.*

Price (L. L.). A SHORT HISTORY OF
POLITICAL ECONOMY IN ENGLAND
FROM ADAM SMITH TO ARNOLD
TOYNBEE. *Tenth Edition. Cr. 8vo.*
5s. *net.*

Reid (G. Archdall). THE LAWS OF
HEREDITY. *Second Edition. Demy 8vo.*
£1 1s. *net.*

Robertson (C. Grant). SELECT STAT-
UTES, CASES, AND DOCUMENTS,
1660–1832. *Third Edition. Demy 8vo.*
15s. *net.*

Selous (Edmund). TOMMY SMITH'S
ANIMALS. Illustrated. *Nineteenth Edi-
tion. Fcap. 8vo.* 3s. 6d. *net.*
TOMMY SMITH'S OTHER ANIMALS.
Illustrated. *Eleventh Edition. Fcap. 8vo.*
3s. 6d. *net.*
TOMMY SMITH AT THE ZOO. Illus-
trated. *Fourth Edition. Fcap. 8vo.*
2s. 9d.
TOMMY SMITH AGAIN AT THE ZOO.
Illustrated. *Second Edition. Fcap. 8vo.*
2s. 9d.
JACK'S INSECTS. *Popular Edition. Cr.
8vo.* 3s. 6d.
JACK'S OTHER INSECTS. *Cr. 8vo.* 3s. 6d.

Shelley (Percy Bysshe). POEMS. With
an Introduction by A. CLUTTON-BROCK and
Notes by C. D. LOCOCK. *Two Volumes.
Demy 8vo.* £1 1s. *net.*

Smith (Adam). THE WEALTH OF
NATIONS. Edited by EDWIN CANNAN.
*Two Volumes. Second Edition. Demy
8vo.* £1 10s. *net.*

Stevenson (R. L.). THE LETTERS OF
ROBERT LOUIS STEVENSON. Edited
by Sir SIDNEY COLVIN. *A New Re-
arranged Edition in four volumes. Fourth
Edition. Fcap. 8vo. Each* 6s. *net.*

Surtees (R. S.). HANDLEY CROSS.
Illustrated. *Ninth Edition. Fcap. 8vo.*
7s. 6d. *net.*
MR. SPONGE'S SPORTING TOUR.
Illustrated. *Fifth Edition. Fcap. 8vo.*
7s. 6d. *net.*
ASK MAMMA: OR, THE RICHEST
COMMONER IN ENGLAND. Illus-
trated. *Second Edition. Fcap. 8vo.* 7s. 6d.
net.
JORROCKS'S JAUNTS AND JOLLI-
TIES. Illustrated. *Seventh Edition.
Fcap. 8vo.* 6s. *net.*
MR. FACEY ROMFORD'S HOUNDS.
Illustrated. *Fourth Edition. Fcap. 8vo.*
7s. 6d. *net.*
HAWBUCK GRANGE; OR, THE SPORT-
ING ADVENTURES OF THOMAS
SCOTT, ESQ. Illustrated. *Fcap. 8vo.*
6s. *net.*
PLAIN OR RINGLETS? Illustrated.
Fcap. 8vo. 7s. 6d. *net.*
HILLINGDON HALL. With 12 Coloured
Plates by WILDRAKE, HEATH, and JELLI-
COE. *Fcap. 8vo.* 7s. 6d. *net.*

Tilden (W. T.). THE ART OF LAWN TENNIS. Illustrated. *Cr. 8vo. 6s. net.*

Tileston (Mary W.). DAILY STRENGTH FOR DAILY NEEDS. *Twenty-seventh Edition. Medium 16mo. 3s. 6d. net.*

Underhill (Evelyn). MYSTICISM. A Study in the Nature and Development of Man's Spiritual Consciousness. *Eighth Edition. Demy 8vo. 15s. net.*

Vardon (Harry). HOW TO PLAY GOLF. Illustrated. *Thirteenth Edition. Cr. 8vo. 5s. net.*

Waterhouse (Elizabeth). A LITTLE BOOK OF LIFE AND DEATH. *Twentieth Edition. Small Pott 8vo. Cloth, 2s. 6d. net.*

Wells (J.). A SHORT HISTORY OF ROME. *Seventeenth Edition.* With 3 Maps. *Cr. 8vo. 6s.*

Wilde (Oscar). THE WORKS OF OSCAR WILDE. *Fcap. 8vo. Each 6s. 6d. net.*
    I. LORD ARTHUR SAVILE'S CRIME AND THE PORTRAIT OF MR. W. H. II. THE DUCHESS OF PADUA. III. POEMS. IV. LADY WINDERMERE'S FAN. V. A WOMAN OF NO IMPORTANCE. VI. AN IDEAL HUSBAND. VII. THE IMPORTANCE OF BEING EARNEST. VIII. A HOUSE OF POMEGRANATES. IX. INTENTIONS. X. DE PROFUNDIS AND PRISON LETTERS. XI. ESSAYS. XII. SALOMÉ, A FLORENTINE TRAGEDY, and LA SAINTE COURTISANE. XIII. A CRITIC IN PALL MALL. XIV. SELECTED PROSE OF OSCAR WILDE. XV. ART AND DECORATION.
A HOUSE OF POMEGRANATES. Illustrated. *Cr. 4to. 21s. net.*

Yeats (W. B.). A BOOK OF IRISH VERSE. *Fourth Edition. Cr. 8vo. 7s. net.*

PART II.—A SELECTION OF SERIES

Ancient Cities

General Editor, SIR B. C. A. WINDLE

Cr. 8vo. 6s. net each volume

With Illustrations by E. H. NEW, and other Artists

BRISTOL. CANTERBURY. CHESTER. DUBLIN. | EDINBURGH. LINCOLN. SHREWSBURY. WELLS and GLASTONBURY.

The Antiquary's Books

General Editor, J. CHARLES COX

Demy 8vo. 10s. 6d. net each volume

With Numerous Illustrations

ANCIENT PAINTED GLASS IN ENGLAND. ARCHÆOLOGY AND FALSE ANTIQUITIES. THE BELLS OF ENGLAND. THE BRASSES OF ENGLAND. THE CASTLES AND WALLED TOWNS OF ENGLAND. CELTIC ART IN PAGAN AND CHRISTIAN TIMES. CHURCHWARDENS' ACCOUNTS. THE DOMESDAY INQUEST. ENGLISH CHURCH FURNITURE. ENGLISH COSTUME. ENGLISH MONASTIC LIFE. ENGLISH SEALS. FOLK-LORE AS AN HISTORICAL SCIENCE. THE GILDS AND COMPANIES OF LONDON. THE HERMITS AND ANCHORITES OF ENGLAND. THE MANOR AND MANORIAL RECORDS. THE MEDIÆVAL HOSPITALS OF ENGLAND. OLD ENGLISH INSTRUMENTS OF MUSIC. OLD ENGLISH LIBRARIES. OLD SERVICE BOOKS OF THE ENGLISH CHURCH. PARISH LIFE IN MEDIÆVAL ENGLAND. THE PARISH REGISTERS OF ENGLAND. REMAINS OF THE PREHISTORIC AGE IN ENGLAND. THE ROMAN ERA IN BRITAIN. ROMANO-BRITISH BUILDINGS AND EARTHWORKS. THE ROYAL FORESTS OF ENGLAND. THE SCHOOLS OF MEDIEVAL ENGLAND. SHRINES OF BRITISH SAINTS.

The Arden Shakespeare

General Editor, R. H. CASE

Demy 8vo. 6s. net each volume

An edition of Shakespeare in Single Plays ; each edited with a full Introduction, Textual Notes, and a Commentary at the foot of the page.

Classics of Art

Edited by Dr. J. H. W. LAING

With numerous Illustrations. Wide Royal 8vo

THE ART OF THE GREEKS, 15s. net. THE ART OF THE ROMANS, 16s. net. CHARDIN, 15s. net. DONATELLO, 16s. net. GEORGE ROMNEY, 15s. net. GHIRLANDAIO, 15s. net. LAWRENCE, 25s. net. MICHELANGELO, 15s. net. RAPHAEL, 15s. net. REMBRANDT'S ETCHINGS, Two Vols., 25s. net. TINTORETTO, 16s. net. TITIAN, 16s. net. TURNER'S SKETCHES AND DRAWINGS, 15s. net. VELAZQUEZ, 15s. net.

The 'Complete' Series

Fully Illustrated. Demy 8vo

THE COMPLETE AMATEUR BOXER, 10s. 6d. net. THE COMPLETE ASSOCIATION FOOTBALLER, 10s. 6d. net. THE COMPLETE ATHLETIC TRAINER, 10s. 6d. net. THE COMPLETE BILLIARD PLAYER, 12s. 6d. net. THE COMPLETE COOK, 10s. 6d. net. THE COMPLETE CRICKETER, 10s. 6d. net. THE COMPLETE FOXHUNTER, 16s. net. THE COMPLETE GOLFER, 12s. 6d. net. THE COMPLETE HOCKEY-PLAYER, 10s. 6d. net. THE COMPLETE HORSEMAN, 12s. 6d. net. THE COMPLETE JUJITSUAN. Cr. 8vo. 5s. net. THE COMPLETE LAWN TENNIS PLAYER, 12s. 6d. net. THE COMPLETE MOTORIST, 10s. 6d. net. THE COMPLETE MOUNTAINEER, 16s. net. THE COMPLETE OARSMAN, 15s. net. THE COMPLETE PHOTOGRAPHER, 15s. net. THE COMPLETE RUGBY FOOTBALLER, ON THE NEW ZEALAND SYSTEM, 12s. 6d. net. THE COMPLETE SHOT, 16s. net. THE COMPLETE SWIMMER, 10s. 6d. net. THE COMPLETE YACHTSMAN, 16s. net.

The Connoisseur's Library

With numerous Illustrations. Wide Royal 8vo. 25s. net each volume

ENGLISH COLOURED BOOKS. ENGLISH FURNITURE. ETCHINGS. EUROPEAN ENAMELS. FINE BOOKS. GLASS. GOLDSMITHS' AND SILVERSMITHS' WORK. ILLUMINATED MANUSCRIPTS. IVORIES. JEWELLERY. MEZZOTINTS. MINIATURES. PORCELAIN. SEALS. WOOD SCULPTURE.

Handbooks of Theology

Demy 8vo

THE DOCTRINE OF THE INCARNATION, 15s. net. A HISTORY OF EARLY CHRISTIAN DOCTRINE, 16s. net. INTRODUCTION TO THE HISTORY OF RELIGION, 12s. 6d. net. AN INTRODUCTION TO THE HISTORY OF THE CREEDS, 12s. 6d. net. THE PHILOSOPHY OF RELIGION IN ENGLAND AND AMERICA, 12s. 6d. net. THE XXXIX ARTICLES OF THE CHURCH OF ENGLAND, 15s. net.

Health Series

Fcap. 8vo. 2s. 6d. net

THE BABY. THE CARE OF THE BODY. THE CARE OF THE TEETH. THE EYES OF OUR CHILDREN. HEALTH FOR THE MIDDLE-AGED. THE HEALTH OF A WOMAN. THE HEALTH OF THE SKIN. HOW TO LIVE LONG. THE PREVENTION OF THE COMMON COLD. STAYING THE PLAGUE. THROAT AND EAR TROUBLES. TUBERCULOSIS. THE HEALTH OF THE CHILD, 2s. net.

Hope (Anthony)—

A CHANGE OF AIR. A MAN OF MARK. THE CHRONICLES OF COUNT ANTONIO. SIMON DALE. THE KING'S MIRROR. QUISANTÉ. THE DOLLY DIALOGUES. TALES OF TWO PEOPLE. A SERVANT OF THE PUBLIC. MRS. MAXON PROTESTS. A YOUNG MAN'S YEAR. BEAUMAROY HOME FROM THE WARS. *All 7s. 6d. net.*

Jacobs (W. W.)—

MANY CARGOES, 5s. *net.* SEA URCHINS, 5s. *net* and 3s. 6d. *net.* A MASTER OF CRAFT, 5s. *net.* LIGHT FREIGHTS, 5s. *net.* THE SKIPPER'S WOOING, 5s. *net.* AT SUNWICH PORT, 5s. *net.* DIALSTONE LANE, 5s. *net.* ODD CRAFT, 5s. *net.* THE LADY OF THE BARGE, 5s. *net.* SALTHAVEN, 5s. *net.* SAILORS' KNOTS, 5s. *net.* SHORT CRUISES, 6s. *net.*

London (Jack). WHITE FANG. *Ninth Edition. Cr. 8vo. 7s. 6d. net.*

Lucas (E. V.)—

LISTENER'S LURE : An Oblique Narration, 6s. *net.* OVER BEMERTON'S : An Easygoing Chronicle, 6s. *net.* MR. INGLESIDE, 6s. *net.* LONDON LAVENDER, 6s. *net.* LANDMARKS, 7s. 6d. *net.* THE VERMILION BOX, 7s. 6d. *net.* VERENA IN THE MIDST, 8s. 6d. *net.*

McKenna (Stephen)—

SONIA : Between Two Worlds, 8s. *net.* NINETY-SIX HOURS' LEAVE, 7s. 6d. *net.* THE SIXTH SENSE, 6s. *net.* MIDAS & SON, 8s. *net.*

Malet (Lucas)—

THE HISTORY OF SIR RICHARD CALMADY : A Romance. THE CARISSIMA. THE GATELESS BARRIER. DEADHAM HARD. *All 7s. 6d. net.* THE WAGES OF SIN. 8s. *net.*

Mason (A. E. W.). CLEMENTINA. Illustrated. *Ninth Edition. Cr. 8vo. 7s. 6d. net.*

Maxwell (W. B.)—

VIVIEN. THE GUARDED FLAME. ODD LENGTHS. HILL RISE. THE REST CURE. *All 7s. 6d. net.*

Oxenham (John)—

A WEAVER OF WEBS. PROFIT AND LOSS. THE SONG OF HYACINTH, and Other Stories. LAURISTONS. THE COIL OF CARNE. THE QUEST OF THE GOLDEN ROSE. MARY ALL-ALONE. BROKEN SHACKLES. "1914." *All 7s. 6d. net.*

Parker (Gilbert)—

PIERRE AND HIS PEOPLE. MRS. FALCHION. THE TRANSLATION OF A SAVAGE. WHEN VALMOND CAME TO PONTIAC : The Story of a Lost Napoleon. AN ADVENTURER OF THE NORTH : The Last Adventures of 'Pretty Pierre.' THE SEATS OF THE MIGHTY. THE BATTLE OF THE STRONG : A Romance of Two Kingdoms. THE POMP OF THE LAVILETTES. NORTHERN LIGHTS. *All 7s. 6d. net.*

Phillpotts (Eden)—

CHILDREN OF THE MIST. SONS OF THE MORNING. THE RIVER. THE AMERICAN PRISONER. DEMETER'S DAUGHTER. THE HUMAN BOY AND THE WAR. *All 7s. 6d. net.*

Ridge (W. Pett)—

A SON OF THE STATE, 7s. 6d. *net.* THE REMINGTON SENTENCE, 7s. 6d. *net.* MADAME PRINCE, 7s. 6d. *net.* TOP SPEED, 7s. 6d. *net.* SPECIAL PERFORMANCES, 6s. *net.* THE BUSTLING HOURS, 7s. 6d. *net.*

Rohmer (Sax)—

THE DEVIL DOCTOR. THE SI-FAN MYSTERIES. TALES OF SECRET EGYPT. THE ORCHARD OF TEARS. THE GOLDEN SCORPION. *All 7s. 6d. net.*

Swinnerton (F.). SHOPS AND HOUSES. *Third Edition. Cr. 8vo. 7s. 6d. net.*

SEPTEMBER. *Third Edition. Cr. 8vo. 7s. 6d. net.*

THE HAPPY FAMILY. *Second Edition. 7s. 6d. net.*

ON THE STAIRCASE. *Third Edition. 7s. 6d. net.*

Wells (H. G.). BEALBY. *Fourth Edition. Cr. 8vo. 7s. 6d. net.*

Williamson (C. N. and A. M.)—

THE LIGHTNING CONDUCTOR : The Strange Adventures of a Motor Car. LADY BETTY ACROSS THE WATER. SCARLET RUNNER. LORD LOVELAND DISCOVERS AMERICA. THE GUESTS OF HERCULES. IT HAPPENED IN EGYPT. A SOLDIER OF THE LEGION. THE SHOP GIRL. THE LIGHTNING CONDUCTRESS. SECRET HISTORY. THE LOVE PIRATE. *All 7s. 6d. net.* CRUCIFIX CORNER. 6s. *net.*

Methuen's Two-Shilling Novels

Cheap Editions of many of the most Popular Novels of the day

Write for Complete List

Fcap. 8vo

535

CPSIA information can be obtained at www.ICGtesting.com
Printed in the USA
LVOW070730290612

288003LV00004B/226/P